SOVIET PSYCHOLOGY

Also by John McLeish:

Evangelical Religion and Popular Education
The Science of Behaviour
The Theory of Social Change
Students' Attitudes and College Environments
Cambridge Monographs on Teaching Methods
The Psychology of the Learning Group
Verbal Behaviour: An Experimental Analysis

SOVIET PSYCHOLOGY:
History, Theory, Content

John McLeish

Methuen & Co Ltd
11 New Fetter Lane, London, EC4

First published in 1975
By Methuen & Co Ltd
11 New Fetter Lane, London EC4P 4EE
Printed in Great Britain
By Cox & Wyman Ltd
London, Fakenham and Reading

© John McLeish 1975
SBN 416 13670 2

Distributed in the USA by
Harper & Row Publishers, Inc.
Barnes & Noble Import Division

To the memory of my father
John Donald McLeish

Contents

Tables

Figures

Preface

This is the first book in any language, including Russian, to provide a detailed analysis of the relationship between Russian philosophy and psychology, as it developed from 1750, and contemporary Soviet psychology. The materials have been collected over a number of years while the writer was teaching at the Universities of Glasgow, Leeds, and Alberta. In each of these places, especially the last, there are exceptional collections of Russian and other East-European materials. The author has also had the opportunity over the years to discuss various questions with East-European psychologists and other colleagues. In the interpretation of the published sources the writer would like to record his particular indebtedness to Jacob Miller of Glasgow, the late Alfred Dressler of Leeds and Metro Gulutsan at the University of Alberta. The final product as well as the interpretations are entirely the responsibility of the author.

This is not an anti-Soviet book. It seeks to present certain unpopular ideas in as clear a form as it is possible to make them. A deliberate attempt *not* to obtrude a personal and negative point of view has been made in the process of exposition. The reader may identify the ideas with the writer, this is a calculated risk which is taken for the purposes of exposition. On the other hand, it is certain that Soviet intellectuals would detect compromise, half-heartedness and bourgeois objectivism in this account of their basic views. Anyone who writes about matters which are of such basic concern to human beings is courting misunderstanding, and even denunciation. The objective in writing the book is to seek to provide the reader with basic information from which, hopefully, he will come to a better understanding of the issues and a more informed judgement of the nature of psychology in general and Soviet psychology in particular. The point of view from which it is written is expanded upon on pp. 2–3, 166–168 and 271–272.

Wherever possible, reference is made to English translations of the works cited as well as to the originals. The author regrets that owing to separation from the source materials when the book was going through the press, it has not always been possible to verify these references. Where the available translations are unsatisfactory, the author has supplied his own.

John McLeish

Edinburgh
October, 1974

Introduction

The Soviet Union has now survived for almost six decades. Throughout this period it has captured attention as one of the most interesting political phenomena of modern times. It was the first country to carry through a long planned for, and much publicized, Marxist socialist revolution. The Bolsheviks, having captured State power, set in train vast social, cultural, economic, and political changes on a scale unknown since Peter the Great. These reforms were not *ad hoc* political expedients but were rooted in a systematic, coherent theory of society and a novel view of the nature of man. The basic doctrine behind these revolutionary changes rejects all the traditional solutions of social and intellectual problems – this explains why 'the Russian Experiment' continues to attract the fascinated attention of outsiders. Marxist ideas have a dynamic quality such that a large number of other nations have followed the Russian model. The question is whether indeed this new form of society and the views which go along with it represent the shape of the future for the whole of mankind.

Soviet psychology shares in this general interest. It has also a unique attraction because here it is that the differences between Soviet views and other ways of thinking about nature, man, and society are maximized. Soviet theories about human behaviour are of great human significance. Following on several decades of embittered controversy, Soviet psychology succeeded in producing an acceptable theory of the human organism and of man's psychological qualities. In content this theory is uniquely different from other view. It originated in the realm of political action rather than in laboratory research. The theoretical framework has given rise to a large body of established knowledge based on empirical studies which use recognized scientific methods. The most important feature of this body of theory is that it is implacably hostile to all other viewpoints. For reasons which will become clear this hostility is directed especially against religious concepts, but in addition Soviet psychology rejects as erroneous any ideas which have any connection with dualism, positivism, phenomenalism, idealism, or agnosticism.

The historical development of this complex view of human nature has to be seen against the backcloth of the special development of Russian thought and Russian society. Its pervasive influence is primarily due to its intellectual appeal as a systematic, coherent, and comprehensive system. But, in addition, Marxism has operated as a political control and as the intellectual organizer throughout the lifetime of the great majority of those living in the USSR. The Communist Party has guided the thoughts, actions, and aspirations of the Soviet people in a way which is impossible for those reared in a liberal society even to imagine. The use of dialectical materialism as a political control leads many people outside the USSR, especially professional scientists, to regard the general theory of Soviet psychology as irrelevant. Particular empirical studies however continue to generate interest, and the theory of Marxism maintains its appeal as a scientific theory.

It cannot be emphasized too strongly that an understanding of Soviet thought presupposes an appreciation of the basic philosophical and social positions on which it is grounded. The story of how Marxism and Pavlovianism came to be the accepted foundation of Soviet psychology, and how this influenced the development of psychology in countries within the Soviet sphere, is the major concern of this book. The remarkable breakthrough of Soviet psychology in the last fifteen years can only be seen in its true light when placed against the backcloth of earlier controversies. In turn, these Soviet controversies can be understood only in relation to the historical development of psychological concepts in pre-revolutionary Russia.

It seems useful to summarize at this point the standpoint from which the writer approaches the study of Soviet psychology. In general terms, Soviet psychology is considered correct in asserting a monistic view of the organism in its environment as the only possible basis for a science of behaviour. Thinking about behaviour must start from the assumption that any dualism (mind–body, spiritual–material, ideal–actual) inevitably leads back to profitless philosophical debates which are anti-scientific in tendency. However, it must also be said that authoritarian dogmatism, associated with the 'cult of personality', held back scientific progress in the USSR and especially the development of psychology. The 'cult' is better described as the subordination of scientific truth to political expediency. For many years, especially between 1935 and 1955, the discussion of psychological theory was reduced to a subjective elaboration of philosophical nuances of a doctrinaire and irrelevant character. However, it must be said that Soviet 'partisanship' does not invalidate the general truth of the scientific 'line' and of many of the scientific principles declared in these discussions. This is shown by the fact that, when divorced from their special terminology and polemical context, the general principles of Soviet psychology are acceptable to a large body of non-Communist psychological opinion.

Two major themes underlie the development of Soviet psychology. The first is the Marxist view that there is no such thing as an unchanging, eternal human essence. This states the theme negatively. Informed Communists believe it possible to transform 'human nature' *to an unlimited extent*. This is done by changing society. The topic of the 'New Man' has been a leading *motif* in Soviet discussions, emerging and re-emerging over the whole period of development since 1917. The emphasis is on *system* and *dynamic change*. Soviet scientists have been concerned primarily with developing a psychological theory which is compatible with an invincible optimism about the possibility of consciously directing social influences to produce a completely new society and a new type of humanity. Pavlov and Lenin are in complete agreement on this principle of infinite flexibility of human beings.

The second major concern is the linking of the philosophical controversies of the eighteen forties, fifties and sixties in Russia with current themes. Soviet psychologists believe that in these controversies, which were devoted not only to philosophical questions but to the problems of social and political change, the basis was laid for the birth of an independent science of human behaviour. Chernishevski is one pillar, Sechenov the other. In his remarkable treatise *Reflexes of the Brain* (1863) Sechenov developed concepts which, properly evaluated, provide the foundation for an objective science of psychology. The true history of these developments, as well as the nature of Sechenov's (and later) Pavlov's scientific contributions, have been obscured since neither the source materials, nor a connected account of Russian psychology, have been available. American behaviourism grossly misunderstood and misrepresented the work of Pavlov: it remained entirely unaware of Sechenov's elaborated views.

Sechenov's programme was about four decades in advance of world scientific thought. For some reason, no translation of his basic writings was available until 1935 in a West European language. His ideas therefore remained dormant until Pavlov, by using the method of the salivary fistula, discovered or invented techniques necessary for investigating cerebral processes in the intact animal. In Sechenov's phrase, 'the reflexes of the brain' became available for scientific study and a new science became possible. In 1917, Lenin and Pavlov respectively took over the pioneer roles which had been rehearsed half a century earlier by Chernishevski and Sechenov.

Part 1 *The Historical Foundations of Soviet Psychology*

The defining characteristics of Soviet psychology are placed in a historical context in terms of the emergence and evolution of a number of basic principles generated in the course of the evolution of Russian social and political institutions.

In this section, a concise summary of this development is provided. An attempt is made to pinpoint the specific differences between the origins of psychology in Russia and parallel, but relatively earlier, movements in West European thought.

The significance of the views of Lomonosov, Radishchev, Belinsky, Chernishevski, and other thinkers discussed in this part will become clear in the light of later developments. In turn, these earlier views will throw light on the later Soviet developments and the controversies about scientific method in the analysis of human behaviour.

Soviet psychology originated and developed within a context of continuing social and political controversies. Its general theoretical principles emerged from a head-on collision between revolutionary, extremist ideas and an entrenched, ultra-conservative set of dogmas about human nature, about the social environment, and about the possibility of change.

Chapter 1 *Social and Political Context*

The origins of scientific psychology can be understood only in the context of social and political developments. Russian society under the Autocrat is almost a perfect example of social equilibrium. Tsarism, as a form of government, was the integral product of evolution within, and diffusion across, a territory of vast expanse, inhabited by millions of illiterate peasants, capable of only a low level of agricultural technique. A type of oriental despotism fitted the objective needs of this situation for long periods, at least as far as the vast bulk of the population was concerned. Had it been possible for the Russian Empire to remain an autarchy, isolated from all other human society, its characteristic institutions – autocratic government; Orthodox religion accepted by, or imposed on, all citizens; serfdom for the great majority; and a bureaucratic routine which maintained the administrative machine as a going concern – could have persisted until the last judgement. But this could not be. A succession of 'Westernizers' – the first being a reigning Tsar, Peter I – opened up avenues for the diffusion of external, exotic materials and productive processes, innovations in government and religion, aspirations towards a different way of life. Among these exotic materials were ideas about what constitutes 'the good life' and about human nature in general.

(i) The Social Background: *Narodnost'*

A discussion of centuries-long standing continues inside and outside the Russian lands. The question is whether these territories, and the peoples who inhabit them, have a special history and destiny or whether they belong to Europe by virtue of common origins and a shared culture. Geographically, the Urals divided the Empire of the Tsars (and now the Soviet Union) into one portion designated 'European Russia', and another designated 'Asiatic Russia'. But the fact is that the schism which tore apart the Christian Church in the eleventh century is of considerably more importance: it gave rise to two distinct ecclesiastical and social cultures which evolved without much interrelation for many centuries. It is true, of course, that the schism itself was a recognition of basic differences which ran deeper than religion.

At a later period, Russia survived the Mongol invasion, only to be subjected to another form of oriental despotism (Tsarism), which survived into the twentieth century. Long after other European nations had abandoned medieval forms of economic and social organization, a retrograde system of military feudalism survived, with the vast majority living as serfs, operating a stagnant economic system. The mass of the population was illiterate and subject to a reactionary Church, which strongly supported other Departments of State in persecuting unorthodox opinions – these including any expression of a modern viewpoint.

Lenin, in his study of the development of capitalism in Russia, points to an essential difference between the Russian system of 'natural' economy and West European capitalism:

> The law of pre-capitalist modes of production is the repetition of the process on the previous scale, on the previous basis. . . . Under the old modes of production, economic units could exist for centuries without undergoing any change either in character or in size. . . . Capitalist enterprise, on the contrary, inevitably outgrows the bounds of the village community, the local market, the region, and then the State.[1]

The relentless and all-powerful influences of custom, the dominant role of conservative social forces like religion, the patriarchal and extended family, the unanimity principle in village government, the communal land relationships and arrangements, the absence of a literate population – these characteristics of Russia under the Tsars all bear the hallmark of the static mode of production referred to by Lenin. Any variation in the seasonal routine carries with it the possibility of a dangerous, perhaps total, breakdown in the process of production, on which survival depends. Likewise, any variation in the thought and behaviour-pattern of the individual is believed to endanger the whole community. It is clear that the economic self-sufficiency of the village, based on the 'natural' system of economy, with its repetitious cycles and the dependence of each subsystem on the proper functioning of the total apparatus of production, is directly related to the subordination of the individual to the family, to the community, and to the State. The ideology of peasant society reflects in detail the static mode of production: it is a kind of analogue model. This is because it is a product of, and, at the same time, a strong support of the prevailing social and economic relationships and systems.

According to the Russian Imperial Census of 1858, the rural population consisted of 51,516,000 adults. The majority of these were serfs; only about nine million being free peasants. The serf population could be classified as shown in the following table:[2]

TABLE I. *Classification of the Russian Serf Population, 1858*

Types of Peasantry	No. of adult 'souls' (both sexes)
1. Crown (State) Peasants	
Palace, Royal and Imperial Family	2,019,000
State lands	16,535,000
Mining enterprises	386,000
Western Provinces	1,773,000
Artisans of the Crown Mines	230,000
Total	20,943,000
2. Landowners' peasants	20,173,000
3. Peasants attached to private factories	518,000
4. Retired soldiers	1,093,000
Full Total	42,727,000

It is clear from these figures that Tsardom was a principal beneficiary and the main support of this system of human enslavement. The landlords, of whom there were 30,000, controlled the lives and destinies of over forty million serfs, settled on twenty million desyatins of land. The ownership of the land was a matter of dispute between the ideologists of the peasantry and the landlords. The peasant theory was that while the landlords owned the peasants, the peasant owned the land. In actual fact, the land was largely mortgaged to the banks, the landlords having contracted a debt of 395 million roubles, more than 53 per cent of the total value of the land.

As far as cultivation was concerned, there was a division into land, which was cultivated by the peasant community, and land cultivated for the landlord in payment for the use of the former.

However, in many cases the payment in labour (*barshchina*) was replaced by a quit-rent (*obrok*) or money-payment. The amount of labour-time, required from the peasant by the landlord, varied according to the district and the quality of the land. Normally it amounted to two or three days in each working week. The landlords had naturally an interest in increasing their income. This could be done by arbitrarily increasing the amounts of *barshchina*, or *obrok*, or by selling their freedom to those serfs who had been able to enrich themselves within the system of serfdom. This they could do by trading on their own account, or by working on contract, or by other means.

Because of the feudal relations between master and serf in the sphere of agricultural production; because of the tribute the landlords exacted from industry in the form of quit-rents paid by their proletarianized peasants, forced to take seasonal town employment to accumulate *obrok* payments; because of the corrupt bureaucracy and backward-looking aristocracy, the Russian economy remained at a low level. A form of protected capitalism had been introduced by Peter in the shape of State monopolies and subsidized industries necessary for his military enterprises. Foreign capital and investment had been attracted to Russia by a succession of Autocrats, especially French and British capital. But there was no social or economic basis for that 'constant transformation of the mode of production, the limitless growth of the scale of production' which Lenin describes as of the essence of capitalism.

The system of taxation, which exempted the great landowners, tended to kill all initiative at the lower levels. The productivity of labour remained low. The population was almost wholly illiterate; the peasantry lacked the basic skills and attitudes necessary for capitalist enterprise. There were certainly changes within the system – for example, the division of labour, which signals and accompanies the breaking-up of the system of natural economy, had been quickened by the Tsarist conquests of the seventeenth, eighteenth and nineteenth centuries. Population changes also occurred. For example, between 1722, when the first census of serfs was taken, and the tenth revision of 1858, the population increased six times. The natural increment in this period was four times; double the original number had been added by conquest. However, about 70 per cent of the Imperial population were serfs of one kind or another; less than 6 per cent of the population lived in towns.

The economic backwardness of Russia dates from the end of the eighteenth century. The political reaction to the French Revolution of 1789, following on Pugachev's revolt of 1773–75, entrenched the system of serfdom and autocratic government in Russia. One result of this was that English and continental capitalism left Russian capitalism far behind during the nineteenth century in terms of growth and diversification. The centre of capitalist development was Tsarist Poland rather than Russia itself.

Serf agriculture was characterized by a permanent and ineradicable crisis. The landlords' interest in intensive farming, derived from English developments in this area, disappeared by about 1840. Even after the Emancipation of the Serfs (1861), and in spite of the growth in population and territory, Russian agriculture showed a stationary yield (1801–70), punctuated by crop failures and widespread famines throughout the nineteenth century. The fact seems to be that there was no possibility of establishing a rational system of agricultural production under serfdom since there was no method of establishing the costs of production with any accuracy. Serfdom concealed the existence of agricultural underemployment on a massive scale. Labour productivity was inevitably low, as under any system of slavery: techniques remained at a primitive level. The system of *obrok,* where the serfs paid rent in lieu of labour-time, had within it the germs of a rational system of capitalism in agriculture. This system gave at least the possibility of a free influx and efflux of labour, a reasonable system of cost-accounting, a basis for credit advances to landlords on a foundation of rational expectations, and a method of primary accumulation necessary for capitalizing farming and industry. But, as late as 1861, 75 per cent of the peasants in the fertile black-earth region (*chernozem* soils) were still *barshchina* serfs. This system of cultivation repaid landlord investment many times over. But the system of *obrok* was typical only of the relatively infertile *podsol* (or clay soil) regions, where the yield hardly repaid cultivation and where rent provided a stable and profitable source of income to the landowner.

The class groupings in Tsarist society originated on the basis of their position as beneficiaries from, or as unwilling contributors to, the system of serf proprietorship. The social, political, and economic views of the different social classes and strata clearly reflected their class interest in maintaining, modifying, or abolishing the serf system of economy. Each of these social groupings had their own developed views about human nature, about social organization, about their origins and characteristics.

The Autocrat was at once the leader, and the captive, of the largest landowners. Their interest continued to dominate State action even after it became clear that the State itself must perish in the general ruin, if change was not allowed. The bureaucracy and its interests were tied to the survival of the Autocracy and the continuance of serf conditions in society at large. The landowners had a vested interest in expressing, as in a wine-press, the last ounce of rent and profit from the peasant. This income was necessary to maintain the system in being – an important element of the system being a rather vacuous social life in the metropolis and an accustomed standard of luxury in the country.

The Orthodox Church operated as an extension and support of the State system. It was a kind of religious 'reflection' of the autocracy and bureaucracy. As far as their social interventions are concerned, Lenin may be quoted to the effect that the priests of the Orthodox Church acted always to safeguard the interests of the oppressing classes. They supported the most conservative State policies, persecuted dissenters and radicals, and fostered anti-semitism. When the need arose the priests acted as unpaid agents of the secret police. If they participated on the side of reform, it was as *agents provocateurs* (like the notorious Father Gapon).

The peasants' economic interest was directly opposed to that of the landlords. It was their purpose to seek to reduce the amount of *barshchina* and *obrok* exacted from them, and to increase the share of the peasant community (the *Mir*) of the land available for cultivation. Although the peasants themselves were lacking a voice and political knowledge, there were many who set themselves up as self-appointed spokesmen for their interests.

The intellectuals had no direct stake in the economic system, nor any recognized function or place in the social system. The Russian word 'raznochintzi' refers to them as falling 'between the social ranks', that is, as 'classless'. They tended to group themselves all along the length of the political spectrum. As individuals, they were ready to place their talents at the service of whichever class interest they could make their own, without doing permanent damage to their moral convictions or ideals.

The merchants were interested in supporting the prevailing autocratic and theocratic system but only in so far as it facilitated their activities in the social and economic spheres. Their inclination was to adapt the system in diverse ways, so as to make possible an extension of their financial operations. In general, they were liberals in their social and political views.

The industrial workers had no independent voice or political influence until the late 70s or 80s. Their interests were largely identical with those of the peasants. To this class they remained attached, physically as well as psychologically, until a late stage in industrial development.

These class divisions constituted the social, political, and economic context within which elaborate theories about psychological processes and functions were developed. As the social classes themselves were, in general, hostile to each other, so their elaborated views about the realities of individual and social psychology were also in violent opposition to each other. The main confrontation was between the conservative, religious, Orthodox, theologically based concepts on the one hand, and the radical, secularist, science-based theories of the progressive intelligentsia on the other hand.

(ii) The Ideology of Conservatism under the Tsars: Autocracy

The policy towards education serves as an index pointing to the reactionary nature of those called to rule the Russian State. The official view, reflected in State action during the greater part of the Tsarist period, was expressed by Shishkov when fourth Minister of Popular Enlightenment. He said in the presence, and with the approval, of the Tsar, 'Knowledge is of value only when like salt, it is used and offered in small quantities in accordance with the people's circumstances and needs . . . To teach the mass of the people or even the majority to read will bring more harm than good.'[3] The Tsar and his advisers were hardly conscious of the fact that they were defending their material interests and specially favoured position. They conceived their task to be something much more important: to prevent the dissolution of society into a jungle where justice would perish, where self-interest would reign unchecked, and where men would give way to every evil influence. These conclusions were the outcome of reflection on a long chain of historical events. The fact that these events were perceived through the prism of dynastic interests, Orthodox religion, and class supremacy was, more or less, apparent to other social groups but not to officialdom. For them was established the absolute necessity for orthodoxy in religious beliefs, with persecution of all dissent; autocracy in government, with the destruction of all opposition by force; and *narodnost'* ('national character') which involved a Chauvinistic rejection of cultural borrowings from all other nations which were believed to be, necessarily, of an inferior type.

According to the official view, every nation-state, except Russia, had forfeited its integrity in every aspect of life. Innovation was the path which others had followed and which must be avoided at all costs. Innovations in religion or in government, 'reforms', could not be tolerated. The parlous condition of European countries, which had 'gone in' for reform, was plain for all to see. To the conservatives, all Western institutions were radically bad. Parliamentary government, trial by jury, freedom of the Press, secular education – all were based on the same lie, namely, the equality of man. In the Russian conservative system of thought, ignorance and superstition were categorically stated to be superior to knowledge and science. They represented an essential natural force of inertia by which humanity was kept to the path of its divinely established destiny, as a ship is steadied by its ballast. To 'civilize' the nation by educating the illiterate, superstitious, poverty-ridden, and uncultured peasant would be to destroy society. Freedom of conscience, which implies the right of criticism, would inevitably lead to criticism of the Autocrat, the divinely anointed foundation of the whole social and religious structure. Such a breach in their faith could lead the whole of society only to the abyss. It was written by a leading Tsarist councillor:

> An old institution is so much more precious, and hence irreplaceable, because it has not been thought out by anyone but created by life itself. It has come into being out of history and is sanctioned in the opinion of the people by that authority which alone history can give. Nothing is capable of replacing this authority, its roots lie deep in that part of our being where the moral ties are most tightly bound and most deeply rooted. Hence, no new idea can be grafted onto the masses. The mass of the people assimilates an idea only through those emotions which arise, and which find their roots, in no other manner than through history.[4]

To the conservatives of the Tsar's court, old superstitions and customs, especially if rooted in Orthodox religious culture, should never be criticized, no matter how grotesque they might appear to an educated man. Ancient customs and long-established beliefs must contain some precious grain of truth. The continued existence of serfdom and illiteracy was proof that they have been sanctioned by history, which is another name for God.

The leading characteristic of this 'Kingdom of Darkness', (that is, official, slave-owning, bureaucratic society), in Dobrolyubov's phrase, was an almost total absence of human feeling. The barriers which social position erected between classes and social groups served also to maintain individuals at a distance. The correct attitude to adopt to other people was defined as a formality which concealed indifference. The dangers of emotionality could best be avoided by immersing oneself in paper-work. Official society under the Tsars lived by paper. It is true that under Alexander certain relaxations were made to the rigours of the Nicholaiyan régime (that 'lead coffin', as even the liberals described it). But there is nothing which could be dignified with the name of a qualitative change so far as basic attitudes to order, system, and lack of human warmth and feeling are concerned. The qualities which Freud associated with the anal personality structure – an obsessional concern with the most minute detail of administration; orderliness, which regards the whole world of human relations as through the eyes of an inspecting orderly sergeant; parsimony, which starves the Empire of essential services – these traits are clearly seen in the whole of official society, modelled as it is on the Autocrat and directly supervised by him in all its manifestations.

The character of Russian society is shown in the ultra-conservative nature of its leaders and the official social theory. In 1843 Uvarov declared the basic ideals of social justice to be Orthodoxy, Autocracy, and National Character (*Narodnost'*). The corollary was the legal persecution of anyone who wished to change any detail of the established religious belief, the political order, or the serf basis of the economy. The distrust of science and popular education, in the interests of a static, formalized religion and a stable society, can be documented from hundreds of incidents and declarations of policy, beginning with the reign of Catherine II and terminating only with the abdication of the last Tsar, Nicholas II.

The restrictions on universities testify to the fear of modern science and modern thought on the part of the official group. It was not only the natural and physical sciences which were confined within a financial and administrative strait-jacket. Such subjects as modern history, constitutional law, and moral philosophy were from time to time forbidden subjects. Professors were dismissed without notice; their chairs were abolished; their students dispersed. Women were not allowed to study at universities except as auditors (*vol'nosluzhateli*). There was a *numerus clausus* which excluded all but a small percentage of Jews. Latin and Greek were the key subjects in secondary schools and universities. Even so, certain parts of Roman history were forbidden as the murder of tyrants and republican sentiments could conceivably give rise to dangerous thoughts. It was the aim and policy of the Autocracy to keep education and science under duel control: that of the gendarmerie and the priest.

(iii) The Concept of Man: Orthodoxy

From the tenth century until the Revolution the dominant thought-patterns of the mass of the Russian population were directly drawn from the teachings of Greek Christianity. As in Europe throughout the Middle Ages, the frame of reference, for the thinker as for the illiterate peasant, was theological. The dogmas of the Church formed the universal matrix within which concepts of science, of art, of literature germinated and developed. Because of the continued association of Byzantine Christianity with the State power, deviations from this pattern remained exceptional, even up to a late date. Innovations in the form of secular knowledge – especially new concepts of nature and of human behaviour – were strongly resisted long after they were commonly accepted in the West. Russia did not benefit (or, as the conservative Slavophils proudly asserted, *suffer*) from either a Renaissance of learning or from a Reformation in religion such as nurtured the free life of the intellect in the countries of Western Europe.

In its basic essentials the concept of man in the Greek Orthodox Church (of which the Russian Church is a branch) was identical to the Roman. Until the Great Schism of 1054 these Churches shared a common life, and (uneasily) a common culture. To someone who belongs to neither, the difference in dogma, doctrine, and ritual represent differences in emphasis rather than differences of substance. The ideas of the Creation, the Fall of Adam, Christ as the Redeemer, the Second Coming, and the Last Judgement were enshrined in creeds accepted by both Churches and drawn from the same inspired Testaments. The essential difference between the two branches of the universal Church consisted in the *orthodox* character of the Eastern Church. This is testified to in the fact that discussion over dogma virtually terminated in the seventh century – the legacy of the Bible and of the Fathers of the Church was regarded as providing a completed body of knowledge necessary for salvation. This knowledge, rather than being developed and interpreted, was required to be preserved intact without admixture and without loss. Religious energies, which in the Western Church were channelled into controversy (and sometimes bloody wars), were concentrated on ritual. This had the function of bringing the individual and the community into direct contact with the Deity. The *ikon* was regarded not merely as a symbol but as a vital link transmitting grace and power to the believer.

It is impossible to divorce the psychological principles of the Orthodox believer from their theological matrix. Russian psychology developed from this original starting point (Christian anthropology), very largely in opposition to it. The concept of man as a union of two principles or substances – *soma* which is material and *psyche* which is non-material or spiritual – is a basic premise. The belief that the psyche is a higher or in some sense a superior category to matter is derived in Orthodox belief from the teaching that the soul partakes of the divine nature whereas the body is of the earth (Genesis ii. VII). Thus the soul is immortal and unchanging, it can be corrupted only by sin. The body (with Satan and the rest of matter symbolized in 'the world') is the source and seat of corruption. Through prayer, and by the merit accruing to man from the Redemption by the Second Adam (Christ), and by means of the sacraments, sinful man can become perfect. This is indeed his task in this world. Life in the natural order is merely a preparation or apprenticeship for the next world where supreme happiness is attained by the ecstatic contemplation of the Divine Essence in paradise. Hence the believer is best occupied in preparing himself for these delights by prayer and Church-going – in general, by conformity to Orthodox customs, rules of behaviour, and conciliation procedures.

According to Orthodox belief, man does not belong in the natural order of development. He did not evolve, but was specially created. Even if all the difficulties in explaining the development of man's body through natural law could be cleared up, the central problem of the origin of man's spiritual (and psychological) life would remain. This is a mystery which only the scriptures can resolve. These testify that God made man 'in His own Image and

Likeness' (Genesis i. XXVI). This text is interpreted to mean that man is a living unity, that the bodily and spiritual spheres are not just stuck together. It means also that man's most important life is that in which he maintains contact with the supernatural order of things. In the formula of the Council of Chalcedon (AD 451), man has two natures, distinct yet perfectly united. The distinction must be made between the true nature of man and the *empirical reality* of man. This means that not only man's spirit but his body as well belongs to both the empirical sphere of reality and to the metaphysical. This explains the violence of the reaction to Peter's *ukaz* against beards. The Orthodox believed that shaving the beard was defiling God's image and likeness, since two of the Trinity were universally pictured as bearded.

An essential difference between the Eastern and Roman Churches is illustrated in the manner of dealing with this text pointing to the dualistic nature of man. The Roman Church, following the rise of scholasticism, claims that arguments such as those of Thomas Aquinas demonstrate the truth of this doctrine through the powers of the unaided reason. For the Eastern Church on the other hand, this doctrine is an original intuition, a primary and simple truth of direct illumination. It is not a construction of the theological reason.

The Orthodox Church places the highest regard on man's feelings, on asceticism and mysticism, in contrast to what it regards as the legalism of the Roman Church. Historically, it has emphasized the social, collective aspect. In addition to the two levels of man's being – the empirical and transcendental – there is a third reality, namely, man-in-the-church. Russian thought, in political theory, in philosophy, and in theology, is steeped in the notion of a mystical, supernatural unity which is generated by communal life – whether this be in the *Mir* or village commune, in the traditional family and State, or in the Church. In the third instance, the additional quality of sanctification through God's grace is added to this mystical union of fellowship which is apparent in all three cases or situations. Man is caught up, and becomes one with Christ and the Church community; he acquires a new holiness (*Sobornost'*, *Gemeinschaftsbezogenheit*, Catholicity). This feeling for the *kollektiv* (which means any group imbued with a common purpose, mutual trust, and empathic unity) is the source of the outrage expressed by the Slavophils (Khomyakov, Kireyevsky, Samarin) as well as the radical Westernizers (Hertzen, Bakunin, Ogaryov) when considering West European individualism. While not denying the individual quality of human beings, Russian culture in all its aspects gives witness to the existence of a super-individual, integral, and social principle.

The metaphysical stability of the person does not derive from the individual personality itself. The source of stability lies in his encapsulation within the living Church. However, the individual is not thereby reduced in value. He is not only a part, but one of the unitary wholes of which the indivisible life of the Church is made up. This is the doctrine of the mystical body of Christ. The essential difference between the Russian and the Roman Church is that the former tends to emphasize the concrete and sensuous reality of the experience of communion with the Saints, whereas the latter takes a more cognitive, almost legalistic view, emphasizing the 'contractual' aspect of belonging to a corporate institution which has both a concrete and a spiritual aspect.

These themes were for many centuries the basic sources of the general theory of the nature of human beings and of behaviour. The idea that it could be possible to develop an account of conduct which started from different, secular assumptions was perforce confronted by the fact that the area it sought to conquer for science was already occupied by an elaborate, coherent, and systematic doctrine which conceded no place for opposition viewpoints.

(iv) The Movement for Change: Reform or Revolution?

The influences which eventually put an end to this monolithic system of state power, ecclesiastical monopoly, and serf exploitation are diverse in origin and complex in historical development. Various movements of religious dissent, beginning with the fifteenth century running in parallel with the Reformation in Europe; the social, military, and industrial innovations of Peter I; the peasant wars of Pugachev and Razin; new concepts of science and freedom of inquiry which were developed by selected students during State-sponsored education abroad – these were major influences in giving rise to an independent secular culture without which a science of psychology is ruled out.

Psychology developed in opposition to Orthodox anthropology. Not only did the basic tenets of religion devalue empirical inquiry in general, but the special problems of psychology had been pre-empted for centuries by theological doctrines about 'the soul'. These views claimed the sanction of Divine Truth and debarred secular investigation. The thoughtful inquirer in this area was immediately involved in a confrontation with all the powers of Church and State, as soon as he began to deviate from the narrow line of Orthodox belief. The religious wars, doctrinal discussions, movements of dissent, martyrdoms, and persecutions which worked themselves out over a decent interval in the West were compressed into a relatively narrow compass of years in imperialist Russia. The first psychologists were, willy-nilly, radicals hardly to be distinguished from revolutionaries. They were persecuted by the authorities; their works were censored and often forbidden publication; they were exiled; they were hampered in their work by lack of material facilities; always they were subject to police surveillance. They were engaged in a war of liberation in which their weapons were pen and ink, reason and logic; on the other side there seemed to be no limit to the official violence which might be used against them.

Paradoxically, however, the main breach in the entrenched system of conservative and Orthodox ideology had been effected by innovatory impulses set in train by the imperialist ambitions of one ruler and the vanity of another. Peter I, regarded by many of his Russian contemporaries as the Anti-Christ, fostered the mechanical arts and Western ways of thought in the interest of military capability. By his draconic application of the criterion of efficient service to the State as the basis of advancement he alienated the old aristocracy; by his personal scepticism and his secularization of State power he (temporarily) removed the official seal of approval from Orthodox belief and fostered a critical spirit in general. After his death, Catherine II, prior to 1789, was responsible for introducing Voltairean ideas into Russia, and for fostering the ideals of the Enlightenment. Shcherbatov associates 'the corruption of morals in Russia' (1786) with these innovations and the personal degeneracy of the Romanov autocrats.

It was Alexander Pushkin who said of Tsar Peter that he had 'cut a window through to Europe'. In pursuit of his Europeanization policy Peter passed decrees making literacy obligatory for children of the nobility and clergy. He established the 'Table of Ranks' by which, through promotion based on service to the State, it was possible to achieve the privileges and titles of nobility; he forced men to shave their beards and women to come out of their oriental seclusion; he introduced the sciences and arts to Russia, especially those technologies having to do with war and the industries which supply the materials of war. Initially supported in these labours by foreigners who had settled in Moscow, Peter soon became the storm-centre which generated a wave of innovation based on the granting of State monopolies and a ruthless drive towards imperialist expansion.

Among the problems bequeathed by Peter to succeeding Tsars was that of controlling the process of change which he had unleashed. The question they confronted was: how can we ensure that necessary changes are introduced 'from above' by decree and not sponsored 'from below' by revolution? Reform as a government-sponsored monopoly, or revolution as an activity of the private entrepreneur – this was the question!

In the history of innovation and secularization of the Russian thought-pattern we cannot exclude Catherine II. For a time, she amused herself by posing as a social critic with tendencies towards enlightened liberalism. In plays, essays, and satirical journals which she established, this German princess entertained her Court and her French *claque* (which included Voltaire) by holding up the laziness and obscurantism of Old Russia to ridicule. She toyed with the ideas of the French Enlightenment and of English Liberalism. Court circles understood that the game was not intended to be taken too seriously. A measure of her sincerity is the fact that she rewarded Bearde de l'Abbaye with a thousand ducats for a prize essay on the emancipation of the peasant serfs whereas it is an historical fact that, during her reign, the number of serfs rose from seven and a half to twenty million. A considerable proportion of this increase consisted of free peasants presented as her personal gift to successful generals, statesmen, and lovers. She forbade landlords to be cruel to their peasants, but simultaneously made the order ineffective by forbidding the enslaved peasants to send her their grievances as had been the custom previously.

After the peasant revolt led by Pugachev, the innovatory impulse passed from the Court to the radical intelligentsia. Dissatisfaction with social conditions, in particular with the system of serfdom and with the condition of the people, was manifest in the writings of Novikov, Fonvizin, and Radishchev. The social disturbance, to which dissatisfaction gave rise, was confined initially to the expression of concern and criticism through the printed word. Radishchev attacked the censorship, and the attitudes and behaviour of serf-owners to their slaves. Novikov satirized the frivolity of the Court and the boorishness of social life. Fonvizin wrote with bitter irony of the laziness and obscurantism of Russian society and expressed his indignation at the condition of the serf.

The way in which Court circles handled these symptoms of disturbance (by death sentence, exile, imprisonment, censorship) effectively put an end to the movement for social betterment which these authors had hoped to sponsor.

Pugachev's revolt (1773–75) shook official circles to their foundations. Catherine imposed a very strict censorship on the printed and spoken word. The French Revolution of 1789 completed her conversion from fantasies of 'enlightened despotism' to autocratic absolutism. Abruptly she abandoned all pretence of liberal ideas. The Freemasons and other voluntary societies were disbanded; many books and journals were suppressed, including Catherine's own writings, in particular her early reform plans which had never been implemented. Novikov was thrown into jail. Radishchev was sentenced to death for his *Journey from Saint Petersburg to Moscow* (1790) in which he describes the condition of the serfs. The death sentence was commuted to Siberian exile. Henceforth critics of Russian society under the Empress confined their remarks to their private journals. Even so, the private papers of influential thinkers, such as Lomonosov and Shcherbatov, were confiscated at their deaths by agents of the government.

European ideas continued to influence Russian life and affairs, but only in the form of literary, domestic, and sartorial fashions. Novel ideas from the West in these restricted fields were quickly assimilated by the minor nobility and landed gentry. But the forces of social inertia, especially peasant illiteracy and religious obscurantism, ensured that the basic values of the vast majority, like the property relations which these reflected, persisted from decade to decade, unchangeable and unchanged. The intellectual currents which strongly affected the thought-patterns of the radical Russian intelligentsia from 1790 through the nineteenth century could find no legitimate expression in any social, political, or educational organization. The censorship of opinion and the police control of social action made impossible any public discussion of social issues. Talk about reforms could be carried on only in small, clandestine groups under conditions of considerable risk. The fate of the Decembrists (1825) set the seal on an era characterized by the total supremacy of the bureaucracy. As far as influencing the decisions of the Tsar was concerned, this meant the exclusion of *all* social classes, other than the great landowners, from any contact with the levers of government power. Social and political initiatives could now be contemplated only in opposition to the Tsar and his bureaucracy.

The war against Napoleon had marked a new phase. Progressive, not to say revolutionary, ideas were exported by the *Grande Armée* to the countries which it overran. Ideas of a constitution for Russia, of democracy, even of a republic, began to be bandied about once more. The conspirators in this case were drawn from the minor nobility: they had picked up their revolutionary ideas in the army. It is paradoxical that under the régime of Alexander I and Nicholas I the military were, for long periods, the most progressive sector of society.

These 'repentant nobles' became known as the 'Decembrists' (*Dekabristy*) because their palace revolution was set for the 14 December 1825. They are significant in the history of Russian thought by virtue of their conception that a bridge must be built between the social élite and the peasant masses. The theme of a social debt which the nobles and intellectuals owed to the people became the inspiration and motive force of most of the attempts to enlighten and liberate the serf and working population of the Empire throughout the nineteenth century. The ironical comment of Count Rostopchin (Governor of Moscow in 1812), when told of the abortive coup, points up the anomalous situation of the revolutionaries: 'Formerly revolutions were made by peasants who wanted to become gentlemen: now gentlemen try to make a revolution so as to become cobblers'.[5]

The historical significance of the *Dekabristy* was the inspiration they gave to the revolutionaries who came after them. Hertzen, Ogaryov, and Sazonov, who organized one of the earliest student circles, the Russian Fourierists (1831–34), counted themselves 'sons of the Decembrists'. The student movement inherited the problem of revolution – or rather, they had it thrust on them by the secret police. To begin with, the embryonic movement consisted of a handful of students who were interested in self-improvement. They set out to study ideal social organizations so as to discover the ethical principle demanded by a clear perception of the 'Good'. The 'movement' existed as 'circles' which discussed, amongst other things, constitutions and ideal societies. It was this aspect of the 'circles' which led the police and Court circles to perceive them as 'conspirators'. It was this kind of organization in the Guards' regiments which had previously been the seedbed of Palace revolts. The Decembrists were still a living memory. Police action against 'conspiracy', as much as theoretical conviction, led the circles to the next phase, namely, propaganda (1853).

The revolutionary impulse expressed itself in a number of

forms in the years 1859–62. It was in this period that scientific psychology originated. At this time the whole of Russian society was in a revolutionary ferment. The Crimean war had revealed the decadence and inefficiency of official Russia. There was the persistent economic crisis in serf agriculture. Continuing rumours of an emancipation decree acted to unsettle the peasants and to maintain them in a condition of anxious expectation. Their unease kept the bureaucracy in a state of fearful apprehension. As a result, the anticipated freedom was withheld. This still further aggravated the unrest. A kind of chain reaction was set up with an escalation in the demands for reform. Their response to these revealed more and more the impotence and inflexibility of the ruling circles.

A useful index of the state of unrest is the number of peasant uprisings. According to the official figures there were 1,186 between 1826 and 1861. In fact, there were certainly more as it was politic not to admit, even within the ranks of the government bureaucracy, the real condition of social unrest. On fourteen esates, a Tsarist commission discovered that peasant disturbances had continued over a period of from ten to forty years. The reason behind the disturbances was clearly economic. Periodically major uprisings took place which involved whole regions. In a period of sixty years (1801–61), as has already been indicated, agricultural production had remained stationary in face of an ever-increasing population. This 'crisis of production' was aggravated by the export of 'surplus' grain by the landlords eager to capitalize on the markets created by the English repeal of the corn laws. Coupled with periodic droughts, this policy gave rise to recurrent famines in Russia.

Conditions in the towns were not much better. The intellectual classes, denied any place in the social hierarchy and any valid social role, in ever-increasing numbers accepted the revolutionary views of Hertzen and Chernishevski. Under the Autocracy, novel ideas on the social question or on religious questions forced the innovator into opposition and then, if he continued 'obdurate', by virtue of the logic inherent in the Russian situation into revolutionary activities. Any discussion, public or private, which ventured outside the limits of Orthodoxy, Autocracy, and Narodnost' ('national character' – that is, the established order of serfdom, patriarchalism, and obedience) was automatically the subject of police action until at least 1905.

Following the Emancipation Decree (1861), with its onerous

conditions which left the peasant worse rather than better off, the political movement, whilst continuing to use discussion, conspiracy, and propaganda, turned to agitation as a tactic in the continuing class struggle. This involved encouraging groups of students, peasants, or workers to react against specific injustices in the here-and-now situation by direct action – for example by a group protest, the withholding of labour, by demonstrating.

Due to the Tsarist censorship on the written and the spoken word, due to police interference which involved the use of *agents provocateurs,* due to the judicial process which decimated their ranks, the revolutionaries were driven to the next step – namely terrorism. The transition to the use of assassination (in 1878) as a political activity represented an 'act of faith' in the revolutionary impulse of the masses. The terrorist groups believed that it required merely an example to set the masses in motion against official society. However, the limited or total lack of response to the assassination of Tsarist officials, coupled with the very detailed preparations required, led to certain rules for survival in this dangerous game being evolved, largely by a process of trial and error. Conventions about dress, behaviour, morality, and social attitudes were developed and accepted as a binding code which the revolutionist must follow. The code and the norms of behaviour ensured group soldarity. They operated in the direction of the survival of the group as well as to protect the individual.

It was within this matrix that the specific features of Russian revolutionary psychology were hammered out. From the 1840s until the 1860s, the various alternatives, and the different stages of development of the revolutionary process, had been analysed by the theoreticians of the 'movement' in terms of the kinds of person capable of enduring the burden of the revolution as well as the 'new men' who would build the ideal society and be generated by it. This is the significance of the social movement for the development of a theoretical psychology on an alternative basis, and for the characteristic emphases in Soviet psychology which perceives itself to be the legatee of this revolutionary inheritance.

In spite of internecine quarrels, splits, and realignments, the Russian 'movement' proceeded to the next phase – organization (1881). This involved the building-up of a large and integrated political movement. In addition to several main centres, there were a number of 'wings' which accommodated the various trends of thought. These could severally 'specialize' in the use of any of the methods they believed to be appropriate in particular situations – whether education, terrorism, propaganda, agitation, or sabotage. Within this loosely knit framework, all sections accepted the common political objective of the transference of state power from the Tsar. Not all were agreed as to what should replace him. The long-prepared-for assassination of Alexander II in 1881, and the disappointing sequel – nothing changed except that police persecution became more vigorous – accelerated the acceptance of a realistic and gradualist programme of building up a public opinion which would accept the need for change and learn how to bring it about.

(v) The Situation of the Intellectual in Tsarist Russia

In Western Europe the process of emancipation of the thought-process from the trammels both of religious dogma and of nationalism was initiated by the Reformation in the first case, and by the Renaissance in the other. By the middle of the seventeenth century an international community of scholars existed. With some few exceptions and limitations, these were relatively free to pursue their inquiries without police or clerical supervision. The history of persecution in Western Europe in the modern period (from 1789) is connected more with the assault on trade-unionism, socialism, and the movement for women's emancipation. Science and philosophy, as such, were not involved in these political struggles since freedom of action had already been granted in these areas. Indeed, scholars as a group had achieved a privileged position in most civilized states to the extent that many achieved high office.

The situation of the scholar – whether historian, scientist, or philosopher – in Russia was vastly otherwise. Intellectuals were, willy-nilly, involved in a social struggle with the ruling class such that it was possible to be sentenced to death for writing a book (Radishchev, 1790), for discussing a letter (Dostoievski, 1849), for distributing a manifesto (Ushakov, 1863). Many scientists were under routine police surveillance. Their journals or books, even private letters, were subject to seizure and censorship. For example, Sechenov was refused permission to publish his physiological monograph *Cerebral Reflexes* under its original title; many passages had to be modified to pass the censor. Following the European revolutions of 1848, all intellectuals were persecuted. University chairs of history and philosophy were abolished – 'all teaching was to be based on religious truth'. Many writers were arrested, beaten, or sent to forced labour in Siberia. Scientists, such as Pavlov, Mendelyeyev and Lobachevski, found conditions of work in universities almost impossible. Professors of unorthodox views were deprived of promotions and facilities. As late as Easter 1917, the Tsarist government appointed the Governor of St Petersburg to censor abstracts of papers to be presented to the first All-Russian Congress of Physiologists, having originally refused permission for the conference to meet in case of political demonstrations.

It is impossible to overlook the influence of this determined war against unorthodox opinions (under which heading must be included scientific knowledge in general and non-biblical concepts of human behaviour in particular). It was waged by the Tsarist Autocracy and the ruling Church on the opinions themselves – regardless of the fact that no *actus reus* had even been contemplated. The act of thinking was itself illegal.

The Russian thought-pattern became polarized effectively into two camps – the radical, atheistic, materialist school versus the ultra-conservative, religious, dualistic obscurantism of the ruling class. Thus were the lines of battle drawn. This was hardly at all a process of peaceful discussion of opposing ideas. At every stage it was marked by official violence. This had become a stereotyped response to novel ideas which threatened existing interests, or which seemed to do so. The official violence was answered by acts of revolutionary terrorism. The search for criteria of truth was helped along by devastating wars (Napoleonic, Crimean, Russo-Japanese, World War One). After 1861, the struggle between official society and the revolution was conducted within a matrix of rapid and radical transformations in the economic basis brought about by war, capitalist development, and imperialist conquest. The stagnant agricultural system was broken up by the liberation of the serfs who were able to emigrate in large numbers to the towns. Capitalist enterprise had made available to it a large supply of cheap labour in the form of liberated serfs no longer guaranteed a livelihood by the system of 'concealed agricultural unemployment' which prevailed up to 1861. The landed proprietor no longer drew his tribute from industry in the form of *obrok* payments, now he had instead massive subventions from his liberated serfs which he could invest in a national cost-accounting based system of agriculture. Liberal capitalist political elements withdrew from the political struggle with Tsarism (as shown, for example, in the break-up of the Sunday School movement in

1862). The main contenders were now the revolutionary students and intellectuals on the one hand and the Tsarist bureaucracy on the other. Caught between the main contenders were numerous liberal, humanistic, uncommitted, neutral tendencies. Basically, these were alien importations from a different world.

The succession of costly wars, the political and constitutional stagnation imposed on the country by a rapacious and corrupt bureaucracy, the general economic and social backwardness, the alienation of the intellectual classes by the military-Byzantine police-state, the contrast with Russia's European neighbours – these factors interacted to produce a condition of general and continuing political crisis. This crisis had revolved for decades around the question of peasant emancipation. This was for a number of reasons. Not the least of these was the fact that the peasantry seemed, to those anxious for a total change, to be the only spontaneous revolutionary force universal enough and powerful enough to overturn the ubiquitous, reactionary forces of Tsardom. The peasant uprisings led by Stenka Razin, Pugachev, and by other anonymous leaders, which had engulfed whole regions of the Empire, served as the direct inspiration of Russian peasant socialism.

It is clear that the Empire of the Tsars, from which the Union of Soviet Socialist Republics was formed, had a peculiar history and a manifest destiny which removed it at an early stage from the main influences which determined the historical development of European states. The development of science, the discovery of the Americas, the colonization of Africa, of the Indies, the religious wars, and the break-up of the universal Church into sectarian movements, the development of toleration and liberal parliamentary government took place *all* without direct Russian participation or involvement. The empirical tradition in philosophy symbolized by the names of Locke, Bacon, Hobbes; the scientific revolution represented in the works of Galileo, Kepler, Newton; the social philosophy of Machiavelli, Vico, Beccaria; the legal innovations inspired by Magna Charta, the Bill of Rights, the commentaries of Blackstone, certainly called forth resonances from within the narrow circle of the Russian intelligentsia. But as they had no defined status in society, so the intellectuals had no influence in changing traditional Russian tempos and motifs of life as did their counterparts in Western Europe. Those formative influences, which nurtured psychological thought and gave it a characteristic mould or impress in the West, were missing in

Russia almost to an absolute degree until the mid-nineteenth century. It is this fact which confers on Russian psychology its specific and distinctive quality.

References

1. V. I. Lenin *Development of Capitalism in Russia* 1957: 45–46.
2. Imperial Russian Census of 1858, in P. I. Lyashchenko 1949, chapter 21.
3. Shishkov: quoted by W. H. E. Johnson *Russia's Educational Heritage* 1950.
4. K. P. Pobyedonoscev *L'autocratie russe* 1927 Paris: Payot; *Memoirs of a Russian Statesman* 1898 London: Richards: quoted by J. Hecker *Russian Sociology* 1934: 15–16, 42–48. For Orthodoxy, cf. V. V. Zenkovsky 1951.
5. Rostopchin: quoted by F. Venturi *Roots of Revolution* 1960: 3.

Reading List

Books in English
Haxthausen, A. F. G. M. (1856) *The Russian Empire: Its People, Institutions and Resources* London: Cassell (2 vols.).
Lenin, V. I. (1957) *The Development of Capitalism in Russia* Moscow: Foreign Languages Publ. House.
Lyashchenko, P. I. (1949) *History of the National Economy of Russia to the 1917 Revolution* (2 vols.) London: Macmillan.
Masaryk, T. G. (1919) *The Spirit of Russia* London: Allen and Unwin (2 vols.) (new ed. 3 vols.).
Vucinich, A. (1967) *Science in Russian Culture: A History to 1860* London: P. Owen.
Wallace, D. M. (1912) *Russia* London: Cassell

Books in Other Languages
Petrovsky, A. V. (1967) *Istoriya sovetskoi psikhologii* Moscow: Prosveshcheniye.
Yaroshevsky, M. G. (1966) *Istoriya psikhologii* Moscow: Mysl'.

Chapter 2   *The Origins of Russian Psychology*

The most distinctive feature of Soviet science in general is the refusal to accept dualistic theories as a basis for the explanation of behaviour. Soviet psychologists adopt a partisan position. They assume that science emerges in the struggle against idealism, dualism, and subjectivism. They perceive their present position as originating with those Russian thinkers who propounded the basic principles of materialism and monism. Although initiated by the 'westernizing' Tsars (Peter I, Catherine II), these views were anathema to the orthodox, servile, and autocratic régime. In its origins, Russian psychology is inextricably entangled with philosophical programmes and counter-programmes as well as with the sociopolitical movement.

It is possible to recognize the development of the scientific tendency in psychology along the line: Lomonosov, Radishchev, Belinsky, Chernishevski, and Dobrolyubov. This constellation made a distinctive contribution parallel to, but independent of, the line in West-European thought which runs from Bacon, through Locke, Holbach, and Feuerbach to Marx.

Introduction : Religious Dissent

The history of psychology in Russia is the history of the war between two main tendencies, two ideologies. In the initial stages one of these was completely dominant. It developed over many centuries to a position of total monopoly of the thought-processes. It prevailed in all the centres of power in the State as the official view. It was impossible, except under very special and exceptional circumstances, even to come into contact with an opposing or a *different* view of society, of nature, and of man.

Any oppositional view had, perforce, to develop from within

the dominant ideology. It was compelled to dissent from the mono-lithic thought-pattern by emphasizing and appealing to certain tenets within the system at the expense of others. In other words the alternative ideology made its appearance in the first instance as heresy. It was the sectarians or schismatics (Raskolniki) who made the first breach in the closed system of Orthodox pre-suppositions about the nature of man. These schismatics criticized the Orthodox reverence for idols, their belief in miracle-workers. They condemned the luxurious Church ceremonial and ritual. Most important of all, they opened the door through which it was possible to advance from their position by criticizing the reveren-tial treatment of the letter of Holy Writ. The appeal to inner free-dom from this worship of the 'God of the Dead', with the new conception of every man his own church, has been categorized by Marx as the beginnings of the ideology of individualism. The social protest of a new economic group (the bourgeoisie) was clothed at this stage in religious form. Following the same line of thought, Engels has said that the revolutionary opposition to feudalism in Europe took three forms: mysticism, heresy, and armed rebellion. The great variety of forms assumed by religious dissent in Russia is indicative of the depth of protest that existed. In their content of ideas these heretical movements represent the first stirrings of a secularized psychology. Historically speaking, dissent was the first unconscious movement towards a new view of the human psyche.

(i) Russian Humanism under Peter –the 'Learned Guard'

The Europeanization process initiated by Peter left the established sociopolitical order untouched, strengthening certain institutions, primarily the State bureaucracy and the autocratic régime, and weakening others such as the old nobility and the established Church. Although Peter's reforms were superficial, touching only those areas of Russian life which inhibited the development and implementation of his 'great power' aspirations, he initiated a process of social change in the same way as did the licence given to Jewish usurers in medieval Christian Europe. Haltingly, and with many compromises, his 'learned guard' subverted the stranglehold of Orthodox conceptions which prevented any secular concept of human nature (or even of animal behaviour) being formulated. Prokopovich, Tatishchev, and Kantemir suc-ceeded in establishing the notion that a science of man was conceivable which would be independent of, but not necessarily contradictory to, theology. Using the concept of natural law they argued for religious toleration, for a secularized curriculum, and especially for freedom of scientific investigation. Whilst remaining orthodox in their profession of Christian belief, they attacked Russian ecclesiasticism for the way in which it fostered idleness, ignorance, and intolerance.

It is of considerable historical interest that the person initiating these attacks was himself a bishop – Theophan Prokopovich (1681–1736). In his sermons and speeches he consistently supported Peter's innovations and celebrated his victories. Like Peter he was a foe of monasticism. After Peter's death a complaint was lodged against him that he:

> . . . abusively refers to orthodox bishops and church dignitaries as scribes and Pharisees. . . . He calls Russian priests gluttons, hypocrites and shamans; he calls monks black peasants and devils. He wants to eradicate monasticism, cloisters and nunneries.[1]

The most important aspect of Prokopovich's strictures on ecclesiasticism was that they originated not from the religious sentiment but from the concrete utilitarianism which Peter applied as a touchstone to all the institutions and social phenomena of his day. The learning of Peter's 'wise heads' differed in its nature from that of the 'long beards' (Peter's term for the clergy). Even in the best cases, the latter were good 'reciters' – they had a store of information and belief culled from the scriptures and devotional literature. The 'learned guard', on the other hand, were intellectuals, well educated in European literature and philosophy. Under Peter's influence, they were encouraged to look at Russian realities (including Orthodox customs and beliefs) with the sceptical eye of science and contemporary European philosophy. Prokopovich was familiar with the works of Pierre Bayle (1647–1706) and followed his lead in advocating toleration of religious dissent – even toleration of atheism. This was in spite of the fact that he wrote a *Discourse* attacking 'the atheist Spinoza' on the grounds that in his philosophical system there was no place for the concept of the immortal soul. As a Uniate priest he had studied in Rome; according to the reports of foreign travellers, his interests and lifestyle were more those of a Renaissance prince than of an Orthodox bishop.

The second member of the 'learned guard' was Antioch

Dmitryevich Kantemir (1708–1744). In the denunciation presented by the holy synod in 1757 to the Empress Elizabeth, *A Report on Books written against our Faith and Morality*, the Church authorities asked for severe punishment for those who wrote or printed anything contrary to the Holy Faith or which was in conflict with accepted belief. Kantemir's translation of Fontenelle's *Conversations on the Plurality of Worlds* was one of the books singled out for attack. Kantemir was not a sceptic, except in so far as he wished to reconcile the religious sentiment with the demands of science. He was criticized for accepting the Copernican theory. In his *Letters on Nature and Man* (1742) he follows Descartes closely, emphasizing that man consists of soul and body which are of different natures or substance; that we have an innate idea of God; that human beings have free will and are therefore responsible moral agents. As a career-diplomat in London and Paris, Kantemir adopted many of the views of the West European Enlightenment, whilst at the same time loyally supporting the autocratic principles of Russian Tsardom.

Tatishchev (1686–1750) was the main ideological support of Peter in his reforms of the educational curriculum, previously monopolized by the ecclesiastics. For theology and metaphysics Peter substituted the applied sciences; education was thrown open to a new class; new secular objectives were defined. Tatishchev justified these changes, as well as the whole concept of education, from a utilitarian standpoint. He attacked the clergy as 'villainous church officials' who sought 'to keep the people in the dark, and to prevent them from understanding any truth, to have them submit blindly and slavishly to their word and command.' However, like Kantemir, his view of human behaviour remained predominantly theological. Whilst arguing in principle for the independence of natural science from theology, he maintained that there could be no conflict between them. He formulated an ethical doctrine based on the principle of utility and believed that sensible egoism (a moderate self-love) was the mainspring of all virtues. The concept of 'sin' he defined in the sense of 'acts harmful to man'. He anticipated many of the ideas of Jeremy Bentham in relation to social questions whilst remaining Orthodox in his conception of human nature. He believed that 'the essence of the soul is the spirit which is devoid of matter and of component parts, consequently indestructible and therefore immortal'. In spite of the Orthodox character of his beliefs, his particular mode of thought remained as a living influence in Russian literature. He was the first to use the scientific approach to historical questions, to social phenomena, and to the lives of ordinary people – their peculiarities, customs, and traditions. Tatishchev, as a member of Peter's 'learned guard' (the phrase belongs to Prokopovich) more than anyone else was responsible for beginning the process of secularization of thought about behaviour which found clearest expression in the 'enlighteners' of the 1860s – Chernishevski and Dobrolyubov.

Tatishchev wrote two treatises which dealt with psychological problems (both published in 1733). The first was entitled *A Conversation on the Usefulness of Science and of Schools*, the second was his *Testament to my Son*. These are unoriginal compilations of materials drawn from West European sources, especially from Walch's *Philosophisches Lexikon* (1726). However, in contrast to the contemporary treatment of psychology in the Peter Mogila Academy in Kiev and the Slav–Greek–Latin Academy in Moscow, derived entirely from Aristotle and scholasticism, Tatishchev introduced a new note from the West by demonstrating that psychological topics need not be monopolized by theology. Leaning heavily on Leibniz, he describes the task of psychology as 'to know the powers and the potentialities of the soul.' His primary concern is to convince his readers of the practical necessity of instruction, and of schools, in the development of human beings.

(ii) Mikhail Vasilievich Lomonosov (1711–1765)

Russia boasts at least one universal genius. Lomonosov is significant in the history of psychology not so much for his direct contributions in this area, but for his approach to reality and his style of thinking. One of the founders of Moscow University, now named after him, Lomonosov was at least a century before his time in his contributions to the natural sciences – chemistry, physics, geography, geology. He also achieved fame as the first truly Russian poet, laying the basis by his poetry, as well as by his linguistic analyses for the Russian literary language. Unlike Peter, he was a Russian patriot in the best sense of the word – unconcerned about military conquest and imperialist expansion, he interested himself in the welfare of the broad mass of the population and concerned himself with the correct interpretation of the history of the nation.

Lomonosov represents the modern spirit of free intellectual inquiry. He strongly supported the principle of scientific investigation of natural and social phenomena, untrammelled by the constraints imposed by the Church and the primitive conceptions of Hebrew and Greek cosmology. In 1760 he suggested a principle which should apply to university teaching: 'That the clergy should not cavil at teachings which demonstrate the truths of nature and which make for improvement and enlightenment; in particular, they should not vilify the sciences in their sermons.'[2]

In his satirical poem *A Hymn to the Beard* he lampooned the priests who covered themselves with beards as 'a curtain for their false ideas'. The holy synod petitioned the Empress to have this and his other satirical verses banned publicly, and Lomonosov to be brought before them for 'exhortation' and 'correction'. He was accused of blasphemy.

It is clear that Lomonosov was a deist, if not an atheist. He belonged to that company of thinkers which had already freed itself from the power of the feudal nobility and the dictatorship of the Church in Western Europe. Modern science, including the science of psychology, was a product of this revolution. Lomonosov, like his European counterparts two centuries previously, boldly challenged the monopoly of truth claimed by the Russian Orthodox Church, demanding freedom of inquiry and of publication for scientific works. In defending himself against the demands of the holy synod that he should suffer severe punishment for suggesting that there may be life on the planet Venus, he said that God had given mankind two books – the first is science, the other is Sacred Writ:

> In the book which reveals the constitution of this visible world, physicists, mathematicians, astronomers and others who elucidate divine actions which influence nature play the same part as do the prophets, the apostles and the teachers of the Church in the second book. The mathematician is not sound in judgement if he wishes to measure the divine will with a compass, nor is the teacher of theology if he thinks that he is able to study astronomy or chemistry from the psalter.[3]

The elements in Lomonosov's thinking which set him in opposition to the prevailing ecclesiastical monopoly of thought may be summarily stated as follows: the appeal to empirical reality as the final criterion of truth; the search for the interconnectedness of processes and things in terms of causes uniformly producing effects (for example, evolution; the law of conservation of energy); the explanation of social phenomena and the history of peoples in terms of forces observable in the here-and-now instead of as the consequences of divine intervention or the arbitrary decisions of Tsars; the immense significance of economics, industrial production, agriculture, and trade on the development of human life and science. These principles appear to us today as truisms. But in the Russia of the eighteenth century, as in Western Europe in the sixteenth, each new scientific conception was evaluated as belonging to the realm of Divine truth (if it seemed to be in conformity with current interpretations of the scriptures) or as a profanation inspired by Satan (if the reverse). The latter case was liable, according to the conceptions then prevalent, to lead to the destruction of Divine Truth as a whole, as one bad apple corrupts the total store.

Lomonosov's deism, expressed clearly in his verses, can be regarded as the formal declaration of his alienation not only from the Orthodox Church but from Christianity. His poetic themes are drawn entirely from the Old Testament – never from the New. In practice, deism is a philosophy which allows the scientist all the benefits of atheism (notably, absolving him of any responsibility for conforming his theories to religious 'truth') whilst saving him from persecution and censorship by the established powers.

It is to Lomonosov's credit that he won the first battle for free intellectual inquiry in Russia. His services to the State enabled successive Empresses to overlook his controversies with the priests, as well as the plain-speaking he indulged in in his 'congratulatory' odes written for royal occasions. The poet Pushkin, writing in 1834, summed up Lomonosov's work and career: 'He was a great man. Between Peter I and Catherine II he was the only original champion of the Enlightenment. He founded the first university (in Russia). To speak more appropriately, he *was* our first university.'[4]

It is of interest to discover the kind of views which, even if innovatory, were acceptable, then and later, to the Orthodox who sought to persecute Lomonosov. Gregory Savvich Skovorodova (1722–1794) was his contemporary, and is honoured as being 'the first Russian philosopher in the strict sense of the word'. A wandering 'pilgrim' most of his adult life, Skovorodova enshrined his teachings in Platonic dialogue form. His themes are similar to those of contemporary Christian existentialism. His central concern was the nature of man. The doctrine he propounded was based in part on his readings in ancient and European philosophy, but more particularly on the psychological views of the ancient

Hebrews. In his wanderings the most essential piece of luggage consisted of the Hebrew Bible. A typical contribution of Skovorodova follows: 'What is the heart, if not the soul? What is the soul, if not a bottomless abyss of thought? What is thought, if not the root, the seed and the grain of all our flesh and blood, and of all other appearance?'[5]

This conception of the heart as the master of all else in man, 'the true man', is the central explanatory principle of human conduct as seen by Skovorodova. He taught that all external appearances were only a mark which conceals not only the soul (heart) of man, but also the spiritual body of man. This is forever mysterious and hidden. All things are to be viewed in this dualistic way – this is the essence of Skovorodova's method. Thus there are not only two bodies, there are two 'hearts' in man. Empirical man is but the 'shadow' or 'dream' of the true man. This true man in us is, of course, the Lord Jesus Christ who is in all of us but remains forever whole and undivided.

Skovorodova's ethics are based on the principle of submission to the 'secret' laws of the spirit – the struggle is with oneself, with the evil within and not with any external reality of evil. 'Accuse not the world, this corpse is not to blame; the root of sinfulness lies in man himself and in Satan.' As befits one who rejects the empirical world and who claims to have hated life, Skovorodova waxed ironical about the notions of progress, of human equality, and of understanding empirical reality:

> We have measured the sea, the earth, the atmosphere, and the heavens; we have disturbed the earth's womb for metals, discovered a countless multitude of worlds. We construct incomprehensible machines . . . Every day brings new experiments and marvellous inventions. Is there anything we cannot conceive or carry out? But the sad thing is that, in all of this, *greatness* is lacking.[6]

Thus, at the very outset, two opposing philosophies are in direct confrontation: Skovorodova represents one pole. Lomonosov the other. The dualistic dogmas of the Church proclaim that the human psyche is not to be discovered by empirical inquiry – not only is the attempt to do so sacrilegious, it is also irrelevant, impossible, and misconceived. Human nature, in all its perversity and rottenness, is best revealed by intensive contemplation of the truth as revealed by God through the prophets, through revelation, and in the works of the Fathers of the Church.

(iii) Radishchev and the Origins of Materialist Psychology

Peter's 'learned guard' were licensed critics of Old Russia, given limited rights by the Autocrat to attack certain aspects of social life which inhibited his work of 'modernization'. Under Catherine, Alexander Nikolaevich Radishchev (1749–1802) took it upon himself to publish a devastating criticism of the whole social system – including serfdom, militarism, censorship, the established religion, even the Empress herself and her favourites. Catherine II, personally involved, if not responsible for the murder of two Tsars, saw in him a man who wished to usurp the sovereign power. She had him sentenced to death, commuting the sentence subsequently to exile to Siberia. In her marginal notes to Radishchev's famous *A Journey from St. Petersburg to Moscow,* written as instructions to the notorious inquisitor Sheshkovsky, she reveals the essentially commonplace nature of her mind.

In this book, as in his other writings, Radishchev reveals himself as a deist, very much influenced by the European Enlightenment. In his student days in Leipzig he assimilated the ideas of writers such as Leibniz, Voltaire, d'Alembert, Montesquieu, Adam Smith, Rousseau, Locke, as well as the classical authors, Plato, Aristotle, Lucretius, Plutarch, and others. If we wished to characterize his thought in terms of his basic assumptions, the most accurate description would be that he was an Aristotelian. His critique of Russian society stems from the concept of natural law, the operation of which can be recognized in man's rational nature which models the divine wisdom. It is the divine wisdom which governs the universe. According to Radishchev the dignity of man, which belongs to him by virtue of his nature as a thinking being, implies freedom. This manifests itself in the rights of religious toleration, including toleration for atheism; free association; freedom of expression without censorship including the publication of so-called 'pornography'; freedom of movement; and due process of law operating without distinction of social rank or status.

In his theory of education Radishchev closely follows Locke, Rousseau, and Basedow. He rejects compulsion of the growing child by adults, substituting for force the principle of unobtrusive guidance towards desirable goals. Children should be allowed to go barefooted and bareheaded to be 'hardened'. A régime of hard work and physical effort with coarse food, 'country fare', is best for the growing child. A neglect of the courtly arts is the ideal, but this does not exclude a knowledge of painting, music, and the art of self-defence from the curriculum.

In his psychological views Radishchev was strongly influenced by Locke, Priestley, and Helvetius, although not simply a copyist of their ideas. Whilst accepting the complete reality and materiality of the external world, he found the doctrine that all ideas arise out of experience of empirical reality unacceptable. The mind is not a clean slate receiving impressions. On the contrary, there are certain innate ideas which develop irrespective of sense impressions, chief of these is the idea of God. Man thinks with a bodily organ (the brain): experience is the basis of all natural knowledge.

But Radishchev makes a distinction between *sense* experience and *rational* experience. Sense impressions are retained in the mind: with the aid of reason, which works on these, we develop clear ideas and are guided towards general principles. In this way the senses and the reason are reconciled: any distinction between them is a matter only of degree and in terms of their origins. Reality is fully knowable by man. Following Priestley in his concept of the dynamic nature of matter, he finds it necessary to defend the materialist position even against him, in asserting that in the analysis of the properties of matter we must ensure that matter itself does not 'disappear'. He asserts the unity of nature: 'Man is kin – born of the same womb – to everything that lives on the earth; not only beast and bird but also plant, fungus, metal, stone, earth.'[7] From Herder he accepts a theory of evolution which links inorganic with organic nature, and man with the lower animals, in a staircase of creation. Man differs from the lower animals by virtue of his rational intelligence and by his limitless power to perfect himself.

These various positions which Radishchev assumed, set within a framework of atheistic materialism, represent the most fundamental presuppositions of Soviet psychology. They were reasserted by Lenin in 1909. Radishchev was the first Russian thinker to provide a comprehensive social and philosophical doctrine independent of ecclesiastical trappings. Whilst accepting the existence of God and the immortality of the soul, he made no use of these ideas in the elaboration and defence of his ideas. He was divorced completely from allegiance to any religious group. His unique synthesis of Western thought was an armoury from which later social critics like Pushkin, Belinsky, Hertzen, and the men of the sixties drew their weapons as social critics and materialist thinkers.

(iv) Belinsky – Founder of Russian Materialism

In the history of Russian Marxist psychology, Vissarion Grigorievich Belinsky (1811–1848) must be considered the forerunner and pathfinder. In his writings after 1840 we find the earliest comprehensive statement of a system of thought which constitutes the basic pattern of assumptions of Soviet psychology. In these writings the camps of militant atheism, monism, dialectical method, and materialism reach the level of self-consciousness; in him the second great philosophical tendency in Russian thought finds a leader. The tendencies are, of course, religious Orthodox Christian philosophy and atheistic materialism.

In his philosophical development Belinsky followed the route traversed independently by Marx. Starting from Hegel and idealism, he graduated to left-Hegelianism under the influence of Feuerbach, from thence to materialism. Belinsky was a literary critic writing for the popular periodical press and seeking through this medium to propagate advanced political and social ideas. Under the influence of Bakunin, he followed a contorted and often contradictory path – from criticism of social realities (especially serfdom) to 'reconciliation' with Tsarist institutions as the embodiment of the rationality of the Absolute Idea, to embittered denunciation of Church and State and the propagation of revolutionary-democratic ideals. His early death from tuberculosis saved him from ending up in the Peter and Paul fortress in St Petersburg where, as he was ghoulishly assured by the governor, Skobelev, they had prepared a 'warm welcome' for him.

Belinsky grew up in the climate of nationalism and patriotism which followed the war with Napoleon. Memories of 1812, the Battle of Borodino, the burning of Moscow, the capture of Paris by Russian troops, remained living realities from the tales he had heard of these great events in his nursery years. A second major source of inspiration was the Decembrist conspiracy of 1825. The participants in this affair thought in a confused way of abolishing serfdom, destroying Tsarism, and introducing a constitutional monarchy. Some thought of a republic and of total revolution.

At the age of nineteen Belinsky was expelled from Moscow University for his revolutionary play *Dmitri Kalinin* in which he attacked the institution of serfdom. Throughout the 1830s he remained a critic of Russian institutions in so far as these were based on inequality and serfdom. But at this time his views were based on idealistic philosophy – until 1837 on Schelling, after that date on Hegel. Under the influence of Hegel's formula – 'All that is real is rational, and all that is rational is real' – Belinsky was able, for a few months, to reconcile himself to Russian realities and preach submission to the will of the Tsar, Nicholas I. Much more lasting in its effects on his thought was his encounter with Hegel's dialectical method. He understood this, in the same sense as Hertzen, as 'the algebra of revolution'. Throughout the forties, until his death, he preached revolution and atheism, attacking the three foundations of the Tsarist régime – serfdom, the Autocratic government, and the Orthodox Church. He was a socialist, drawing inspiration not only from German philosophy but from French Utopian social critics, especially Saint-Simon and Leroux. In a letter to Botkin, dated 28 June 1841, he says, 'There has developed in me a kind of wild, frenzied, fanatical love of freedom and the independent human personality, which are possible only in a society founded on truth and virtue.'[8]

The characteristic features of Belinsky's philosophical views in the 1840s – all of which set him in opposition to the reigning powers – were: (i) his belief in the power of reason and of scientific understanding; (ii) his deeply expressed hostility towards any theological or idealistic theory of man; (iii) a social critique based on revolutionary humanism and concern for the individual; and (iv) the attempt to develop and apply a dialectical and objective method as a basis for understanding reality. He accepted development, by which he meant the transition from lower to higher forms of being, as an absolute law or principle which operates in all spheres of existence – in nature, in society, and in human consciousness. Following Hegel, and paralleling the thought of Marx, he believed that the source of development must be sought *within* phenomena. In other words, the principle of contradiction is at the root of change. In controversy with the Slavophils he asserted:

These people would like to assure themselves and others that stagnation is better than movement, that the old is always better than the new, that living in the past is real, true life filled with happiness and morality. They agree, although very reluctantly, that the world has always changed and has never stood long at the moral freezing-point: but they regard this as the cause of all the evils in the world.[9]

Belinsky's writings, partly due to the conditions of censorship and the Tsarist persecution of dissident opinions, were mainly in the field of aesthetics and literary criticism. Under Nicholas, this was the only medium through which, using a special terminology to refer to forbidden authors and forbidden ideas, it was possible to express social, political, or religious criticism. For reading a letter from Belinsky to Gogol, expressed in clear terms, twenty-one members of Petrashevsky's circle (which included Dostoievsky) were led out for public execution, only to be reprieved and exiled to Siberia at the last moment. It was in this way that the war against ideas was waged. Belinsky himself was under constant police surveillance.

More than anyone else, the development and acceptance of the 'realistic' movement in Russian literature must be placed to his credit. Demanding that the world be taken as it is, in its materiality and unity, he sought to convince his generation that this approach corresponds not only to the demands of science but of practical life.

His psychological conceptions draw their strength from the same source. According to Belinsky, psychology must rest on the foundation of physiology and anatomy. The activity of the mind is the result of the activity of the cerebral hemispheres. Pure thought, mind without flesh, is a logical dream, a lifeless abstraction. But this does not imply that mental activity can be explained solely in terms of physiological laws – on the contrary. Mental activity has its own specific features which can only be studied in the activities of mind itself. Nevertheless, he maintained, 'Psychology which is not based on physiology is as unsubstantial as physiology that knows not of the existence of anatomy.'[10]

In other words, Belinsky asserts the unity of the human organism. He denies the independent existence of a non-material soul. Man's spiritual nature can be studied only in inseparable connection with his physical nature, and in relation to his environment. Thought cannot be *identified* with matter, although it cannot take place in the absence of matter. Following in the tradition of Lomonosov, he claimed that 'factual' knowledge (derived from empirical experience) and 'philosophical' knowledge (based on ratiocination and abstraction) must be combined and any contradiction between them resolved by practical activity. The essence of cognition is the 'understanding of facts'. Truth is concrete but is, at the same time, relative. This contradiction is at the roots of

our understanding of reality: it is resolved in the recognition that
cognition is a historical process:

> Pure absolute truth is merely a logical abstraction; all living
> truth always bears the impress of the provisional, the tenta-
> tive. . . . Truth develops historically, it is sown, watered with
> sweat and is later reaped, threshed and winnowed: a great deal
> of husk must be blown away to get at the kernel.[11]

In his celebrated 'Letter to Gogol', Belinsky laid out a programme which was taken up and developed by later thinkers and
scientists belonging to this tendency:

> Russia sees her salvation not in mysticism, nor asceticism, nor
> pietism, but in the successes of civilization, enlightenment and
> humanity. What she needs is not sermons (she has heard enough
> of them!) or prayers (she has repeated them too often!) but the
> awakening in the people of a sense of their human dignity lost
> for so many centuries amid the dirt and refuse: she needs rights
> and laws conforming not with the preaching of the church but
> with common sense and justice, and their strictest possible
> observance.[12]

In all that he wrote Belinsky expressed himself with warmth,
passion, sincerity, and conviction. In the moral and intellectual
wilderness of Nicholas I's Tsardom he passionately proclaimed
the ideals of education, humanism, the rejection of rewards and
punishments in social and educational life, the principle of active
participation of the ordinary man and woman in life and government. He preached the virtues of hatred and intolerance of oppres-
sion and of the oppressor.

(v) Chernishevski – the Materialist Basis of Psychology

As the opponent and victim of Tsarism, an honourable place must
be reserved for Nikolai Gavrilovich Chernishevski (1828–1889).
The second half of his life (after 1862) was spent in prison, penal
servitude, and in exile. He was sentenced for publishing articles
which had been previously passed by the censorship in a trial which
offended even wide sections of conservative society as being a
mockery of justice. In the course of his brief career as a writer (he
described himself as a 'journalist') he set out various positions in
philosophy and psychology which he had reached independently
but which are now taken to be the special postulates of Marxism.

Although Marx was familiar with Chernishevski's writings (having learned Russian so that he could study his economic writings) it is clear that Chernishevski owed little, if anything, to Marx's direct influence.

In a summary characterization of the history of the revolutionary movement, Lenin places Chernishevski as follows:

At first – nobles and landlords, the Decembrists and Herzen. This was a narrow circle of revolutionaries, very far removed from the people. But they did not work in vain. The Decembrists awakened Herzen. Herzen launched revolutionary agitation. This agitation was taken up by the revolutionary commoners (raznochintzy) beginning with Chernishevski and ending with the heroes of the 'Narodnaya Volya' (the 'People's Will'). The circle of fighters widened, they established closer contacts with the people. 'The young helmsmen of the impending storm', Herzen called them. But as yet it was not the storm itself. The storm is the movement of the masses themselves. The proletariat, the only class that is revolutionary to the end, rose at the head of the masses and for the first time aroused millions of peasants to open revolutionary struggle.[13]

This thumbnail sketch indicates Chernishevski's historical position and circumstances. After 1861, along with Hertzen, he found himself isolated from liberal opinion as the sponsor of peasant emancipation through a socialist revolution to be undertaken by the peasants themselves. He takes his place as a link between the aristocratic constitutionalists and rebels of 1825 and the mass revolutionary movements of 1905 and 1917. It is now clear that it was Chernishevski's novel *What is to be done?* (following the shock of his elder brother's execution) which first served Lenin as the introduction to, as well as providing the detailed model for, the life of a dedicated revolutionary. Intending the novel (which was written in prison awaiting trial and sentence) to be his testament for future revolutionaries, Chernishevski has been justified by history inasmuch as Lenin represented the new man he specified and predicted. Similarly, Chernishevski's essays played a considerable role in forming Lenin's philosophical ideas.

Chernishevski was compelled by the conditions of the censorship to write in an oblique and 'Aesopian' language. For example, it was impossible to refer by name in print to Feuerbach, or Radishchev, or to a great number of other proscribed writers, both Russian and European. Serfdom could be discussed only obliquely, in terms of Negro slavery in the Southern States of America. Even the social position of women, and the question of female suffrage, then being written about by John Stuart Mill in England, were forbidden topics. As a result of these prohibitions Chernishevski's major writings, such as *The Anthropological Principle in Philosophy* (1860), are now almost unreadable owing to the elliptical, often incoherent and semi-serious, style he was forced to adopt to put over his basic ideas. Nevertheless, there is no difficulty in identifying his views as belonging to the school of militant philosophical materialism and atheism. In literary style Chernishevski was forced to compromise with the censorship, but he did not compromise in terms of ideas.

The 'anthropological principle' is defined by Chernishevski as follows:

A man must be regarded as a single being, having only one nature; a human life must not be cut into two halves, each belonging to a different nature; every aspect of a man's activity must be regarded as the activity of his whole organism, from head to foot inclusively, or if it is the special function of some particular organ of the human organism we are dealing with, that organ must be regarded in its natural connection with the entire organism.[14]

This basic assumption of psychophysical monism was the central thesis of Chernishevski's philosophy which he developed in the course of the guerrilla war he was waging against the liberals, the Slavophils, and the Orthodox Establishment. What was being asserted, in the face of very considerable opposition from all these quarters, was that human behaviour, consciousness, and morality were amenable to scientific study – 'exact scientific analysis' is the phrase he used; that man was part of the natural order, close kin to other animal species, and subject to the general laws of nature, like every other species – this was Chernishevski's teaching. In this regard he anticipated Darwin and Huxley. He goes on to say: 'Psychology and moral philosophy are emerging from their scientific poverty: they now possess a considerable amount of wealth, and if they don't know something or other they can afford to say frankly: 'We do not know.'[15]

As an instance of what psychology definitely knows, Chernishevski notes that all the phenomena of the psychic life (or 'moral world') originate from one another, and from external circumstances, in conformity with the law of causality. He calls for an alliance between science and philosophy and between physiology and psychology. In opposition to the prevailing tendencies he explains that human nature forms an integral unity, based on the material life of the body. Thinking is a function of the living brain. It is based on two elements: an external object which gives rise to sensation and a being that is conscious of the sensation. Our sensations are a true and adequate reflection of the objects which cause them. He notes the role of activity in perception and recognizes *human practice* as the criterion of truth: 'Practice is the great exposer of deception and self-deception, not only on practical matters but also in matters of feeling and thought. That is why science accepts practice as an essential criterion in all controversial points.'[16]

As a general explanation of human motive Chernishevski put forward the theory of *rational egoism*. This is the view that all men are prompted in their actions, not by general abstract principles which are essentially alien to them, but by self-interest. This does not necessarily divorce the individual interest from the public interest – Chernishevski does not advocate a *laissez-faire* system. The ethics of rational egoism demand that the individual be aware of the common good. In repudiating freewill, Chernishevski states the principle that an action is evil when it is not in harmony with the common good. But it is not the individual so much as the given social organization which is responsible when any such conflict arises. 'Normal' social conditions (by which Chernishevski means socialism), when achieved, will consist of a social structure such that behaviour, which will still necessarily be based on egoistical calculations, will be at the same time altruistic.

In other words, Chernishevski was a Utopian socialist. In philosophical matters he was strongly influenced by Feuerbach; on social and political questions he found inspiration in the French school. But he differs from Feuerbach in that he remains acutely hostile to all forms of religion – even the 'religion' of love. He had a more concrete vision of man than did either the German Left-Hegelians or the French Utopians, coming very close to a statement of the materialist conception of history. One of his main differences with the liberals was their rooted dependence on the concept of liberation of the serfs 'from above' – that is, that emancipation must be carried out in the name of the Tsar. According to Marx, this was precisely the illusion which beset the Utopian socialists – that the emancipation of social classes could come about only as the result of 'good-will', and the intervention of higher powers. Chernishevski taught that such an intervention would change only the forms of servitude whilst preserving the content. His programme for social change included emancipation 'from below'. The peasants would change society by wielding their axes against their oppressors. But in political matters he remained a Utopian in so far as he believed that socialism in Russia could develop within the matrix of the village community (the 'obshchina'). This belief separates him from Marxism. According to the principles of historical materialism, the Emancipation Decree of 1861 marks the beginning of the era of industrial capitalism in Russia. The primitive village commune was one of the first casualties in this new development – as Alexander II himself declared, the 'communistic principle' must be abolished on liberation of the serfs. But on philosophical questions Chernishevski developed the themes proclaimed by Belinsky and Hertzen to the level, as Lenin has said, of 'an integral philosophical materialism' hardly to be distinguished from Marxism. He is regarded as one of the main pioneers of that concept of man as a social organism which lies at the roots of Soviet psychology.

(vi) N. A. Dobrolyubov (1836–1861) – 'the struggle against depersonalization by an immoral society'

Chernishevski's principal associate after 1857 was the young Dobrolyubov – he died at the early age of twenty-five. Like Chernishevski, he was an ex-seminarist and the son of a priest; unlike him, Dobrolyubov passed directly from religious orthodoxy to materialism, dialectics, and revolutionary conceptions. In essence, his views on philosophy were identical with those of Chernishevski. His revolutionary ardour was expressed more forcefully. Politically he strongly supported Chernishevski's break with the liberals after 1859.

The Russian radicals followed a path parallel to that of Marx and Engels in the West. Chernishevski and Dobrolyubov were precursors of Marxist thought in Russia. They can be criticized from the Marxist standpoint only in so far as they failed to discover Marx's conception of historical materialism. Their materialism is not entirely free of remnants of Utopian socialism in the form of a belief in the possibility of Russian society continuing to survive as collectives in the form of village communes. This idea survives in their thinking from Fourier and other Utopian theorists. However, they give due emphasis to the fact that man is a social animal with a history. Unlike Feuerbach, and in line with Marx, they do not 'overlook' the class struggle in society. Neither do they divorce their theoretical principles from practical revolutionary activity, nor do they seek to establish a new religion of humanity.

In the division of labour on the journal *Sovremennik* (*The Contemporary*), which Chernishevski edited, Dobrolyubov was assigned to write about ethics, pedagogy, aesthetics, and literary criticism. Consequently his ideas are more clearly relevant to empirical psychological questions than are Chernishevski's. The latter are more concerned with the foundations of psychological inference, being more like programmatic declarations than detailed discussions of particular questions. As a publicist, Dobrolyubov's objectives were derived from (i) his conviction of Russia's need for a social revolution; (ii) his belief that a materialistic and evolutionary (dialectical) conception of nature, society, and man was alone adequate as a lever with which to move and change society; (iii) his view that the propagation of materialism involved destroying the credibility of idealism and the metaphysical mode of thought.

Like Marx and Engels, the 'men of the sixties' used the method of criticism: their positive views are implied rather than developed systematically. The conditions of the censorship also make it difficult for the modern reader to interpret some of their writings. However, the problem is less serious than with Marx and Engels since the Russian radicals, having their own press, could return again and again to a theme and develop it from a number of perspectives. They were writing, too, more directly about specific problems – the central themes being serfdom and autocracy and the kind of interpersonal relations which these generated.

Dobrolyubov's views on psychological topics are much more developed (perhaps because he received his academic training at the Central Pedagogical Institute in St Petersburg and not at the University). In a series of quite remarkable essays he presented an extraordinarily perceptive analysis of the psychological and moral effects of serfdom and of autocratic government, and of the ways in which these relations worked to corrupt society. His main contribution, presented in the form of an analysis of the plays of Ostrovsky, was the detailed demonstration of how values, habits of thought, and behaviour are conditioned by the environment.

In all his analyses he laid emphasis on the *interdependence* of social phenomena. It could be said that his insight, like that of Marx, was to perceive the operation of *systems* where others saw only disconnected and unrelated phenomena. Together with Belinsky, even more than Chernishevski, Dobrolyubov was responsible for fostering the understanding of realism in Russian literature. When we speak of the 'psychological novel' as one of Russia's contributions to world culture (Gogol, Goncharov, Tolstoy, Dostoievski, Turgeniev) we should remember that Dobrolyubov was one of the main interpreters of these and other artistic creations (Ostrovsky, Saltykov, Vovchok). It is his analyses, in fact, which provide the psychological insights (in the Soviet sense) rather than the creations themselves. Similarly, his analysis of the activities of Peter I can be regarded as a worthy contribution to the corpus of psychological literature, remarkable for its period. He states his own basic approach as follows:

> Help me to understand the character of a phenomenon, its place among the rest, its meaning and importance in the general course of life, and I assure you that in this way you will help me to form a far more correct opinion about the matter in hand than you will with all the syllogisms you may choose to prove your cases. . . . Everywhere and in all things the synthesis reigns; people say that a certain thing is useful and then they go hunting around for arguments to prove that it is useful; they stun us with a maxim and then they condemn everything that does not comply with that maxim.[17]

This appeal to the concrete historical reality and his emphasis on the interconnectedness of the phenomena were characteristic of Dobrolyubov. In speaking of 'man' he referred not to some abstraction removed from space and time co-ordinates but to a socialized historical figure, living under specific historical conditions. This marked his line of division from liberals such as Turgeniev and Kavelin – their protest against the existing Russian realities was muted by a sentimentalism which to Dobrolyubov was an evasion of reality. Thus, a gaping void became apparent between the principles proclaimed and the things which were actually being done by the liberals. The following sentence by Dobrolyubov might have been written by Marx: 'In all everyday relations the material side predominates over the abstract side; people who lack material security attach little importance to abstract rights.'[18]

According to Dobrolyubov, this false and sterile idealism, which ignores the reality of life whilst stating the most abstract and pleasant-sounding principles, is nowhere so clearly expressed as in

the sphere of education. Like Pirogov and other liberal critics of
Russian education in the period following the disastrous Crimean
War (1854–1856), he attacked the 'unnatural system' of 'obtuse
pedagogical officialdom' in vogue. He condemned the attempts to
din into children's heads an enormous amount of abstract concepts totally alien to their experience and understanding. Positively,
he advocates that we recognize the 'rights of infant nature' against
pedagogical tyranny. He proposes the substitution of a method of
learning through experience in place of the rote-learning of abstract and lifeless schemata. Dogmatism, superficiality, and life-
lessness lead the teacher to use a method where 'training' the
child, like an animal in a circus, is substituted for a valid system
of education in which the rationality of the child is encouraged
to question, to analyse. It is only through such a rational approach
that the child can be brought to love truth with sincerity, to stand
up for it fearlessly, and to be free and candid with his teachers:
'We demand that teachers should show more respect for human
nature and try to develop and not suppress the *inner man* in their
pupils; that the object of education should be to make a man
moral not by habit, but by consciousness and conviction.'[19] It was
in terms of the actual implementation of these principles that
Dobrolyubov attacked the liberals for their policy of compromise
with Tsarist realities. Whilst professing the loftiest principles they
became vague, vacuous, tame, and trivial when confronted by
actual issues – such as serfdom, the subjection of women, corporal
punishment, arbitrary police action, anti-semitism.

In education the issue lay between Dobrolyubov and Pirogov.
Unfortunately, in spite of his critical articles *Questions of Life*
which had made him the hero of progressive Russia in the first
flush of Alexander's reign, Pirogov helped to draw up and gave
assent to rules concerning transgressions and punishments for
pupils in the Kiev Educational Region. These included the advocacy of flogging and 'slaps in the face' for violations of the school
rules by pupils. In two articles in the *Sovremennik* in 1860–1861,
Dobrolyubov attacked these 'Pan-Russian illusions'. He sought
to demonstrate in these and in other essays that such methods were
the means by which children were forced to conform to the
corrupt social system by developing personalities characterized by
obsequiousness, insincerity, and tolerance of injustice. Thus
children were forced to grow up 'forcibly tied to the corpse of the
obsolete past'. In the eyes of the radical intelligentsia, Pirogov
took his place amongst those 'liberals and reformers who base

their schemes on legal subtleties and not on the groans and cries of their unhappy fellow-men'.

Dobrolyubov saw himself as the implacable opponent of 'Oriental survivals' in Russian life. He believed that crime was the result not of human nature but of a man's abnormal relations to society which resulted from upbringing and from the nature of the environment. In a classic series of essays on *The Realm of Darkness* he characterizes this environment as follows:

> External submission and dull, concentrated grief that reaches the stage of downright imbecility and the most deplorable obliteration of personality are interwoven with slavish cunning, with the most despicable deception and the most shameless perfidy. Here nobody can trust another: at any moment you may expect your friend to boast about how skilfully he has cheated or robbed you; a partner in a profitable speculation may get hold of all the money and documents and get his partner locked up in the debtors' prison; a father-in-law will cheat his son-in-law out of his dowry; a bridegroom will cheat the matchmaker; the bride will deceive her husband. Nothing is sacred, nothing is pure, there is no justice in this savage world; the savage unjust tyranny that reigns over them has driven all sense of honesty and justice from their minds. Those cannot exist where tyrants have shattered and have arrogantly trampled upon human dignity, the freedom of the individual, faith in love and happiness and the sacredness of honest toil.[20]

In spite of this terrible legacy from the past, Dobrolyubov remained optimistic about man's ability to change this environment. Piecemeal reforms will not serve – his admiration for Peter is based on 'the complete renunciation of the past, the total and instantaneous transformation accomplished by the will of one man over against popular habits and instincts'. Literature is a prime mover, but 'it serves as the mouthpiece of the concepts and strivings of the educated minority and is accessible only to this minority'. The intellectual classes are a non-starter as a political lever – 'where and when has any real improvement in the life of the people come about simply as the result of convictions held by clever people?' Education takes too long – 'the number of people who think independently grows slowly, almost imperceptibly, from generation to generation'. Only the labouring people, the inarticulate masses, are capable of overthrowing this 'kingdom of darkness', only they have preserved sufficient energy and courage to accomplish this task. In 1859, after battling with the censorship for permission to publish, Dobrolyubov was allowed to make the point obliquely:

> Yes, among these people there is a force for good, which certainly does not exist in that corrupt and half-mad society which claims to be educated and capable of something serious. The masses are unable to speak eloquently: so they cannot – and do not want to – stick to words, enjoying the sound of their words as they float away in the distance. What they say is never empty. It is expressed by an appeal to facts, and as a condition for immediate action.[21]

In his short working life of five years Dobrolyubov accomplished an enormous amount of work. This was directed to a single objective – the destruction of the idea of 'platonic love' in social activity. His message, transmitted through hundreds of pages of social, literary, and philosophical criticism was simple – one's every act should correspond to one's idea of 'the good', which must involve a love for all mankind. In the course of these writings, he developed a number of basic principles which persist as the central theses of Soviet psychology.

(vii) The Opposition to Materialism in Psychology

In a famous passage, concluding his analysis of a particular trend in philosophy, Lenin says:

> It is impossible not to see the struggle of parties in philosophy, a struggle which in the final analysis reflects the tendencies and ideology of the antagonistic classes in modern society. Recent philosophy is as partisan as the philosophy of two thousand years ago. Concealed behind the sham-scholarship of new terminology or a half-witted non-partisanship, the contending parties are, in essence, materialism and idealism . . .[22]

Whatever may be said about West European philosophy over the past two thousand years, it is certainly true that philosophical thought in Russia over the past two hundred bears the character attributed to it by Lenin.

Beginning with Radishchev, the Autocracy, representing the interests of the feudal state and the landowning classes, persecuted all innovations in philosophy. Any tendency adjudged hostile to Orthodox religion or to autocratic government was officially proscribed. From 1826 until 1863 it was forbidden to teach philosophy at all in Russian universities. After 1863 instruction was permitted in the form of public lectures, these being limited to commentaries on certain texts of Plato and Aristotle. The lectures were super- vised by representatives of the Church (and by agents of the secret police) stationed in the classrooms. Philosophical thought per- force developed outside the universities. The original contribu- tions were by literary men who, at great personal risk, developed the classic themes of Russian philosophy – the nature of good and evil in social life, the meaning of existence, the philosophy of his- tory. These individuals were liable to denunciation by the priests; their writings were censored and often totally forbidden publica- tion. They took the risk of being declared insane by the Tsar, or exiled to a distant province, or confined in a fortress-prison. If noblemen, they could be deprived of their rank and drafted into the army for life as a private soldier. In the case of the Petrashevsky circle, as we have seen previously, twenty-one members were sen- tenced to death for reading a forbidden letter. Dostoievski described the macabre scene of the elaborate preparations for public execution and the theatrically arranged last-second reprieve on the scaffold and subsequent exile to Siberia.

This is what is meant by 'partisanship in philosophy'. These are the risks which Sechenov, for example, was running in 1863 when he sought to publish his study *An Attempt to Establish the Physiological Basis of Psychical Processes*, the founding charter of Russian psychology. A year previously, Chernishevski had been subjected to the public ritual of 'civic execution', a realistic simu- lation of the real thing, and sent to penal servitude in exile for similar writings in the same journal to which Sechenov submitted his work. Sechenov was well aware that he was engaged in a war in which he could expect no quarter: his only weapons were ideas, his only ally, public opinion. Any teachings which made a sub- stantial break with Orthodox religious conceptions (as these were understood by a semi-literate priesthood), or which provided an interpretation of history hostile to religion or to Tsarism, any theories about man which led to a denial of his supernatural origin and destiny, any thoughts adjudged to be 'dangerous' for any reason whatsoever were forbidden publication.

Having run the gauntlet of the Tsarist censorship and arriving in print in a mangled condition, unorthodox ideas – or those re- garded as such – were subjected to a withering volley of criticism from the established schools of thought. The critics ranged themselves along a spectrum from solidly Establishment-based guardians of truth and morality ('gendarmes-out-of-uniform' – Hertzen), through chastened radicals-turned-conservative, to aristocratic liberals acting the role of rather frightened or disgruntled 'fellow travellers' in the radical movement. The views of some sophisticated opponents of a secular, scientific conception of behaviour will now be considered, but briefly, since their contribution of original ideas is modest, these being drawn from the legacy of Orthodox Christianity. They make no direct impact on current Russian thought, although the themes they discuss remain central influences in the Russian approach to social reality.

A   PETER YAKOVLEVICH CHAADAYEV (1794–1856)

Chaadayev was one of the casualties of the Tsarist régime. In 1836, one of eight *Philosophical Letters* he had written was published in a journal. Chaadayev was immediately and officially declared to be insane by the Tsar. He was placed under daily medical surveillance, and forbidden ever to write again. The censor who passed the article (the Rector of Moscow University) was dismissed and deprived of his pension. The journal was suspended. No comment of any kind on this famous letter was allowed in print until after the 1905 Revolution. Chaadayev lived in Moscow until his death in 1856, the first of the 'superflous men', a type which subsequently became a well-worn theme in Russian literature. He was also the first of the so-called 'Westernizers' in literature. Being an intensely religious thinker, he advocated reunion of the Orthodox Church with the Church of Rome as the only basis on which Russia could enter on the path of civilization.

Chaadayev is memorable in the history of Russian psychology for his notion that man's rational nature and human qualities are the product of the social environment. This basically correct formula is qualified by the idea that human rationality was originally derived from the Divine Illumination. Chaadayev denies that man can be wholly included in nature and society. Man is a spiritual being living in two worlds, only one of which can be known to science. The human group preserves and transmits the light of reason, but the true origin of man's rational understanding dates from his conversation with God on the day he was created:

God's word to man transmitted from generation to generation, leads man into a world of consciousness and transforms him into a thinking being . . . There is no truth in the spirit of man other than that which God placed there with his own hand at the time when he drew man out from nothingness.[23]

In a unique synthesis, Chaadayev developed a systematic philosophy around the concepts of human freedom, the collective nature of human consciousness, and the existence of a world consciousness as the basic reality. The latter is a kind of ocean of ideas in which we are all immersed and from which each of us draws. Although his philosophical views and historical judgements are quite unacceptable to modern Soviet thinkers, many of his themes – man's dependence on the social environment, his responsibility for historical events, the unity of the human person, the criticism of narrow individualism and the lauding of the collective – have become perennial in the Russian thought-pattern. Hertzen gave a very positive evaluation of Chaadayev in his memoirs as a man who 'knew how to write an article which thrilled all Russia and which was a turning-point in our understanding of ourselves'. He remembered Chaadayev as 'an incarnate veto, a living protest', 'a grievous rebuke against the dark background of Moscow high society'. Chaadayev's influence on Russian thought after 1836 was mediated through his conversation and example: the manuscripts of the remaining letters setting out his developed philosophy were discovered only one hundred years after his first (and last) ill-fated publication.

B ALEKSEI STEPANOVICH KHOMYAKOV (1804–1860)

Khomyakov was a nobleman who, after a short spell of military service, settled on his country estates, living the life of a dedicated Orthodox Christian, writing on historical and theological topics. He was the recognized leader of the Slavophil tendency in Russian thought, believing that Russia had a unique destiny which entailed that she should preserve her special characteristics and culture uncontaminated by foreign ideas, institutions, and ways of life. Khomyakov took the Orthodox Church as the central element or core of this uniqueness. His basic theme is the spiritual life of the congregation by which, and through which, truth is discovered. This is the conception of *sobornost'*, the organic union of the faithful which generates the highest and truest forms of knowledge.

In place of abstract, rational processes Khomyakov relies on a collective intuition – an unconscious, instinctual, immediate apprehension of the living truths of existence and of the supernatural life. It is spiritual pride which induces a man to seek the truth through his individual powers of cognition – inevitably, in isolation from the collective, he falls into grievous error. The vital paradox of human psychology, according to Khomyakov, is that, through faith in Orthodox Christianity, the individual freely chooses a vocation in which he becomes a slave whilst remaining free. There is an analogy between the individual participating in choral singing in Church and life: the musical consensus of the group is made up of individual, uncoerced contributions from the individual. Seen from this perspective, serfdom did not really worry the Slavophils. They considered the Russian institution of the *obshchina* (or village community), within which the bound peasant lived his daily life, to be a kind of social analogue of the Church community, an exemplar in everyday life of that combination of necessity and freedom characteristic of life within the Church.

Khomyakov decisively rejected the idea that 'man is a concentrated reflection of the external world'. Indeed, the theory of causal determinants of really human behaviour was unacceptable to him. Man is characterized by free will; this for Khomyakov is basic to the very idea of reason. But freedom is not an absolute, nor is it universal. It is a gift which belongs only to the spiritual sphere and is mediated through the organic Church illuminated by the spirit of God:

> Everything moves according to the law of cause and effect; everything is equally subject to necessity. Freedom can be no more than relative, that is, in relation to one given force, but in no case in relation to all. Whence, then, has arisen the recognition of free-will? Strictly speaking, as I have already said, it defines the limits of human subjectivity in relation to objectification or internal representation. It indicates to man what in himself comes *from* himself, distinguishing it from what does not come from himself.[24]

To understand Khomyakov's message and his influence it must be understood that he does not place authority in the Orthodox Church as an institution. On the contrary, the Church is primarily a facilitator, bringing together the community of believers. It is they who generate warmth, and illumination, through their mutual love and 'togetherness' (sobornost'). This is one of the most basic differences between Orthodoxy and Romanism. In the Eastern Church, truth about doctrine, dogma, and the spiritual life is a matter for conciliar consensus ('sobor' means a council); in the Roman Church the final authority is derived from Papal infallibility. Any group, however small, of Orthodox Christians can determine religious truth which is binding for them. Orthodoxy is maintained by virtue of the fact that the smaller groupings perceive themselves to be part of the living Church, in spiritual communion with the community of believers, living and dead. This is the dialectical contradiction of freedom and constraint to which the believer is committed.

The relevance of this for psychology is that, according to Khomyakov, the truth about man cannot be discovered by empirical inquiries and the unguided reason. The nature of reality can be discovered only by an organic community of thinkers, bound to each other and inspired by love. Knowledge cannot safely be separated from the moral principle: the attempt to do so leads to the untruth, heresy, error, and other corruptions characteristic of Western Europe, especially of the Roman Church since the Schism of 1054. The initial stage of knowledge is an act of faith by which we achieve an immediate and total union with reality. These perceived data are then 'turned over' to the rational processes for analysis:

> I give the name 'faith' to that faculty of reason which apprehends actual, real data and makes them available for analysis and awareness by the understanding. Only in this area do the data still have the fullness of their character and the marks of their origin. In this area, which precedes logical consciousness and which is filled with a living awareness that does not need demonstrations and arguments, man realizes what belongs to his intellectual world and what to the external world. Here, by the touchstone of his free will, man perceives what in his objective world is produced by his creative, subjective activity and what is independent of it.[25]

According to Khomyakov therefore, cognition is a process which begins with faith, continues through logical analysis and the other rational processes which are illuminated and permeated with valuations, and is completed in the 'total reason' which embodies the wholeness of living knowledge. Thus he makes a distinction between 'logically possible' and 'actual' truths – only the former are available to rationalism and, obviously, must be 'corrected' within a context of Orthodox belief.

In 1847, Khomyakov expanded these views with special

reference to science. Science does not consist of 'truths', the same everywhere, established as objective and external realities. On the contrary, scientific method is essentially an analysis of facts as these are perceived by the mind. Consequently, the direct know-ledge of facts is always accompanied by a 'hidden synthesis'. This is directly dependent, amongst other things, on the nationality of the observer. Therefore, for different reasons, neither England nor Germany is capable of developing a worthwhile body of scientific knowledge.

These ideas were repeated and developed in a more official form in 1856 by Samarin in the Slavophil journal *Russkaya Beseda*. The universal character of scientific laws is now admitted. But the influence of national differences on such studies as eco-nomics and history is brought out to support the general propo-sition of the futility of attempting to transplant Western science in Russia.

Despite efforts by Khomyakov and other Slavophils to influ-ence the student movement by the formation of 'circles', their direct influence was almost zero. However, their ideas, completely secularized, remain extremely influential, and an active force, in Soviet thought of the present day.

C NICHOLAS IVANOVICH PIROGOV (1810–1881)
Representative of the liberal trend, hostile to revolutionary ideas and to materialism in psychology, we cite the well known military surgeon, Nicholas Ivanovich Pirogov. Following a brilliant career before and during the Crimean war, Pirogov published a series of articles on *Problems of Life* (1856), in which he criticized the Russian system of education. His standpoint was very similar to that of the Christian Socialists in England, although the connec-tion was not obvious to his readers. The following might have been written by F. D. Maurice:

> Contemporary education fails to take measures to imbue in us the most lofty human convictions; it makes us jurists, scientists and soldiers, but not men. And men act by chance, following the leadership of the mob, first in one direction, then in another, because the inner man is not educated and receives no training in basic convictions. But no one can have convictions who has not been taught from the earliest years to look deeply into himself, to love truth sincerely, and to stand up for it like a rock.[26]

The passion with which these articles were written, rather than their content, created a kind of shock-wave which ran through Russian society. His articles were a trumpet-call to action following the defeat suffered by Russia in the Crimea. The fact that Pirogov had spent ten months in the field, operating on and organizing the care of the wounded under the most revolting conditions, gave his ideas and his protest against the morally debilitating influences of the educational system an immediacy and authenticity which electrified public opinion. In the view even of later admirers, such as Bervi-Kaidanova, there was nothing original in Pirogov's articles. The same ideas had been expressed by Belinsky, Pisarev, and Dobrolyubov.

In his diaries, published in 1910, the basis of Pirogov's critical comments on Russian society is made clear. It is in fact Christianity slightly modified by remnants of a pantheistic deism surviving from his university days. Pirogov attacked materialism for its superficiality, in particular its failure to pay due attention to the *mysterious* qualities of matter. In place of materialism he substituted a doctrine of 'universal life' and 'universal thought'. Conceding that the body, and particularly the brain as the organ of thought, evolved by natural processes, Pirogov maintained that the 'self' is inserted from the outside into this cunningly devised apparatus as a particular manifestation of the universal mind. Having chosen the universe as its 'organ', this universal mind manifests itself as individual 'selves'. This is achieved by taking advantage of a special mechanism contained in the human nerve-centres. 'We do not of course know how this takes place'[27]

The universal consciousness is infinite and eternal: however, like matter, it undergoes change. Therefore, Pirogov sees the necessity to posit in addition to this universal reason an immutable and absolute foundation. This, of course, is God.

Recognizing the existence of God lays the basis for the distinction between faith and reason. The trouble with reason is that, although it is 'consistent' with itself and with reality, it does not link us with the ideal, with God. This is the function of faith: it liberates our spirit from the consistency of reason. In a manner very similar to Khomyakov, Pirogov claims that faith initiates cognition and leads us to 'total truth'. This is a truth which incorporates the ethical sphere. There is no doubt that simple particular truths are available to the 'consistent' reason. But reason cannot be relied upon in such questions as whether man has freewill. To the mind unaided by faith the consciousness of inner freedom appears to be an illusion. Illuminated by faith, however, we recognize that this is the most basic fact about human beings.

Pirogov takes the view that knowledge, which is based on empirical reality, cannot give us the truth about reality. Knowledge must be distinguished from truth.

Our perceptions of space and time, and of life, are based on a primary sense: they are given to man, not developed by him. Sense data need to be corrected by meditation: 'empiricism' needs to be rounded out by critical reflection. In this way our thinking is enlarged to become a function of our integral 'self' which thus becomes prepared for the gift of faith. By means of faith we are attuned to the absolute. Pirogov seems to picture the process of cognition as taking place within a matrix of unconscious mechanisms which process the data of sense perception, first of all by reflection, secondly by what he calls the 'illusions' of faith. These 'illusions' are really higher truths granted to us as immediate realities – 'intuitions' would perhaps be a happier word. They appear to the inner self as though suffused with light: they disappear when subjected to analysis. Reflection, working on the empirical data of sense perception, interconnects all our separate perceptions to provide us with factual knowledge in the form of separate truths. The 'illusions' of the spirit kindle the light of faith which transforms these simple atomistic truths about reality into total truth. Thus *pravda,* which is the integral union of truth and justice, is granted to man. In this way, every man is capable of discovering truth for himself.

As regards man's nature, Pirogov is very close to Dostoievski. 'Base, evil, and miserable impulses' are concealed in the 'underground' of the human soul, as in a deep pool. We are involved in a continuous struggle with the forces of evil within us. But we are free in that we can dominate these impulses and direct our own lives.[28]

Having been 'taken up' during the incumbency of one 'liberal' Minister of Education, Pirogov was unceremoniously dismissed by his successor in 1861. The last twenty years of his life were passed in relative obscurity on his estate, his fate being reminiscent of that of Chaadayev.

The scene has now been set for the story of the development of scientific psychology in Russia. We date the birth of this activity from the publication in 1863 of Sechenov's *Reflexes of the Brain.* Amongst other consequences of this publication we can point to the establishment in 1885 (five years after Wundt's laboratory in Leipzig) of the first psychological laboratory in Russia at the University of Kazan by Bekhterev.

References

1. G. V. Plekhanov *Sochineniya XXI* 1923–29: 32–33, 45 ff.
2. B. N. Menshutkin *Russia's Lomonosov* 1952: 84.
3. Menshutkin 1952: 148.
4. A. S. Pushkin *Pol. Sob. Sochineniya* Moscow: State Publishing House. 1936, **6**: 198.
5. Skovoroda *Sochineniya* (ed. Bronch – Bruyevich) St. Petersburg 1912: 238; cf. Zenkovsky 1953, **1**: 112, 242.
6. 'A conversation between five travellers about life's true happiness' in *Sochineniya* 1912: 224; J. M. Edie *et al* 1965, **1**: 41 from Skovoroda *Tvori* **1**.
7. A. N. Radishchev *Sochineniya* 1907, **2**: 149.
8. Belinsky's letter to Botkin of June 28, 1841: J. M. Edie (*ed.*) *Russian Philosophy* 1965, **1**: 306; V. G. Belinsky *Selected Philosophical Works* 1948: 503 ff.
9. V. G. Belinsky *Selected Philosophical Works* 1948, **2**: 415.
10. V. G. Belinsky *Selected Philosophical Works* 1948: 369, 385.
11. V. G. Belinsky, *op. cit.*
12. V. G. Belinsky *Selected Philosophical Works* 1948: 536–546.
13. V. I. Lenin *Selected Works* (2 vols.) 1946, **1**: 633–638.
14. N. G. Chernishevski *Selected Philosophical Works* (in English) 1953: 132–133.
15. N. G. Chernishevski *Selected Philosophical Works* 1953: 95–96.
16. N. G. Chernishevski *Selected Philosophical Works* 1953: 29.
17. N. A. Dobrolyubov *Selected Philosophical Essays* 1948: 564.
18. N. A. Dobrolyubov, 1948: 583.
19. N. A. Dobrolyubov, 1948: 19.
20. N. A. Dobrolyubov, 1948: 247–248.
21. *Collected Works*: 138; E. Lampert *Sons against Fathers* 1965: 259.
22. Lenin, Materialism and Empirio-Criticism in *Collected Works*, **14**: 343.
23. Peter Chaadayev, Letter VI, in R. T. McNally *The Major Works of Peter Chaadayev* University of Notre Dame Press 1969: 124.
24. J. M. Edie *et al.* 1965, **1**: 264.

25. J. M. Edie *et al.* 1965: 251, 239, 243, 245; Khomyakov's second letter to Samarin, cf. Hertzen 1965: 557; V. V. Zenkovsky 1953, **1**: 202.
26. N. I. Pirogov, quoted by Bervi-Kaidanova *An Historical Outline of Russian Education:* 20–21.
27. N. I. Pirogov *Sochineniya* Kiev, 1910, **2**: 20.
28. N. I. Pirogov *Sochineniya* 1910: 207, 209.

Reading List

Books in English

Edie, J. M. *et al.* (eds.) (1965) *Russian Philosophy* (3 vols.) Chicago: Quadrangle Books.

Lampert, E. (1965) *Sons Against Fathers: Studies in Russian Radicalism and Revolution* Oxford: Clarendon Press.

Mathewson, R. W. (Jr.) (1958) *The Positive Hero in Russian Literature* New York: Columbia University Press.

Monas, S. (1961) *The Third Section: Police and Society in Russia under Nicholas I* Cambridge, Mass.

Venturi, Franco (1966) *Roots of Revolution* New York: Knopf.

Yarmolinsky, A.)1962) *Road to Revolution: A Century of Russian Radicalism* New York: Macmillan.

Books in Other Languages

Ambrogio, Ignazio (1963) *Belinsky e la teoria del realismo* Roma: Riunti.

Plekhanov, G. V. *Sochineniya* (1923–29) (30 vols.) (ed. David Ryazanov), **20, 21, 22** (Istoriya russki obshchestvennoi mysli) Moscow: State Publishers.

Zenkovsky, V. V. (1951) *Das Bild von Menschen in der Ostkirche* Stuttgart: Evangelische Verlagswerk.

Part II *The Methodological Foundations of Soviet Psychology*

To evaluate Soviet psychology as it exists in reality, it is necessary to accept that there are two systems of thought, not one, in relation to the subject matter and methods of psychology. In spite of the existence of a number of different tendencies, Western psychology exhibits certain well-marked features: (i) it developed under the aegis of empiricism, that is, it is based on experiment; (ii) in the main, it is concerned with the individual, his qualities, traits, abilites, etc.; (iii) it is characterized by an eclectic outlook, seeking to build up a general theory inductively from experimental data; (iv) it seeks to avoid any 'contamination' with philosophical *a priorism*. On the other side, Soviet psychology presents a picture noticeably different in texture: (i) whilst empirical in method, being experimental, Soviet psychology rejects empiricism as a principle of organization of scientific data; (ii) it attempts to explain experimental data within a context of presuppositions about the nature of man and of society – these assumptions derive from Marxism; (iii) it is concerned with the individual, but not as an abstract, isolated human being; (iv) it rejects eclecticism as a sign either of intellectual incompetence or of an intellectual compromise based ultimately on ideological self-interest.

Part II is devoted to developing this theme, seeking to connect the two basic pillars on which Soviet psychology is poised – on the one hand Marx, Engels, Lenin, on the other Sechenov and Pavlov.

Chapter 3   *The Origin of Objective Psychology*

Russian psychologists of the present generation deny that the science of psychology was founded by Wundt and other European scientists. The radical intelligentsia, especially Belinsky and Chernishevski, were the pioneers of a materialistic monism, the only possible foundation for a science of man. These views were developed by progressive Russian scientists working within the limitations of Tsarism.

The monistic theory was the basis of a programme of physiological research, elaborated by Sechenov (1863). This laid the natural-scientific foundation for Soviet psychology. As far as Wundt is concerned, his priority in setting up a psychological laboratory at the University of Leipzig (1879) is not denied. But similar developments, on a firmer basis, can be recognized in Tsarist Russia – for example, Bekhterev's laboratory at Kazan (1884). This monistic trend was, however, most firmly established in the work and concepts of behaviour developed by Pavlov. This constitutes the natural-scientific basis of the science of behaviour, regarded as higher nervous activity.

Marxism is the other great foundation stone without which a positive science is unthinkable for Soviet intellectuals. Lenin's development of the views of Marx and Engels, together with the Russian physiological school (Sechenov–Pavlov) made an objective science of the human psyche possible.

(i) Ivan Mikhailovich Sechenov (1829–1905)

In the indictment prepared by the St Petersburg Censors' Committee against Sechenov in 1866, he was charged with putting forward views in his book *Reflexes of the Brain* which are described as follows:

This materialistic theory reduces even the best of men to the level of a machine devoid of self-consciousness and free will, and acting automatically; it sweeps away good and evil, moral duty, the merit of good works and responsibility for bad works; it undermines the moral foundations of society and by doing so destroys the religious doctrine of life hereafter; it is opposed both to Christianity and to the Penal Code, and consequently, leads to the corruption of morals.[1]

This book, published originally in 1863 as two journal articles, is in reality a scientific treatise which seeks to establish that voluntary movements are in fact reflex actions in which there is some discrepancy between the stimulation and the normal response evoked. More than any other work, it can be said of it that it heralded the establishment of an objective science of psychology. It was welcomed by Russian scientists and violently attacked by Russian philosophers. It led quite directly to the establishment of 'reflexology', claimed to be the objective science of behaviour by Bekhterev; more importantly, it provided Pavlov with his scientific programme of forty years' work on higher nervous activity ('behaviour'). Indirectly, it fathered American behaviourism and the whole movement in world psychology away from philosophical analysis and subjectivity in the direction of experimental science and objective methods.

Sechenov worked in the laboratories of Helmholtz, Du Bois Reymond, Ludwig, Bunsen, and Magnus in Germany, with Brücke in Vienna, and with Claude Bernard in France. He was certainly familiar with the famous pact entered into by Helmholtz, Brücke, Du Bois Reymond, and Ludwig that they would establish and compel the acceptance of this truth: that 'no other forces than common physical and chemical ones are active within the organism'. Sechenov extended this principle in a novel way to include the 'so-called psychical activity' (the phrase is Pavlov's). He did this, not in the sense of reducing psychic events to laws of physics and chemistry but by demonstrating that the three concepts of: (1) the organism-in-its-environment; (2) the tri-member reflex; (3) the process of inhibition and/or intensification of response provided a model perfectly adequate to explain all animal and human behaviour.

In 1863, he was far in advance of West European thought. The social and political blight of Tsarism had the effect of polarizing opinion: views presented within a climate of compromise, hesitancy, and temporizing in Europe were developed by Russian thinkers to their extremist, logical conclusion.

Wöhler's synthesis of urea from inorganic materials in 1828 overthrew the theory that some special 'force' distinguished living processes from non-living. The principle of the unity of all chemical processes, 'organic' and inorganic, was joined in 1847 by Helmholtz's declaration of the law of conservation of energy. Darwin's theory of evolution by natural selection in 1859 gave the death-blow to all teleological explanations in natural science. Vitalism and dualism were in retreat in all branches of science. Sechenov was then thirty years of age. This was the scientific milieu in which his formative years were spent. His social and political views were formed in the period when Hertzen and Chernishevski were calling for radical changes in Russian society and for a new foundation for philosophic thought, purged of the subjectivity and spiritualism of Hegel and Schelling.

Even in his doctoral thesis *Data for the Future Physiology of Alcoholic Intoxication* (1860) Sechenov put forward a consistent materialist viewpoint. In this work, in addition to his experimental studies of alcohol and other chemicals in the blood, he stated the various principles which guided him later in his writings on psychic processes. These were: the unity of the organism and the conditions of its existence; the unity of the forces of organic and inorganic nature; the need to unravel the mysteries of consciousness by objective methods.

For materialism, the recognition of the primacy and existence of the objective world, external to man and independent of his perceptions, wishes, and very existence, is absolutely basic. This is the great dividing line which distinguishes materialism from all other philosophical viewpoints. Under the influence of Beneke's *Psychological Sketches* and *Theory of Education*, texts which he studied out of interest whilst a student at Moscow University, Sechenov became an extreme idealist – 'the whole picture of psychological life came out of the primary forces of the soul'. But under the influence of his German teachers he was led to adopt materialism as his basic premise.

Recognizing the objectivity of the external world, Sechenov claimed that *all* our psychic activity is the result of environmental stimulation. In other worlds, the initial cause of every human action lies outside of man. Not only that, but in his psychic and motor activity man is subject to the same laws as appertain to the material world. Contrary to idealism, there is only one set of causal laws: these govern not only man's bodily functions but apply to his psychic life as well. This does not mean that chemical and physical laws are adequate to explain psychic processes; rather, in explaining psychic processes we cannot assume that their uniqueness absolves them from operating under the restraints of scientific law. To be specific: the most general scientific law is causality; next are the laws of conservation of mass and of energy. In the natural sciences we have the law of development from lower to higher forms of life. In physics, chemistry, biology, and physiology, particular laws refer to specified situations. We must assume that these relationships apply in the study of man, *unless there is specific scientific evidence to the contrary*. The scientific study of human behaviour must, and can only mean, the establishment of causal relations in this area. It is only on this basis that a science of psychology is possible.

> It may be that psychology will shed some of its brilliant and universal theories; huge gaps may appear in its actual knowledge; instead of explanations we will get in most cases the laconic phrase: 'We do not know' . . . And yet psychology will have made a tremendous advance. It will no longer be based on erroneous reasoning prompted by the misleading voice of consciousness; it will rely on positive facts, on verifiable propositions. Its generalizations and deductions, strictly confined to real analogies, will no longer depend on the taste and whims of the investigator, which in the past brought psychology to transcendental absurdities; they will acquire the character of truly objective scientific hypotheses . . . In short, psychology will become a positive science.[2]

The principle that the organism is inseparable from its environment was developed by Sechenov in various forms, since it is basic to an understanding of behaviour. In the first place, given the fact of this dependence and interrelationship, it is nonsense to talk about man as a 'free spirit'! There can be nothing autonomous about the psychic life; it is *organically* interconnected with bodily process; these in turn are inseparably linked to the environment. Man's psychic life can be divided into two aspects, the mind and the feelings: this distinction is made by 'common psychology' (that is, by introspection). Sechenov is prepared to accept this as a working model. Sensation, perception, memory, thought appertain to the mental sphere; to the emotional belong fear, pleasure, love, enthusiasm, ecstasy. These phenomena of the psychic life are all engendered by the functioning of the brain within the body system. The initial impulse which starts off these trains of psychic acts comes invariably from the environment.

The entire psychic life of man is associated with the nervous system: this is stimulated, perceives, and reacts to, changes in the external reality which surrounds the organism. Psychic life is inconceivable without external stimulation of the sense organs. There is also, of course, a process by which the nervous system responds to changes in man's internal environment – that is, the organs, muscles, tendons, etc. which constitute the body. The law which governs all these phenomena, and nervous processes in general, is, of course, the law of causality. There is nothing random, chance, uncaused, in man's psychic life. Acts take place in the mind always as an effect, never as an arbitrary act of the free will:

> The question of whether the most voluntary of all voluntary actions of man depend on external and internal conditions has been answered in the affirmative. From this it inevitably follows that given the same internal and external conditions the activity of man will be similar. Choice of one of the many possible ends of the same psychical reflex is absolutely impossible; its apparent possibility is merely a delusion of self-consciousness.[3]

Thus man's psychic life is a process of interaction with the objects of his external environment. In the course of this interaction, beginning in childhood, a complex, evolutionary development takes place. In his *Reflexes of the Brain,* Sechenov sought to demonstrate from an evolutionary account of individual development how thought and consciousness originate as the result of inhibition or suppression of the last member of a reflex reaction to an environmental stimulus. The ability to think, to meditate, to reason, is signified by the chain of interconnected notions and concepts which exist in man's consciousness at any given moment and which are *not* expressed in any external manifestation. 'A thought is the first two-thirds of a psychical reflex'.[4]

The capacity to inhibit particular responses is a learned activity: it is acquired by means of reflex associations in the course of human life. For Sechenov the concept of inhibition is absolutely central (no pun intended); from the point of view of the development of his theory of psychic activity it is as basic as excitation. In the history of physiology his name will always be associated with the discovery of 'central inhibition'. This process can be demon-strated by placing salt on the cut end of the spinal cord of a de-capitated frog: spinal reflexes, previously obtained by pinching the frog's leg (reflex withdrawal being the response), are com-pletely suppressed.

By an extension of the argument to man, he deduced that spinal reflexes can be, and are, inhibited by the cerebral cortex: the brain acts in basically the same way as the grains of common salt. Sechenov thought of localizing the process in an inhibitory centre ('Sechenov's centre') in the brain. The essence of his theory is that *all* conscious and unconscious acts are reflexes. The so-called 'higher mental processes' characteristic of human beings are the product of the inhibition of the motor response characteristic of reflexes at the *spinal* level. Consciousness, which distinguishes man from the animals, arises on this basis 'as a kind of mirror, reflecting the surrounding reality'.[5] It seems to have no beginning and no end; the picture it presents is ever-changing, extremely variegated, not to say chaotic.

Consciousness can hardly be regarded as the ideal object of study. Neither can introspection be considered the method of choice in studying the thought-process. Because many of the links in the sequence of psychic acts, as these appear in consciousness, are missing, thoughts appear to be the original products of con-sciousness. This is the main error which necessarily results from the use of introspection as a method of investigation. It leads to the second basic error – that of concluding that the thinker has some choice of alternative courses of action. The real relationship between psychical activity and the external agents which initiate it, and influence it as cause, must ever remain obscure to intro-spection. This is because the 'subjective method' cannot isolate the basic unit of scientific study, namely the psychic act. 'The concept of a psychical act as a process or motion having a definite beginning, course and end, must be retained as fundamental'.

This leads to the proposition that there is an affinity between psychical acts and nervous processes. The reflex arc is the basic unit of physiological analysis; the psychical act is the basic unit of consciousness. The psychical act is simply a cerebral reflex. In certain cases the response termination may be *suppressed* (as in thinking); in others it is *intensified* (as in emotion). Thus, all acts of conscious or unconscious life, without exception, can be cate-gorized in terms of one or other of these processes.

Hence, the essence of Sechenov's teaching is that three separate mechanisms control man's psychic activity – the reflex arc, the inhibitory mechanism, and the intensification mechanism. All talk about 'Special Forces' is not only idle chatter, it represents a return to animistic ways of thinking:

> The essence of all philosophical theories concerning the body, the spirit and the objects of the external environment is based (according to Tylor) on real but wrongly interpreted facts. For our particular purposes we could add: 'on the facts of life wrongly interpreted, because the savage is too ready to accept the voice of consciousness.' Actually the philosophy of primitive man starts out from the same basic psychical predispositions as the philosophy of the thinker of today who is guided solely by the voice of consciousness.[6]

Idealist psychologists, such as Kavelin, with whom Sechenov engaged in controversy, imagine that there is some kind of inner vision. This originates from an alleged facility with which the soul divides itself into two parts, one critically looking at the other. The idealists teach that the human psyche is in this way unique and bears no resemblance to any organism. In the same way they used to teach that organic objects bear no resemblance to inorganic materials; this was before Wöhler.

Sechenov takes this argument as the *reductio ad absurdum* of psychological method (introspection). He takes the view that physiology alone has the objective, scientific method essential for studying not only 'the material substratum of consciousness' but psychical activity as well. The object of study is in both cases the same, namely, the reflex action. The method of analysis is to discover the objective connections between psychical acts and surrounding reality.

(ii) Ivan Petrovich Pavlov (1849–1936) – A New Science

Sechenov's *Reflexes of the Brain* was some forty years before its time. He had a number of predecessors but no one had anticipated him in his daring identification of the thought-processes with the reflex arc. In fact, it was only after his discovery of central inhibition that it became possible even to speculate about the physiological processes underlying thought. There was a materialist tradition in Russian physiology represented by Muchin, Dyadkovsky, and Filomafitsky at Moscow University: this prepared the ground for Sechenov's teachings about higher mental functions and their dependence on the brain as the organ of thought. In 1874, the British neurologist Hughlings Jackson, a disciple of Herbert Spencer and a contemporary of Sechenov, expressed the view that the reflex arc concept could be extended to the functioning of the cerebral cortex. He was indebted to an Edinburgh Professor of Medicine, Laycock, for the idea. The conscious process develops when the higher nervous centres are stimulated. But Jackson accepted from Spencer a view of mental process (psychophysical parallelism) which precluded him from making the intellectual leap which Sechenov accomplished.

As he had no direct predecessors, so also Sechenov had no successors for almost half a century. After distinguished physiological research on the circulation of the blood, and later, on the digestive system, Pavlov was attracted into the area of cortical functioning as a direct outcome of his work on digestion. Once involved, he made the discovery, through actual attempts to use it, that the prevailing psychological or 'subjective method' led only to scientific sterility and fantasies which became more and more divorced from the results of crucial experiments. He was compelled to adopt the methodology Sechenov had suggested in 1863. This was to maintain the role of the 'objective, external observer and experimenter, having to do exclusively with external phenomena and their relations'. This constituted a scientific revolution.

Pavlov was involved in studying the effect of stimuli at a *distance* from the organism, and with responses which called in the higher mental processes. In the terminology then current, he was engaged in investigating the 'psychical stimulation of the salivary glands'. The initial observation was that the animal began to secrete a flow of saliva at the sight of food. Pavlov recalled that humans salivate even in response to talk about food, indeed even at the thought of it. He had the temerity to extend the objective method of collecting and measuring saliva produced in response to this so-called 'psychical stimulation'. This method meant, in practice, that attempts to explain behaviour from the standpoint of some 'internal world' – of thoughts, feelings, desires – could be ruled out in favour of the physiological model of excitation-inhibition, reflex arc, stimulus and response. The discovery of this method of actually entering into the central nervous processes constituted Pavlov's first and greatest contribution to the science of psychology. Sechenov's genius had delineated the model: it was given to Pavlov actually to execute the design. As far as general methodology is concerned Pavlov accords priority to E. L. Thorndike whose experiments on animal learning (1898) preceded Pavlov's on conditional reflexes by two or three years.

Pavlov's work on conditional reflexes can be divided into five distinct phases, or periods, covering a total of forty years. Three of these relate to the period prior to the Revolution of 1917.

A FIRST PHASE (1897–1903): ORIENTATION

In this period Pavlov was switching his activities from the study of the functioning of the digestive system to that of the higher nerve centres. He had discovered the method of associating an originally neutral stimulus (for example, a light, bell or metronome) with the act of feeding the dog. Establishing by surgery a chronic salivary fistula in the experimental animal, he was able to collect and measure the amount of saliva secreted under varying conditions of stimulation of the nerve centres. The major significance of his methodological innovations was that (aside from the fact that the salivary gland was now outside the animal's mouth) experimental access was obtained to the functioning of the cerebral hemispheres in terms of an objective measurement made on an intact organism in a known environment.

His creative genius had been fostered by a twelve-year study of the circulatory system and sixteen-year study of the digestive system. It was in the course of this work that he elaborated the method of the 'synthetic experiment'. In place of electrical stimulation or extirpation of parts of the hemispheres, it became possible to study brain process as a whole under natural conditions.

His assistant, Dr Snarsky, was given the task of explaining the results in terms of the subjective state of the dog, basing his interpretations on the analogy of human experience. As these anthropomorphic accounts became more and more incompatible with the actual results of experiments and observations on the dog's behaviour, it became clear that this dualistic approach would have to be abandoned. The use of explanatory principles, such as 'attention', 'pleasure', 'disgust', 'remembering', 'forgetting', became more and more confusing and contradictory as the experiments proceeded. It was impossible to make any prediction of anticipated results on the basis of these categories. On the other hand, the physiological concepts of excitation and inhibition of nerve centres proved entirely adequate in this regard. Pavlov decided to drop all subjectivism and dualistic explanations in interpreting the dog's behaviour. In place of dualism, he set out to develop a theory of behaviour in terms of brain functioning, causality, and the absence of special 'forces' such as 'intention', 'desire', 'memory', or other subjective states. His purpose was to discover the operation of the established laws of physiology, in particular the characteristics of nerve functioning at the cortical level.

To illustrate the inadequacy of the subjective ('psychological') explanation, Pavlov instanced the fact that one would predict that 'an ardent desire' for food would excite the salivary or gastric glands. This conclusion is based on introspection. However, the following experiment falsifies this prediction. A hungry dog, shown dry bread at a distance, produces abundant saliva, whereas it does not salivate to the sight of moistened meat. This is explicable in terms of the other experimental observation, that dry food in the mouth produces a great flow of saliva, moist food only a weak secretion, or none at all. In his very first report on the experiments on conditional reflexes (*uslovniye refleksy* is better translated *conditional reflexes* than conditioned reflexes) Pavlov stated:

> The first and most important task before us, then, is to abandon entirely the natural inclination to transpose our own subjective condition upon the reaction of the experimental animal, and instead, to concentrate our whole attention upon the investigation of the correlation between the external phenomena and the reaction of the organism.[7]

In addition to the principle of association (a response can be shifted from a natural stimulus, such as food in the mouth, to any other stimulus and repeated presentation), Pavlov discovered the principle of reinforcement (that repeated association strengthens the link between the originally neutral stimulus and the response, which otherwise disappears).

Having abandoned the subjective explanation of behaviour, Pavlov interprets the phenomenon of the shifting of the response (saliva in the mouth) from the natural, unconditional stimulus (food) to some originally neutral stimulus (a given metronome beat) in terms of ongoing processes in the nervous system. The simultaneous excitation of two points on the cortex (one in the food centre, the other in the auditory centre) establishes a connection between them such that when one is excited (the auditory point) the other is activated (the food point). The general significance of these temporary connections is that it is through this mechanism that the activity of the organism and the changing environment are brought into a fine and ever-changing adjustment. For this purpose it is as essential that non-reinforced connections die out as it is that a relationship is established between meaningful signals from the environment and the vital activities of the organism.

B SECOND PHASE (1904–1909): CONSOLIDATION

In the first phase of his activity, Pavlov was, so to speak, establishing the ground rules which should apply in this new field of investigation. The decision to abandon subjectivism, and to forget the word 'psychic', except to communicate with the unenlightened psychologists and physiologists of the period, led him back to the basic assumptions of physiological thought. These he developed in a unique Russian synthesis. From Claude Bernard he inherited the idea of the organism as a system in dynamic equilibrium ('homeostasis'); from Charles Darwin the concept of adaptation to the environment through the processes of nature; from Botkin the idea that the cerebral cortex was the ultimate controller of all bodily functions ('nervism'); from Sechenov he inherited the idea that the functioning of the cortex could be investigated according to the same rubric as spinal reflexes; from George Henry Lewes he inherited associationism; from the general philosophical tradition in nineteenth-century medicine and the Russian intelligentsia of the 60s he inherited atheistic materialism. This last was a necessary spur, as even amongst physiologists of that period, there was a feeling that any attempt to investigate psychical processes, even at the level of the dog, constituted some kind of desecration, or sullying, of the unique and exalted life of the soul.

The second phase of his work on conditional reflexes consisted in working out the implications of the monistic approach in terms of experimental procedures and data. During this period he conceived the prime task to be that of ascertaining completely how a living being maintains itself in constant equilibrium with the environment. He sought to demonstrate that conditional reflexes show exactly the same properties as the natural, or unconditional, reflexes, and obey the same laws of extinction and restoration. In a series of experiments carried out with the assistance of a growing band of collaborators, he proved that temporary connections could be established in the cortex to all imaginable stimuli, the only condition being that the animal is able to detect the stimulus as some novel signal from the environment. Using this method, he found it possible to discover the limits of the dog's power to discriminate sounds, shapes, colours (the dog is, in fact, colour-blind), and so on. He began to use the concept of inhibition as a process the reverse of excitation. He engaged in controversy with Bekhterev (who had followed Pavlov into this field, producing results which appeared to contradict some of Pavlov's findings). He enunciated the law of irradiation-concentration as one of the first scientific discoveries using the new method.

In an early experiment (1904), he discovered that a conditional reflex established at a distance can be quickly extinguished by various means. For example, dry bread at a distance induces a strong flow of saliva; when meat is exposed simultaneously the flow stops. Similarly, actually giving the dry bread to a hungry dog causes the saliva to flow even more; giving it to another dog stops the flow of saliva. These facts would appear to be impossible to explain on the basis of subjective states of the animal. Pavlov explains the stoppage of saliva in both of these cases as the result of the transfer of stimulation from the salivary to the motor centre. In both cases this transfer of excitation is accompanied by inhibition of the cortical area which is normally excited by the stimulus of meat or dry bread.

The law of irradiation-concentration was given as the explanation of the way in which a particular conditional response is originally elicited by a great number of related stimuli (for example, a metronome beating at different frequencies); and then, assuming that only one specific stimulus (for example, a beat of sixty per minute) is reinforced again and again by feeding, the response is elicited by only this stimulus. Again the explanation is given in terms of a physiological model. Initially a wave of excitation travels over the auditory area (irradiation-phase), centred in the point on the cortex which is excited by the metronome beat of sixty. The process is rather similar to the production of waves which travel from a focal point on dropping a stone into a pool. Subsequently, the excitation concentrates around this single point: the waves retreat back to the focus rather like a film running backwards. Saliva is then elicited only to the beat of sixty per minute.

In the Huxley Memorial Lecture delivered in London in 1906, he referred to the possibility of studying human psychology on the basis of the same assumptions and methodology:

Mankind will possess incalculable advantages and extraordinary control over human behaviour when the scientific investigator will be able to subject his fellow men to the same external analysis as he would employ for any natural object, and when the human mind will contemplate itself not from within but from without.[8]

In his controversy with Bekhterev, Pavlov succeeded in showing that the differences between them resulted from poor laboratory techniques on the part of Bekhterev's students and the carelessness with which Bekhterev treated scientific fact.

C THIRD PHASE (1909–1916): DEVELOPMENT

In the third phase, his activities were, like everything else, seriously interrupted, not to say disrupted, by the outbreak of war in 1914 and Revolution in 1917. Pavlov elaborated certain findings made earlier, and worked out new interpretations of phenomena which attracted his attention. He expressed the view that *all* the nervous activity of the dog is reflex activity. He described reflexes of the second order, observing that they were weak and transitory. He realized that the experimental animals had various types of nervous system. He described several kinds of inhibition, including dis-inhibition. He put forward theories about the nature of sleep and of the hypnotic trance. He demonstrated that the law of irradiation-concentration is related to the two processes of excitation and inhibition. He associated the law of generalization – differentiation with the action of inhibition which acts during the second phase, that of concentration. He developed the concept of the 'analyser'. He stated the law of mutual induction. He defined consciousness as a localized area of heightened excitation in the brain, not fixed but in motion. The concept of the brain as a system in dynamic equilibrium was developed.

In declaring that all the nervous activity of the dog was reflex in character, Pavlov was returning to the earlier formulation of Sechenov. But he enriched the views of the latter by recognizing the nature of the physiological mechanisms involved. These he described as the permanent and inborn connections which unconditionally link certain everyday stimuli with pre-established responses. On this foundation of natural reflexes it is possible to develop a second kind of temporary link established conditionally on the basis of association of two stimuli in time. Like Sechenov, Pavlov included voluntary actions under this general rubric of reflex response, although he did not elaborate on this particular point until much later. In Sechenov's (1863) formulation, the explanation of voluntary movement is as follows:

> When the external (Pavlov would probably have added at this time, 'or internal') influence (i.e.) the sensory stimulus, remains unnoticed – which occurs very often – thought is even accepted as the initial cause of action. Add to this the strongly pronounced subjective nature of thought, and you will realise how firmly man must believe in the voice of self-consciousness, when it tells him such things. But actually, this is the greatest of falsehoods: the initial cause of any action always has an external sensory stimulation, because, without this, thought is inconceivable.[9]

Pavlov, during this period, expressed an interesting view of consciousness. This he took to refer to a nervous activity situated in a certain part of the cerebral hemispheres, the remaining parts of the hemispheres being in a state of diminished excitability:

> In the region of the brain where there is optimal excitability, new conditional reflexes are easily formed, and differentiation is successfully developed. The outlying parts with their decreased irritability are incapable of such performance. . . . The area of optimal activity is, of course, not fixed; on the contrary it is perpetually migrating over the whole extent of the hemispheres.[10]

The investigation of cerebral functioning by counting the drops of saliva elicited by presenting exactly defined stimuli in controlled experimental situations yielded the law of mutual induction, at least in a rudimentary form, during this period. Pavlov recognized that a focus of strong excitation in one part of the cerebral hemisphere resulted in a considerable decrease of irritability in the other parts. In other words, excitation in one area of the cortex induces inhibition in the other parts.

During this period Pavlov revised his classification of the types of inhibition which he had found in these experiments. He recognized sleep as a kind of generalized inhibition which shuts down the activity of the central nervous system almost completely. Hypnosis had a very similar effect, except that it was only partial. The closing-down affected only defined and limited areas of the cortex. External inhibition is that inhibition which results from the fact that various stimuli affect the organism at the same time as the conditional stimulus; these interfere with and inhibit the reflex then in operation. In external inhibition the interfering stimulus may come from inside or from outside the organism.

Internal inhibition he now recognizes to be of four types. The common defining feature is that there is some special relationship between the conditional and unconditional stimulus which results in the conditional reflex disappearing. First of all, if the stimulus is applied several times at short intervals without the connection being reinforced (for example, the metronome signal being given, say, twenty times with the animal never being fed) the response will suffer *extinction*, that is, it will disappear. Secondly, if there is a delay between the application of the conditional and the unconditional stimuli – the effect is called *retardation* – the response again disappears. The third kind is called *conditional inhibition*. This is where a neutral stimulus is combined several times with the conditional stimulus (for example, a bell and the metronome beat), and the response to the latter by itself dies out. Fourth is *differentiated inhibition*. Here stimuli similar to the conditional stimulus (for example, metronome beats of say 50, 55, 65, 70) at first produce an effect similar to the conditional stimulus (a metronome beating at 60 per minute). But they soon become inactive if not reinforced.

The interesting feature of these four cases is that the inhibition can be removed immediately by introducing any additional agent which provokes the orienting reaction (looking, listening, etc.). For example, putting dilute hydrochloric acid in the mouth will immediately restore the response to the metronome beat. This phenomenon is called *dis-inhibition*, or inhibition of inhibition.

Pavlov also concluded that inhibition and excitation are complementary parts of a single process. It appeared that they obeyed the same laws. Both are involved as mutual complements in the law of reciprocal induction. Like excitation, inhibition operates in accordance with the law of irradiation-concentration; the period of concentration of excitation is characterized by the irradiation of inhibition which takes over more and more of the peripheral parts of the cerebral area in which concentration is taking place. Thus, differentiation of response, as a consequence of discriminating between stimuli, is based on the dynamic relationship between these polar opposites, excitation and inhibition.

Pavlov from his earliest days – in fact, even before he became a physiologist – thought in terms of complex dynamic systems. At this point in time (1916) he had elaborated the first approximation to a working model of the cortex. He conceptualized it as a complex system in dynamic equilibrium, functioning in accordance with certain definite rules or laws. In its totality, the system could be described as being made up of two kinds of mechanism – the reflex arc and the sensory analysers. The former concept he had taken over from Descartes and the physiological tradition which culminated in Sechenov. The latter had also spoken of 'analysers' in the sense that hearing, vision, the muscle sense, etc., were physiological devices suited to the analysis of sound, shape, movement, etc. They could be conceptualized on the analogy of Helmholtz's resonators which functioned in such a way as to pick out and identify the elements of a complex tone. Pavlov extended this notion, the analyser being for him not only the sense organ but also the nervous connections to the brain and the cerebral 'end' where the stimulus was presented to consciousness. The analysers act as special transformers, converting one kind of energy external to the organism – for example, the metronome beat – into nervous impulses. Their function is to decompose the complicated external world into its smallest possible integral parts or units, its elements. There are also analysers which deal with the enormous complexity of the inner phenomena which arise within the organism. Working together, these analysers, in conjunction with the reflex arcs, maintain the organism in a moment-by-moment, dynamic adjustment. Thus is achieved a unity between the organism and its conditions of life. The chief instrument through which the organism, including man, is maintained in closest relationship with the changing external conditions of life is the central nervous system. All external and internal changes are, so to speak, 'reported to', 'monitored by' and 'decided upon', in the last analysis, by the cortex.

Lastly, in this pre-revolution period, Pavlov noted that there were various types of dogs. At this stage, he observed merely that the process of inhibition (manifested in the fact that some dogs went to sleep on the experimental stand) was more pronounced in some cases than in others. This was a theme which would receive systematic treatment later.

At this stage, before the outbreak of war, and as the product of a dozen or more years of scientific activity, Pavlov had established on an experimental basis a completely new approach to the behaviour of organisms. By choosing the dog as the experimental animal Pavlov had, with deliberation, thought to discover psychological principles which could be generalized to human beings. His first, and it remains his chief, discovery was that it is impossible to account for behaviour in terms of the categories provided by subjective analysis. The concept of the 'psyche', as an independent entity, provided nothing that was of any value as an explanatory principle. After centuries of introspective analysis of subjective states, psychology and the other studies which dealt with man's inner life had come up with nothing in the way of scientific laws, causal explanations, even real understanding of any aspect of the psychic life. Pavlov therefore decided to explain behaviour without reference to inner psychological states or forces. It was his belief that the objective methods characteristic of science, by taking man as the object of study, would in relatively short order discover the fundamental laws which underlie the fearful complexity of our internal world. In crucial experiments he had demonstrated the extreme unlikelihood that the human mind, contemplating itself from within in search of causal relationships, was capable of generating anything but fantasies. Only the systematic application of a purely naturalistic method of thinking, based on the ordinary canons of scientific inquiry, was capable of generating knowledge of behaviour – whether animal or human.

Up to this watershed in time – the Great War of 1914–1918 – Pavlov had established as a set of working hypotheses: (i) the integral character of the inner organization of the animal and its inseparable unity with the environment, in other words, psychophysical monism; (ii) the reflex theory of behaviour as learned, or inborn, responses to changes in the environment, in other words, the principle of association; (iii) the leading role of the central nervous system, in particular, of the cortex, in the regulation of the life-processes of the organism and its response to stimuli; (iv) the operation of specific laws of cerebral functioning – as, coupling of cells stimulated simultaneously; mutual induction; irradiation-concentration; (v) the dependence of excitation on inhibition, and of inhibition on excitation, as opposite aspects of a single process.

(iii) Pavlov and Lenin – the Theoretical Basis of Soviet Psychology

At this point, the relationship between Pavlov's conceptions of psychic processes and Lenin's theory of reflection will be examined. These have undoubtedly been the most formative influences in the elaboration of Russian psychology since the Revolution. Marxism has been more important than Pavlovianism. Marxism not only serves as the criterion of truth, but Marxist 'anthropology' arrived, so to speak, fully developed, as the most progressive tendency in European philosophy. Pavlov, on the other hand, was still in the middle of his empirical enquiries when the Revolution occurred, with the status of an indigenous prophet who still had to make way. This status was changed radically when Lenin, as Chairman of the Soviet of People's Commissars, signed an edict in January 1921 granting Pavlov exceptional privileges 'in consideration of his extraordinary scientific services which have enormous significance for the workers of the whole world'.[11] This was an affirmation that Pavlovianism and Marxism were compatible, that they were indeed closely akin.

The central problem common to Marxism, to Pavlovianism, and to psychology, concerns the basic assumptions about the scientific method we must implement to ensure progress in understanding the object of investigation. The questions which arise here may be posed in this form: do the basic presuppositions of Soviet psychology contradict each other? Do they distort the general character of psychology as a science? Other questions to be raised in connection with the basic foundations of Soviet psychology are as follows: which of the views of Lenin and Pavlov can be used as the frame of reference for the solution of psychological questions? What is the acceptable method and the agreed content in the sciences which deal with behaviour – physiology, psychology, and psychiatry? What common tradition underlies these views? Is there perhaps some incompatibility between the views of Lenin and Pavlov on scientific method? And the most significant question of all must be raised: is there some basic incompatibility between the methods of Lenin and Pavlov and scientific method in general?

It might not always be easy, but it would be quite possible to demonstrate a historical link between any two thinkers chosen at random from the history of European thought. There is an evolutionary continuity in human thinking, which grips all of us mentally, as in a vice. Even our rejection of a specific element in the tradition is normally in terms of some other part. As regards Lenin and Pavlov there is no necessity to force a historical link. A clear and organic connection exists. Both were nourished in the same stream of thought. They were both materialists; both were atheists and monists; both were radicals, optimistic about the reformative and redemptive character of scientific knowledge on human society and on individuals. Pavlov was not a political revolutionary, although he was radical in his opinions, and prepared to express them. Nor was he a Marxist, although his characteristic style of work and his mode of thought, as we shall see, were very compatible with Marxist procedures.

Fig. 1 The basic tradition

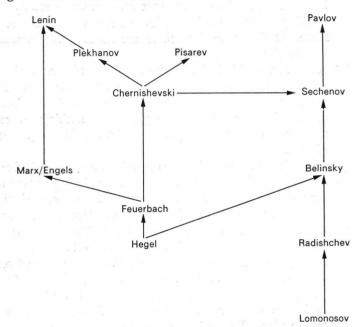

Lenin derived his views, through Marx and Engels, from the revolutionary left-wing of classical German philosophy. In common with Marx and Engels, he described his philosophy as dialectical materialism. This system of thought claims to subsume what is true in all previous philosophical schools, and to reduce the remainder (described rather loosely as 'metaphysics') to the status of museum curiosities. In particular, it claims to provide the most general principles of scientific method and scientific truth. These can be summed up in quasi-axiomatic form, as follows:

   (i) All reality is material in nature. All phenomena, whether physical, mental, or social, are the product of matter in motion.
   (ii) Matter is objective and primary; the human spirit, psyche, or 'soul' (so-called) is secondary and derivative from matter.

The psyche has no independent existence: it is a property of highly organized matter.

(iii) Reality is fully knowable. Truth is the reflection in the human brain of the actual objects and connections existing outside of us. Science yields laws which reflect causal sequences. The fact that we know the real world is proved by human practice – that is we can transform reality by working on it to achieve a known and predictable outcome. At the same time there are no absolute, eternal, unchanging truths.

(iv) All nature – this includes the physical universe, society, and the individual – forms an interconnected whole. Nothing is 'locked away' or separated absolutely from other objects or processes. In particular, nothing can remain isolated from the operation of the universal process of change.

(v) There is nothing absolute or eternal. The apparently fixed character of boundary lines, and the enduring nature of certain categories, are arbitrary constructions of the human mind which projects these divisions into nature.

(vi) Development is not the result of a uniform process of gradual change or evolution. There are periods of revolutionary change when evolution proceeds by leaps from one stage to another qualitatively different from the first. These periods of violent change may be followed by quiet periods when apparently no, or minimal, changes are taking place. But quiescent periods are those when vast revolutionary changes are being prepared: change *is* actually taking place but on a reduced scale, and often in terms of inscrutable operations.

(vii) All change is the result of a conflict between opposing tendencies. Thesis begets antithesis; as a result of conflict and mutual interpenetration, a synthesis comes into being. This is the law of the negation of the negation. Change, or development, normally follows this pattern. But this principle is qualified by the recognition of 'non-antagonistic contradictions', whereby development proceeds as the result of an interaction between aspects or 'sides' of reality which differ from each other, but which are not necessarily hostile. This is an important qualification in relation to Pavlov's work, although made without reference to it (by Marx who stated it as a general principle in 1845).

In discussing the methodology appropriate to psychology these axiomatic principles serve at once as a set of constraints, and as guide-lines, clarifying the nature of problems and the road to their solution. The basic source is Lenin's work on philosophical problems undertaken in preparation for his polemic with the party group associated with Maxim Gorki – Bogdanov, Bazarov, and Lunacharsky. In addition to *Materialism and Empirio-criticism* (1909), there are his *Philosophical Notebooks,* first published in 1929. The argument of these contributions can be stated, as follows:

> Materialism, in full agreement with natural science, takes matter as primary and regards consciousness, thought and sensation as secondary, because in its well-defined form sensation is associated only with the higher forms of matter (organic matter), while 'in the foundation of the structure of matter' one can only surmise the existence of a faculty akin to sensation.[12]

Materialism in Lenin, as in Marx and Engels, has become sharply aware of itself and has developed a spirit of partisanship. The most basic truth for Russian Marxism is that 'consciousness, in general, reflects being'. Thus materialism recognizes the existence of 'objects in themselves', existing outside the mind. Ideas and sensations are copies, images, reflections of these objects and their interrelationships. Idealism, on the other hand, claims that objects do not exist except as 'combinations of sensations'. Lenin argues that there is no difference between the phenomenon and the 'thing-in-itself', and that there can be no difference. The only difference is between what is known about the object and what is not yet known.

It is claimed that the verification of these basic assumptions is to be found in the whole history of science and technology. For example, alizarin was an unknown thing-in-itself before it was abstracted from the madder plant by man for use as a dye. At this point it became a thing-for-us. When alizarin was synthesized as 1:2 dihydroxyanthraquinone ($C_{14} H_8 O_4$) its objective existence and the truth of man's perception of it were simultaneously demonstrated. This is the test of *practice* which, according to Marx's earliest writing (*Thesen über Feuerbach*, 1845), proves the reality, the 'this-sidedness' of our thinking. The standpoint of practice, of life, should be first and fundamental in the theory of knowledge. This approach leads inevitably to materialism, brushing aside the endless fabrications of professorial scholasticism, as Lenin puts it.

According to Lenin, there are no more comprehensive concepts for the theory of knowledge than the opposed pairs being and thinking, matter and sensation, physical and psychical. One or the other must be taken as primary. It is this decision which irrevocably divides materialists such as Feuerbach, Marx, and Engels from the idealists and agnostics such as Hume, Berkeley, Mach, and Avenarius. But even the antithesis of matter and mind is relative, not absolute. What is miscalled 'the mind' is, in fact, a property which emerges historically at the point where matter has reached a certain level of complexity. Mind is inseparable from matter; Duns Scotus's question of whether matter can think is quoted approvingly by Marx.

In face of the developing crisis in physics, represented in his day by the development of non-Euclidean geometry, the discovery of radioactivity, the electron theory of matter, the quantum theory and what is called the 'disappearance of matter', Lenin points out that this has no relevance to the epistemological distinction between materialism and idealism. What Lenin is claiming is that the difference between these two tendencies arises from their respective answers to the question of the *source* of our knowledge, and of the relation of such knowledge to the physical world. The question of the structure of matter, of atoms and electrons, is a question that refers only to this physical world, it has no bearing on the question of the relation between matter and the psyche in general. The crisis in modern physics, associated with the quantum theory and 'the principle of indeterminacy', is produced by the scientific community deviating from a direct, resolute, and irrevocable recognition of the objective value of its theories. It represents a breakdown of nerve in face of the breakdown of old-established concepts. The question for materialism is whether the source of our knowledge of these connections is objective natural law or whether they are simply properties of our mind, of its innate faculty of apprehending certain *a priori* truths, and so forth.

The importance of all this is clear. From the basic proposition that 'consciousness reflects being' there follows the proposition 'social consciousness reflects social being'. The attitudes and relationships of the individual are not something generated spontaneously from within – on the contrary, they reflect an existing reality. By conceding to the idealist tendency that 'social life in all its manifestations is a consciously psychic life',[13] Bogdanov was abandoning objective truth and making of class consciousness an idiosyncratic reaction of certain radical thinkers, a personal foible, a fantasy, if you will. In this connection Lenin said: 'From this Marxian philosophy, which is cast from a single piece of steel, you cannot eliminate one basic premise, one essential part, without departing from objective truth, without falling a prey to a bourgeois-reactionary falsehood.'[14]

According to Marxism, social being is independent of social consciousness. The latter is secondary and reflects the former. Now reflection is not the same as *identity*: the reflection may be an approximately true copy, but to speak of identity is absurd. Where class interests divide a society, the reflection is particularly distorted. The real relations between man and production, between the social classes, and between knowledge and reality is twisted out of all recognition. Men develop a false consciousness; another name for this is *ideology*. As Marx and Engels put it in *The German Ideology* (1845):

> Hitherto men have constantly made up for themselves false conceptions about themselves, about what they are and what they ought to be. They have arranged their relationships according to their ideas of God, of normal man, etc. The phantoms of their brains have gained the mastery over them. They, the creators, have bowed down before their creations. Let us liberate them from the chimeras, the ideas, dogmas, imaginary beings under the yoke of which they have been pining away.[15]

This implies that there are degrees of enlightenment and that an accurate, objective reflection of social reality and of real human relationships is possible. Class consciousness is, of course, the instrument or tool by which the distorted images of ideology can be corrected. For the exploited, that is, for the mass of humanity, this tool is Marxism. Starting from a partisan standpoint, and using the dialectic method in thinking about the real data, it is claimed that it is possible to develop an objective science: further, that it is *only* by these procedures that an objective science *is* possible. Man is not a contemplative being, and truth is not obtained by withdrawing from action. Truth is something to be *made* at the same time as it is being *understood*: it is only understood in the process of being made. In the final analysis, the only way to correct ideology is not by criticism of its false conceptions nor by a descriptive exposition of the nature of the realities – only transformation of the actual social relations, by revolution, will put an end to the false and tendentious reflections. This is what is meant by partisanship. In attempting to change reality, man discovers its true nature and his own. Passive contemplation can generate only a sterile scholasticism which is cut off from the real world. Thus, in changing reality man also changes himself: understanding is the product of practical-critical, that is, revolutionary activity.

The actual laws of dialectic were taken over from Hegel. But Marx stripped them of their mystic form and related them to the actual developments in the world of nature and human history. According to Engels, the laws of dialectics are not 'built into nature, they are discovered in it and evolved from it'.[16] They are nothing but scientific laws of development of the greatest degree of generality. There are three such laws: (i) the unity of opposites; (ii) the transformation of quantity into quality; and (iii) the negation of the negation. In Lenin's hands, the formal exposition of these laws characteristic of Engels' popularizations of Marxist philosophy gave way to an attempt to apply dialectical ways of thinking in the day-to-day situations that confronted him as a party leader. In his article on *The Teachings of Karl Marx,* published in the Granat encyclopaedia in 1914, he provides a classic statement of this mode of thinking, rich in its implications for developmental psychology:

> A development that repeats, as it were, the stages already passed, but repeats them in a different way, on a higher plane ('negation of negation'); a development, so to speak, in spirals, not in a straight line; a development in leaps and bounds, catastrophes, revolutions; 'intervals of gradualness'; transformation of quanity into quality; inner impulses for development, imparted by the contradiction, the conflict of different forces and tendencies reacting in a given body from inside a given phenomenon or within a given society; interdependence, and the closest, indissoluble connection between *all* sides of every phenomenon (history disclosing ever new sides), a connection that provides the one world-process of motion proceeding according to law – such are some of the features of dialectics as a doctrine of evolution more full of meaning than the current one.[17]

The relationship between Pavlov's and Lenin's conceptions is a very close one. Indeed one might speak of the two sets of concepts as isomorphic. This basic similarity, or identity, of viewpoints arises from the fact that both inherited a particular method of thinking about reality, in terms of *systems*. A system is a complex unity made up of interconnected parts which are related to each other so that changes of condition take place without the system losing its integrity. Continuing adjustments are made which maintain the system in a condition of dynamic equilibrium. This is the concept of society which Lenin inherited from Marx: it is also the concept of the organism which Pavlov inherited from Claude Bernard. The consequence of this relationship is that, on the one hand, Pavlov's investigations represent the translation of the principles of dialectical materialism into practical laboratory work, while Lenin's contribution can be seen as the application of natural-scientific ways of thinking to the analysis of social phenomena.

Pavlov's unique contribution to human thought is his conception of the organism as an integral whole. He understood this integrity in three senses. First, all the parts and the physiological functions of organisms are interconnected to form a single system which is in continuous interaction with the environment. It is an enduring system, in mobile, unstable equilibrium. Man too, being a physical organism, is conceptualized in the same form of 'self-regulating system'. The second thing to be said about the functional unity of the system is that it operates in such a way as to integrate the external and internal activities of the organism. In other words, the overt and covert responses to stimuli connect the organism with the changing conditions of its external environment and at the same time relate these to the activity going on within it (the *internal* environment). Thus, the internal and external environments represent an integral totality to which the organism responds. The unity of environment and organism is brought about through the operation of the central nervous system (the Botkin–Pavlov concept of 'nervism') which receives, monitors, and co-ordinates the signals from these two sources. Thirdly, the human organism is one being, not two. There is an integral unity of mental and somatic. Throughout his life Pavlov was a persuasive exponent of psychophysical monism. He constantly criticized scientists like Sherrington, Köhler and Claparède on the grounds that they were confused by quasi-religious conceptions and dualistic in their thinking. Statements like the following abound in his writings:

A single and indivisible nature expressed in two different forms – material and ideal: a single and indivisible social life expressed in two different forms – material and ideal – this is how we should regard the development of nature and social life. .... The development of the ideal side, the development of consciousness, is preceded by the development of the external conditions: first the external conditions change, and then consciousness, the ideal side, changes accordingly.[18]

This is actually a quotation from Stalin's *Anarchism and Socialism* (1903), illustrating the close parallel that exists between Pavlovianism and Marxism. The concept of adaptation of the organism to its conditions of life runs through the whole of nineteenth century biology, from Lamarck. It crystallized in Darwin's theory of natural selection, and became the common intellectual currency between the natural sciences and Marxism. But both Pavlov and Marx go beyond Darwin – Pavlov by applying the systems concept in detail to *individual* organisms, Marx by emphasizing the *creative* aspects of man's interaction with the environment. The character of the environment changes the functioning of the organism, says Pavlov; yes, says Marx, and the organism, by its activity, changes the character of the environment.

The conception of the organism as a system in equilibrium, unstable and self-regulating, is the first principle of Pavlov's physiological scheme. It is to be found clearly expressed from the Marxist point of view by Engels, as follows:

In the living organism we see continual motion of all the smallest particles as well as of the larger organs resulting in the continual equilibrium of the total organism during the normal period of life, which yet always remains in motion, the living unity of motion and equilibrium.[19]

His second principle is the theory of reflexes. This states that the complex and subtle interrelations between the organism and the external environment, as well as the internal interactions between the various organs and parts of the system, are brought about through the operation of a system of reflexes. Some of these links are inborn, some acquired. The theory of reflexes in its turn involves three basic concepts: the principle of determinism, the principle of analysis-synthesis, and the principle of structure.

The principle of determinism, as we have seen, is entirely basic to Pavlov's work. It is stated most cogently about human behaviour in his article *A Physiologist Replies to Psychologists*:

Man is of course a system (more crudely, a machine), and like every other in nature is governed by the inevitable laws common to all nature. But it is a system which, within the present field of our scientific vision, is unique for its extreme powers of self-regulation.[20]

Determinism is, of course, an essential presupposition of Marxism. But it is qualified in Hegel's sense that the understanding of necessity makes man free. Lenin quotes Engels with entire approval:

> Freedom does not consist in the dream of independence of natural laws, but in the knowledge of these laws, and in the possibility this gives of systematically making them work towards definite ends. This holds good in relation both to the laws of external nature and to those which govern the bodily and mental existence of men themselves – two classes of laws which we can separate from each other at most only in thought but not in reality. Freedom of the will therefore means nothing but the capacity to make decisions with real knowledge of the subject.[21]

In another place, Lenin argues, in exactly the same way as Sechenov and Pavlov, that this definition of causality and of human freedom in no way invalidates the principle that human beings are responsible for their actions and in no way reduces their status as persons.

The principle of analysis-synthesis is a statement of the fact that the cortex performs two functions, or that two functions are represented in it. First is the discriminatory function – for example, the fine discrimination of tones, odours, etc. Second is the synthesizing activity. This is made essential because of the separation in space of the analysers (that is, the sense organs and their cortical representation). These two activities go on all the time in the brain; thus the cortex, like the whole organism, is also a system in dynamic, unstable equilibrium. This dynamic system has therefore the appearance of a mosaic of interpenetrating functions. The mosaic is made up of the physical disposition of the processes of analysis-synthesis and also of excitation-inhibition. The mosaic is continuously changing, its boundaries fluctuating from moment to moment like a kaleidoscope. This conception of how the cortical system actually works is absolutely compatible with the principles of dialectics.

The principle of structure, which takes account of the different organs and systems within the brain, is necessary to explain how the forces represented in the cortex are distributed in space, how the different functions of the cortex are associated with different kinds of structure, and vice-versa. This way of conceptualizing these problems leads to the study of the 'architectonics' of the central nervous system. By this Pavlov means the study of the brain, spinal cord, and the nervous connections of the central nervous system as an integrated system with dominant and subordinate levels of functioning. The conception of 'levels' of functioning and of the distribution of matter and energy in space as an explanation of the different cortical processes might have been written by Engels.

The third general principle of Pavlovian theory is derived from the theory of 'nervism'. According to this view there are levels of organization within the central nervous system: the highest of these is the cortical level. In addition to the most general laws of nervous functioning the cortex obeys laws which are specific to it. This is explained as follows: the *general* laws of nervous function are common to all animals with a nerve-net – this includes everything from sponges to man. The laws in question are conduction, summation, induction, etc. These appertain to all nervous functioning. In animals with the same kind of nervous system as man, that is, the vertebrates which have a central nervous system with various levels dominated by the highest level, the cerebral cortex, there are laws which are specific to the spinal level and other laws which are specific to the cortex. The laws which relate to the spinal level of nervous activity were discovered by Flüger around 1850 and restated by Sherrington. These are: the law of homonymous conduction (movement is on the same side of the body as that to which the stimulus is applied); the law of bilateral symmetry (that if excitation spreads to the other side of the body it affects the same muscles as those responding on the side of the stimulus); the law of unequal intensity (in the latter case, the reaction to the stimulus is unequal); the law of distal-proximal movement (that is, the irradiation of the reflex impulse is in the direction away from the head). Sherrington added to these, laws relating to co-ordination, latency of response, after-discharge, reciprocal innervation and others. In his classic treatise *The Integrative Action of the Nervous System* (1906) he gives an exhaustive account of spinal reflexes.

The laws describing the mode of functioning of the cortex were discovered by Pavlov. They are: the law of irradiation-concentration; the law of mutual induction; the mosaic of activities in dynamic equilibrium; the coupling function (that is, conditional reflexes in the narrow sense); analysis-synthesis. In addition to these, man differs from all other animals with a central nervous system in having a 'second signalling system'. By this Pavlov means human speech. Although Pavlov does not mention this specifically, it seems to be implied in the structure of his general conceptual system that the 'second signalling system' conforms to the general laws of nervous activity, to the specific laws of cortical function, and in addition operates according to special laws of its own. In his *Dialectics of Nature,* written between 1872 and 1882, but published only in 1927, Engels writes:

> The Hegelian distinction, according to which only dialectical thinking is reasonable has a definite meaning. All activity of the understanding we have in common with animals: *induction, deduction,* and hence also *abstraction, analysis* of unknown objects, *synthesis,* and as a union of both, *experiment.* In their nature, all these modes of procedure – hence all means of scientific investigation that ordinary logic recognises – are absolutely the same in men and the higher animals. They differ only in degree of development of the method in each case. On the other hand dialectical thought – precisely because it presupposes investigation of the nature of concepts – is only possible for man, and for him only at a high level of development.[22]
>
> (slightly abbreviated)

The fourth Pavlovian principle is that of the unity of the subjective and objective. This is directly in line with Lenin's conception of 'reflexion'. Pavlov did not deny the existence of inner mental experience. On the contrary, he regarded it as higher nervous activity. In his day, and as a result of his influence, the methods of introspective psychology were declared to be barren in explaining behaviour. Thousands of years of subjective analysis had contributed little or nothing to an understanding of mental processes: absolutely nothing had been recorded about their 'material substratum', the functioning of the nervous system. An amalgamation of the science of psychology, as it was then understood, and of physiology seemed to be indicated. Pavlov spoke in this strain referring to 'the legitimate marriage of psychology and physiology'. In such an amalgam – if it were really 'legitimate' – the *objective* data obtained by controlled experiment must be prior to, more decisive than, and provide the analytical tools used in the interpretation of subjective data. In concrete terms this means that the laws of cortical functioning discovered by Pavlov,

and others to be revealed by future investigation, must be the basic
concepts used in organizing and explaining psychological data. In
contrast, such data and principles as are provided, for example,
by the Freudian corpus, are useless in a scientific study of behaviour. They are not the result of objective experimentation but
of subjective analysis of subjectively obtained data. Pavlov declared in 1906, and he never subsequently made any concessions
on this point, nor did he retreat from this position:

> In the end all data of a subjective character must pass over into
> the field of objective science. A mixture of the subjective and
> objective methods of investigation is harmful. The attempt must
> be made to analyze phenomena from the purely objective
> standpoint.[23]

He was speaking as a physiologist, but the principle was intended
to be of general application. At the time he made this declaration,
it should be recalled that certain physiologists were advocating
the use of introspection as the preferred *physiological* method in
problems of perception (for example, Hering, working in the field
of vision.)

It is clear that a detailed comparison of Pavlov's concepts with
the basic principles of dialectical materialism reveals no conflict
between them. Indeed Lenin's ideas and Pavlov's go hand-in-
glove. It is this fact which probably accounts for the special facilities provided for Pavlov after the Revolution, beginning with
Lenin's decree of 1921. This decree ordered that Pavlov's work
must have priorities of one kind and another, including extra
rations for himself and his wife. The special treatment he received
eventually reached such a scale that Pavlov expressed embarrass-
ment, fearing that his laboratory might not produce results com-
mensurate with the amount of money being given him for
research.

The question remaining, whether the principles stated by Pavlov
and Lenin are in conflict with science and scientific method, is
one which will be answered ultimately according to personal predilection. Expressing a personal view, it may be said that, stripped
of their ideological aura and emotion-charged terminology, the
principles of dialectics, as well as Pavlov's basic assumptions,
appear to be compatible with the commonsense assumptions
which scientists make with regard to scientific procedures in the
course of their work.

References

1. I. Sechenov *Selected Physiological and Psychological Works* 1952: 581.
2. I. Sechenov 1952: 135, 198.
3. I. Sechenov 1952: 135.
4. I. Sechenov 1952: 116.
5. I. Sechenov 1952: 422.
6. I. Sechenov 1952: 163–164.
7. I. P. Pavlov *Lectures on Conditioned Reflexes* 1928, **1**: 37.
8. I. P. Pavlov 1928: 50.
9. I. Sechenov 1952: 118–119.
10. I. P. Pavlov, 1928: 221.
11. Lenin's edict on Pavlov of January, 1921, printed in Asratyan 1953: 32.
12. V. I. Lenin *Materialism and Empirio-Criticism* 1909: 32; Lenin, Philosophical Notebooks in *Sochineniya* 1947, **38**.
13. Bogdanov quoted: V. I. Lenin 1909: 329 (Russ edit. p. 308)
14. V. I. Lenin *Materialism and Empirio-Criticism* 1909: 332.
15. K. Marx and F. Engels, Preface, *The German Ideology* 1947.
16. F. Engels quoted: *Anti-Dühring*. Moscow: Foreign Languages Pub. House, 1962.
17. V. I. Lenin *Teachings of Karl Marx* London: Lawrence and Wishart 1934: 14.
18. J. V. Stalin, Anarchism and Socialism, in *Collected Works* 1952, **1**.
19. F. Engels *Dialectics of Nature* 1955: 170.
20. I. P. Pavlov, A Physiologist Replies to Psychologists. *Psychological Review* 1930, **37**. Reprinted in *Lectures on Conditioned Reflexes* 1941, **2**: 409–447.
21. V. I. Lenin *Collected Works* 1938, **13**: 185; F. Engels *Anti-Dühring* 1962: 128.
22. F. Engels *Dialectics of Nature* 1955: 203.
23. Pavlov, 1906: in *Lectures on Conditioned Reflexes* (Eng. trans.) N.Y.: International Publishers. 1928, **1**: 81–96.

Reading List

Books in English
Babkin, B. P. (1951) *Pavlov: A Biography*. London: Gollancz.
Brožek, J. and Slobin, D. (1972) *Psychology in the USSR: An*

Historical Perspective White Plains, New York: Int. Arts and Sciences Press.

Frolov, Y. P. (1937) *Pavlov and his School* London: Paul, Trench, Trübner.

Lenin, V. I. (1947) *The Essentials of Lenin* (2 vols.) London: Lawrence and Wishart.

Sechenov, I. M. (1965) *Autobiographical Notes* Washington, DC: Am. Inst. Biol. Sciences.

Sechenov, I. M. (1952) *Selected Physiological and Psychological Works* Moscow: Foreign Languages Pub. House.

Books in Other Languages

Hippius, R. (1945) Zur Psychologie des russischen Volkes, chapter 4 in *Die Russentum und der Bolschevismus* (Microfilm: University of Alberta).

Koyré, A. (1950) *Études sur l'histoire de la pensée philosophique en Russie* Paris: Libraire Vrin.

Rubinstein, S. L. (1955) Psikhologicheskie vozzreniya I. M. Sechenova. *Voprosy Psikhologii* 1 (5): 26 ff.

Part III *The Content of Soviet Psychology*

Chapter 4   *The Revolution and its effects:*
1917–1929

The unique chaos and disruption in which the Revolution of 1917 took place meant that it was impossible to devote much thought or attention to reconstruction on the 'philosophical front' (Lenin). Until about 1921 'idealism' as a self-conscious and declared intellectual trend persisted in universities. Following a protracted discussion devoted to the anti-scientific nature of this philosophical tendency, idealism (which was, of course, closely associated with religious thought) was discredited in 1923–4 by Blonski and Kornilov. Institutional support was withdrawn; many intellectuals were forced to emigrate, others were forced into retirement.

Four alternative theories were presented in the period 1924–9 for consideration, and possibly official recognition, as Marxist psychology. These were: (i) Kornilov's 'reactology' which was class-conscious, interested in human reactions, especially in work. Theoretically it was considered to have borrowed too heavily from Feuerbach, Plekhanov, and Bukharin and other thinkers outside the mainstream of Bolshevik thought. It was condemned as dualistic, being a form of psychophysical parallelism. As a system, it was criticized for the failure to recognize the transformative influence of changing conditions on human characteristics; (ii) Bekhterev's 'reflexology' was a cosmic system which attempted to derive psychological and social laws from general considerations about energy. In turn, this system was condemned as 'mechanical materialism, degenerating into idealism'. Lenin had previously condemned a very similar theory, Ostwald's 'energetics', in 1909 in similar terms; (iii) Pavlov's *conditional reflex* system was regarded as inadequate as a basis for Marxist psychology because of its 'canine' basis – Pavlov's work with humans not being very well known as he published preliminary results only in 1939. Pavlovianism was known only to psychologists in its distorted American behaviourist form. This was considered to be too crude and erroneous as a basis for a scientific psychology; (iv) Vygotski's 'cultural-historical' views were discredited on the grounds that he borrowed too heavily from Western psychology: he was also heavily involved with 'pedology' which was already under attack.

(i) Social and Intellectual Background

In considering the influence of the Russian Revolution it is convenient to mark off the period beginning in October 1917 and ending with the discussions at the Sixteenth Party Conference in April 1929 which took place in connection with the adoption of the First Five Year Plan. In this period the Communist Party settled its accounts with the various other political parties and opposition movements in the course of assuming power, withdrawing unilaterally from the war of 1914–18, defending the revolutionary seizure of power in the wars of intervention, and emerging as victor in the Civil War. Essentially, 1917–29 was a kind of interregnum period when the various interested groups (including the numerous political parties, counterrevolutionaries, and foreign interventionists) struggled for the right to determine the future of the Russian people, first with arms, then in terms of political power, finally with ideas. It ends with the establishment of the absolute hegemony of the Bolshevik Party under the Party secretary Stalin, and with the decisions to re-equip and reorganize the whole of industry and agriculture on the basis of Marxist socialism.

These events may seem remote from the development of academic studies such as psychology. But, in fact, the process of total war and revolution radically transformed the scope and content of this subject. In the case of psychology, in addition to the transformations to be expected from war and almost total destruction, we must take account of the calculated decision of the Communist government to revolutionize this study, in common with all other academic disciplines, to remove it from its normal limits, and to place it at the service of the Revolution and the task of industrializing a predominantly peasant economy.

There is no great problem in differentiating phases of development in Soviet psychology. This is because, with intellectual matters, as with political questions, manifestoes and decrees are issued which clearly mark the origin and demise of particular schools of thought. There is considerably less divorce between theory and practice under Communist rule. This means that the discussion of theory takes account of the effects of particular ways of doing things and of looking at things, inculcated by the theory, on practical outcomes. Having criticized or condemned the underlying theoretical principles, the associated practical activities are banned at the same time. Soviet psychology develops in a Hegelian or Marxist pattern of revolutionary catastrophic change, not according to the Darwinian model of uniform and gradualist evolution.

The essential similarity between Lenin's conception of 'the Party' and the way in which academic studies develop in the Soviet Union is not only an analogy. Both bear the stamp of their Russian origin. Both belong to a certain historical tradition and appear to be congenial to the national character of the Russian people. Russian institutions traditionally work on the basis of a group consensus. Individualistic views are not tolerated to the same degree as in liberal societies. Thus, Soviet discussion of scientific or political questions would be clearer to Western observers and students of Soviet affairs if they were considered in the context of Lenin's principle of 'democratic centralism'. This principle is derived from Marx's practice as the leader of the Communist political movement in Europe (in the First International), as well as from the traditional Russian folk practice in the Mir or village commune. The principle of 'democratic centralism' consists in an organized discussion in which all are encouraged to participate as equals up to the point where a clear and decisive majority viewpoint emerges. The vote is then taken. The members of the group who are then in the minority are expected to reconsider their standpoint with a view to making the decision unanimous. In any case, everyone must implement the majority decision loyally: neither is further discussion tolerated when a definitive vote has been taken. In Old Russia, according to Kovaleski, in the village commune members of the minority, if they continued contumacious, were beaten with rods until they agreed with the majority view.

(ii) Phases in the Development, to 1929

In the twelve-year period 1917 to 1929 it is possible on the basis of declarations to discern three clearly marked phases. These phases represent natural divisions of the history of this subject, singling out the effects of political decisions and of new forms of social organization on intellectual processes.

PHASE I: IDEALISM IN PSYCHOLOGY

The first phase is initiated by the Revolution and lasts from 1917 until 1921. At the beginning of this period psychology in Russia is not noticeably different from psychology anywhere else. A confusion of schools exists; there is a welter of conflicting theories. This is characterized as 'a methodological crisis' by Russian psychologists, since there is an absence of clarity about the real object of study, the method appropriate, and the level of generalization it is possible to reach in drawing conclusions. The proliferation of schools, the overt and more subtle influences of theology, Kantianism, and other philosophical tendencies are regarded as symptoms of an extremely unhealthy state, leaving little prospect of the development of a valid science. Psychology is in a very weak state, being still in thrall to theology and philosophy. At this time there are no professional chairs in psychology. There is a single institute of psychology (in Moscow). But it is not viewed very favourably by the ruling powers since it was founded and led by the idealist philosopher Chelpanov. This backwardness of psychology in Russia cannot wholly be attributed to Tsarism, although as we have seen there was very considerable interference with the attempts to develop the natural and social sciences by State and Church. It corresponds, in a general way, to the condition of psychology in most other places at that time with the exception of America and Germany. Probably a greater degree of backwardness than that which existed in Britain at this time can be recognized because of the religious obscurantism fostered by Tsarist conditions. On the other hand psychological medicine was well advanced having long had university status and a network of clinical institutions. For this fact the tradition of Russian humanitarianism and the close association between medical science and the military needs of the State must be given credit. For example, Pavlov, Sechenov, and Bekhterev were, at various times, professors in the Military Medical Academy.

The feature which distinguishes this phase of Soviet psychology from subsequent developments was the existence of frankly idealistic trends. University teachers like Vvedenski, Lossky, and Frank, who belonged to philosophical tendencies openly hostile to materialism, continued to be tolerated. In 1923 over one hundred intellectuals were expelled from Soviet Russia as obscurantists and saboteurs; these included Bulgakov, Lapshin, Lossky, and Frank and others whose views were totally anti-pathetic to Marxism.

Alexander Ivanovich Vvedenski (1856–1925) is classified as a neo-Kantian. He argued that it is impossible for us to know external reality (the 'thing-in-itself') except that it exists. In addition to our ordinary knowledge, which is based on *a priori* judgements rather than on sensation and experience, there is another kind of cognition, namely *faith*. This is a kind of special faculty or sense which we have in addition to our ordinary, physical sense organs. This special sense is exercised on data appertaining to the sphere of moral judgements. In his book *Psychology without Metaphysics* (3rd ed., 1917) he expressed the view that psychological experimentation was completely inane and pointless. Chelpanov, on the other hand, attempted to subordinate experimental psychology to his metaphysical, philosophical system. In discussing the question of introducing the teaching of psychology in secondary schools at the First Conference on Educational Psychology (1906) he came out against the idea of introducing experimental work into these courses on the grounds that 'without the metaphysical element psychology loses half of its charm for students'.

Nicholas Onufriyevich Lossky (1870–1965) was concerned mainly 'with the task of working out a system of metaphysics necessary for a Christian interpretation of the world'. In his book *The World as an Organic Whole* (1915) he wrote that reality is made up of certain beings who live outside of space and time, having being created by God in his own Image. Their activities, like God's, are free and creative. Some among them have chosen the paths of righteousness, but others have freely chosen not to enter the kingdom of heaven and are therefore ordained to live in a fallen condition at a lower level. They are bound by time and space in this material world. But through self-creative activity and by reincarnation, through successive stages, these agents can improve their spiritual status and become united with their peers. Lossky is also well known for his theory of intuitionism whereby he hoped to overcome the dichotomy between subject and object created by Descartes. According to this theory, the object of cognition enters the knowing subject's consciousness *directly*, 'so to speak in person'. It is apprehended immediately, intuitively, as a whole – quite independently of the act of knowing (*sic*).

Simon Ludwigovich Frank (1877–1950) is considered by the White Russian *emigré*, Zenkovsky, to be the most profound thinker in the whole history of Russian philosophy. In the period when he lived in Russia, whilst Professor at Moscow University, he published two works, *The Object of Knowledge* (1913) and *The Soul of Man* (1917). Frank is an idealist of classical vintage.

For him, 'the spiritual reality of primary thinking' (which he calls *cogito*) is a more basic reality than the world of fact – in truth, it is because of *cogito* that there is a world of 'objective reality' at all. The primary sources of his own thought are Plotinus (205–270 AD) and Nicholas of Cusa (1401–64), the Roman Catholic Cardinal and mystic.

In addition to these openly expressed idealistic views, the psychology to be found in Russia at this time included a considerable number of theoretical systems borrowed from abroad. For example, Watson's behaviourism had a tremendous vogue at this time; the Gestalt psychology of Wertheimer, Koffka, Köhler, and Lewin was also highly regarded since it was believed to exemplify methodological principles which were considered to be compatible with Marxism. Even the psychoanalytic schools of Freud and Adler owned a few adherents.

This dependence on Western viewpoints arose from the fact that many Russian scholars of ability before, and even after the 1917 Revolution, spent some time studying abroad, under the foremost representatives of European science. The Russian intellectual has always shown incredible diligence in assimilating the last word in European science and social and political theory throughout the nineteenth and early twentieth century. Indeed, the tradition of borrowing the scientific and technical knowledge of the Western world is one which goes back to Peter the Great. At the same time, there has always been another group which has tried to emphasize the native traditions and the fact that many discoveries have been made independently by Russian scholars.

With the anticipated end of the Civil War and the wars of intervention at the end of 1920, attention was directed more and more to the enemies of the 'proletarian dictatorship' at home. In this connection, the Bolsheviks under Lenin recognized the fight on what he called the 'philosophical front' as having an importance only second to that of the fight on the military front. Under the influence of the continuing Revolution, a reconstruction of the intellectual life on the basis of Marxism was recognized as being more and more pressing. Lenin wrote in 1922:

We must understand that no natural science, no materialism whatever, can hold out in the struggle against the onslaught of bourgeois ideas and the restoration of bourgeois philosophy without a solid philosophic basis . . . unless we do this, the great investigators in natural science will be as helpless in their philosophical deductions and generalizations as they have been here-tofore.[1]

In 1922 and 1923 the campaign against religion reached new heights, culminating in the expulsion of many university teachers as irreconcilable enemies of the Soviet régime and thought-pattern. In accordance with Lenin's technique of isolating the main enemy before dealing with the successively weaker ones, attention was first directed to exposing the errors of 'idealism' as a self-conscious and declared movement. 'Idealism' in this context includes not only a tendency in philosophy; it is identified with a covert form of religious belief which was included in the same enemy camp.

PHASE II: BLONSKI, KORNILOV, AND 'IDEALISM'

The second phase opened in 1921 and came to an end in 1923 with the discrediting and liquidation of the idealist school as an independent movement. Blonski's *Essay on Scientific Psychology* (1921) is considered to have given the death-blow to the conciously idealistic school in psychology.

This book was the first attempt by a Soviet psychologist to con-struct a system of materialist psychology based on Marxism. Pavel Petrovich Blonski (1884–1941) was a social-revolutionary who was converted to Marxism by the influence of Krupskaya, Lenin's wife. In 1920 he published *The Reform of Science* which shows evidences of his changing viewpoint. But it was in the *Essay on Scientific Psychology* (1921), especially in the brief historical sur-vey chapter, that he developed the argument of the scientific sterility of the 'science of the soul' and the insubstantiality of its metaphysical method. He proposed the materialistically based 'science of behaviour' as a natural and social science firmly linked to evolutionary biology and the materialist conception of history of Marx and Engels. He proposed the methods of observation of human behaviour, experiments, questionnaires, mathematical analysis of data, including correlation studies, introspection (although this presents difficulties). He proceeds to summarize the state of the science at this time.

Kornilov is given the credit for having finally swept idealism into oblivion in 1924. In his book *Contemporary Psychology and Marxism* he attempted to assimilate contemporary psychology within the conceptual framework of Marxism. There is little originality in this work: it is only of historical interest. It reiterates the basic principles of Marx's view of human nature set down in his notebook on Feuerbach in 1845 and in the works he published against the Hegelians. But, in the situation that existed in 1921–23 and in the light of subsequent developments, Blonski's and Kornilov's two monographs are important texts since they mark the direction along which advance was to take place. Indeed the principles set down by Blonski and Kornilov are reiterated again and again, even as the central themes in recent discussions. The central idea stated by Blonski was that 'in a class society, "man in general" is an empty abstraction, for man's social behaviour is determined by the behaviour of his class'.[2] This was, of course, the key principle in the Marx–Engels critique of the Left-Hegelians, stated most succinctly by Marx in these terms: 'Feuerbach consequently does not see . . . that the abstract individual he analyses belongs in reality to a particular form of society'.[3] The originality of Blonski consisted in his seeing the need for psychology to base itself on the principles set out by Marx and developed by Lenin. Speaking of this principle, Teplov, in his review of thirty years of progress in Soviet psychology, asserts, 'The history of Soviet psychology is in reality the history of the mastery of the Marxist–Leninist method by the Soviet psychologist . . . Each new step forward is a witness to a new stage in the creative mastery of Marxism'.[4] This is a statement typical of the interpretation of the development not only of psychology but related intellectual Soviet disciplines. Shmaryan in a similar review article, speaking of psychiatry and neurology, asserted:

> Soviet neurology and psychiatry are based on the stable foundation of the teachings of Marx, Engels, Lenin and Stalin. Since the October Revolution the best representatives of our science and practice carried on an active struggle against all varieties of idealism filtering through to us along with foreign theories. Soviet neurologists and psychiatrists played an active part in the philosophical discussions of 1930–31, and in the unmasking of these idealistic errors had their place as representatives of our native neurology and psychiatry. Soviet neurology and phychiatry, integrated in a single entity by the theory of dialectical materialism, produces fruitful conceptions, usefully revealing the nature of different phenomena.[5]

In a more recent history (1967) it is stated: 'Substantial facts in the history of psychological science in the U.S.S.R. must be considered in the light of the struggle of the Communist Party for dialectical materialism as the basis of Soviet Psychology'.[6] It is clear that Blonski, as a leading psychologist in his day, must be credited with initiating a process of development which still goes on: his writings formally initiated this line of thought.

Another major principle of Soviet psychology – that it must unreservedly place itself at the service of the Communist Party in the struggle to establish socialism – was stated first by Kornilov in this period, as early as 1923. He declared that psychology must not shun the practical questions of everyday life and the demands of socialist construction. With Blonski he is consequently entitled to an important place as a pioneer of the point of view which prevails in Russian psychology at the present time.

The main outcome of the discussion of Blonski's and Kornilov's views was twofold. Blonski's theses: (i) that, in adopting a framework for psychological investigation, declared anti-materialist schools must be excluded as possible choices; and (ii) that a generalized psychology of 'human nature' which ignores class divisions is an empty and useless abstraction, were accepted as correct in principle. They were taken as indicating the direction in which Soviet psychology must develop. The second result was the acceptance of Kornilov's assertion that only Marxism is adequate as the basis for a scientific psychology.

In later discussions of the nature of psychology and of the methods appropriate for advancing it, these principles are never seriously brought into question. The problem as it is posed by all protagonists in later discussions is whether the assumptions, methods, or data under debate are or are not consistent with Marxism, and whether the psychology in question is the *only* one which logically translates Marxism into psychological language basis for a scientific psychology.

It should be remembered in connection with these discussions, as in the analogous case where various groups of Soviet politicians were discredited, that the controversies in which various psychologists were criticized were played out according to rules accepted and applied rigorously to others by all the competitors. The losers, therefore, have no claim on our sympathy because they lost, except in so far as we may indulge ourselves by feeling sympathy for the under-dog. There is a marked tendency for Western observers of Soviet affairs to demand a change in the rules *after* the protagonists they favour have been defeated. Unless we have indicated in advance that we think the game too rough this demand cuts no ice. There is a predilection in Western evaluations of Soviet controversies to favour the loser always. No regard is paid to what this commits us to in accepting the positive theses of the discredited protagonist.

An important point about Soviet discussion is that the criterion of practice is invariably used to evaluate the truth of particular theories. Discussions always centre on two main issues: the practical usefulness of particular views, as well as their conformity with objective reality.

PHASE III: ALTERNATIVES TO 'IDEALISM'

The third phase follows logically on the second and consists of a close scrutiny of various theoretical frameworks which their authors presented as being the only acceptable formulation of Marxism in psychological clothing. Kornilov played a major part at this time in demolishing the claims of certain of these schools. He had been appointed to a key post in psychology as Director of the State Institute of Experimental Psychology (GIEP) in Moscow on its reorganization in 1923. This institute was originally the Shchukina Psychological Institute, associated with Moscow University, with Chelpanov as Director from 1912. It was reconstituted and officially reopened in 1914, Chelpanov still being Director. On 15 November 1923 Chelpanov handed over the directorship to Kornilov. This phase can be regarded as the most formative in the history of Soviet psychology in that all the competing schools (with the exception of the 'idealistic' tendencies which had been eliminated in previous encounters) were given a fair run for their money. Some notable advances were made in eliminating blind alleys by testing different viewpoints in a variety of concrete settings. There was considerable criticism of the available theories and methods. But the debates were not indulged in solely for the sake of 'abstract truth'. The different theories and viewpoints were certainly assessed from the point of view of objective truth. But, as in all Soviet discussions, the social implications of particular conceptions were very much to the fore. The question was posed in this form: what are the practical applications of the opposing psychological principles?

The tasks imposed by reconstruction and the laying of the foundations of a socialist society were the practical tests applied to the special standpoints and methods under discussion. The test was applied by allowing the various psychological and industrial research institutes to experiment freely along the lines suggested by the director and staff of these institutes. When it became obvious to all concerned that any particular viewpoint had no practical value (the pragmatic test is high up in the hierarchy of criteria of truth in Marxist philosophy) the institute or research team would be invited either to choose a different basis on which to work or they would be assimilated into other organizations. In fact, psychological theories were *tested* by putting them to work. Those which failed were discarded: the conclusion seemed irrefutable – if, given the best conditions, a theory was shown to have no practical value, it must be false. Once tested and shown to be false in this way, a Soviet theory tends not to survive. The psychologist who attempts to revive a discredited theory is regarded as reactionary in just the same way as a politician who attempts to reopen a closed political issue is regarded as violating the principle of 'democratic centralism'. Attempts to organize a 'platform' hostile to majority decisions are classed as treason. This suggests that Soviet psychologists take psychological theory seriously. It is not regarded as being just an afterthought or an appendage to certain empirical results collected haphazardly. Theory, and the *correct theory*, is a prerequisite for intelligent research.

In this phase, which lasted from 1923 until 1929–30, four main schools struggled for supremacy: Kornilov's reactological school, Bekhterev's reflexological school, Pavlov's school of conditional reflexes, and Vygotski's cultural–historical theories. The final result of their mutual opposition was that *none* was considered adequate for the new tasks posed by the success of the October Revolution.

(a) *Kornilov's 'reactology'*
As we have seen, Konstantin Nicholaevich Kornilov (1879–1957) was one of the two main leaders of the attack on 'idealism in psychology'. His positive views, as well as his criticisms of other tendencies, came closest in expression to classical Marxism of any of the contending parties. On behalf of the Bolsheviks, he was consciously conducting a struggle on two fronts: (i) against Chelpanovian idealism, entrenched at the beginning of the period in Moscow University, and (ii) against Bekhterev's school, which had its centre in the influential Reflexological Institute for Brain Research, founded by Bekhterev in Leningrad in 1917.

There were two main positions of Chelpanov to which Kornilov took exception. Firstly, there was the 'metaphysical' view that an empirical psychology (that is, a theoretical empiricism as well as a procedural empiricism) was compatible with the principles of

Marxism. Secondly, Chelpanov claimed that the method appropriate to psychology was the study of mental states by the technique of introspection, completely divorced from the study of physiological processes. On the other hand, against Bekhterev and his disciples, Kornilov deprecated the attempt to reduce the data of psychic processes to the laws of biology and physics. In other words, he attempted to steer a middle course between the Scylla of 'no physiology at all' and the Charybdis of 'nothing but physiology'.[7] In this connection as principles of method he suggested: (i) that the objective, experimental method was fundamental. But he did not limit this method to reflexology as Bekhterev attempted to do: he was prepared to sanction all available methods of scientific study of the living organism. He suggested: (ii) that the data elicited by objective techniques must be considered to be the primary data of science, in this manner echoing the views of Pavlov. In addition: (iii) he allowed the method of introspection a secondary role, recognizing that observations obtained by its use, although not acceptable by themselves, could often be used to supplement or support those obtained by objective techniques. The struggle against Bekhterev – who was in fact much closer to Kornilov's position than was Chelpanov – was waged with more intensity and heat than was the struggle against the declared idealist. The controversy with Bekhterev was regarded as a fight for the very existence of psychology as an independent study.

As a positive contribution, Kornilov attempted to establish a complete scheme of the nature of the human psyche. In this he leant heavily on Feuerbach, Plekhanov, and Bukharin in addition to the recognized and established Marxist classics. From an elaborate analysis of their views he claimed to deduce that the proper sphere of psychology could be correctly defined as 'reactology'. By this he meant 'the study of human reactions in their biosociological setting'. This was intended to direct attention especially to *working* behaviour and the influence of social class in determining the individual reactions. These two areas, according to Kornilov, should receive prior investigation by empirical methods.

A very elaborate programme of research for the analysis of movement in the laboratory and work situation was developed. Use was made of standard Western psychological equipment, such as the Hippchronoscope, the dynamoscope, and motorgraphic method. A classification of the main types of reaction and some 'laws' dealing with the expenditure of energy were worked out. But the whole thing smelled of the study and laboratory rather than of the factory and real life. It was much too programmatic (words rather than performance) in character. In following Bukharin, Plekhanov, and Feuerbach instead of Lenin, Engels, and Marx as his primary sources, Kornilov fell into the error of psychophysical parallelism, the view that mental or bodily processes are mutually independent, although proceeding along parallel lines.

His approach was also condemned as being eclectic. By this was meant that he was insufficiently critical of the techniques and formulations drawn from non-Marxist sources. In fact, it is clear that his main methodological blunder consisted in his considerable dependence on the American school of 'human engineering'. His abstract schematism was said to lead to a disregard for the influence of consciousness. In particular, in the condemnation of his tendency, it was alleged that he failed to give due emphasis to the possibility of modifying reactions by social processes, including those of education and social change. This could be blamed on Feuerbachian 'anthropologism' – the emphasis on man as a biological organism being allowed to obscure the fact that his abilities and 'nature' are conditioned by the kind of society he belongs to, as well as by his 'activity'. Thus he was guilty of 'mechanism' which was considered a very dangerous error in relation to the practical task of educating the developing Russian proletariat. On the reorganization of the GIEP in 1931 Kornilov ceased to be Director. But he continued to do important work and was highly regarded. He was one of the three editors of a definitive textbook of psychology as recently as 1948; he was a founding editor of the Soviet psychological journal *Problems of Psychology* in 1955. He died in 1957.

(b) *Bekhterev's 'reflexology'*
The second important school was that of Bekhterev. Much more than any of the other psychologists considered here Vladimir Michailovich Bekhterev (1857–1927) was guilty of trying to build up a completely new system of thought. This practice had been roundly condemned by Engels as a besetting sin of his German compatriots. Bekhterev aspired to proclaim scientific laws which should have cosmic validity. He based these laws on a generalization of his work on the 'associated motor reflex' – built upon the defensive withdrawal by the dog of a forepaw subjected to electric shock. An incredibly industrious and erudite scientist, he is said to have composed more than 600 scientific works based on his researches on the brain in relation to psychiatry. According to

Babkin, who worked for a time in his laboratory, his tremendous output was based on exploitation of his students and his slipshod approach to truth.

Like Pavlov, Bekhterev belonged to the radical and generally materialist group of Russian scientists who set themselves the task of developing the teachings of Sechenov. In this connection, it is interesting to learn that the professional association of Russian psychiatrists (Bekhterev was a psychiatrist) was the first organization to offer its services to, and declare its support for, the Bolshevik Government in 1917. His first important work was an elaborate monograph on the *Functions of the Brain* (1903–1907). In his *Psychic Activity and Life* (1904) he took issue with the prevailing idealism in psychology and philosophy, developing his 'energy' principle in opposition to these views. In psychology he is chiefly remembered for his work on the associated reflex. This work was based on Pavlov's experiments on the conditional salivary reflex in dogs. The method of the chronic salivary fistula (that is, bringing the salivary gland by operation to a permanent position on the outside of the face) – the technique used by Pavlov – seemed to Bekhterev to be quite unsuited to the study of 'behaviour' as the psychiatrist interpreted this word. For one thing (until the invention in America of Lashley's funnel which collected saliva without the need for operation) it could not be used with human beings. In any case, Pavlov's methodology seemed to Bekhterev capable of giving only the most trivial information about behaviour because of the unimportant psychological role of salivation in the total life of the organism. In other words, those very characteristics of the method of the chronic salivary fistula which seemed to Pavlov to single it out as *the* uniquely efficient way of studying the functions of the cortex condemned it in the eyes of Bekhterev. He had, of course, defined the purpose of his research very differently from Pavlov.

In 1907, four years after Pavlov's first report on the new method, he reported on 'artificially associated respiratory motor reflexes' where dogs had been used as subjects. In the following year he reported similar experiments with human subjects. In the next few years (1908–1910) he developed the method of the associated motor reflex. Here a defensive withdrawal of the hand or foot in response to a slight electric shock is associated with an originally indifferent stimulus in the manner made historic by Pavlov. The term 'reflexology' to describe the methods and results of these investigations was introduced.

Unlike Pavlov, Bekhterev immediately attempted to generalize his work. Indeed in the course of time he included *all* aspects of human development under the single rubric of 'reflexology'. He named various branches of 'the science of reflexology'; he wrote programmes of work which gave an outline of these branches of knowledge; he set up research centres for the working out of these programmes; and carried on a number of controversies (for example, with Pavlov) in which he sought to demonstrate that reflexology was 'the only strictly objective scientific discipline which studies human personality in its outer manifestations in objective correlations with its environment'.[8]

In 1925 in his *Psychology, Reflexology, and Marxism* Bekhterev tried to show that the 'crisis' in Soviet psychology could be solved only by adopting his energy standpoint, as set out in his various 'laws' of associated reflex activity. These laws could be deduced from the general cosmic process of energy-transformation first expounded by him in 1904! He maintained that reflexology was not in any way contradictory to dialectical materialism.

But he was judged by his contemporaries: the decision went against his system. It was described as 'vulgar mechanical materialism fast degenerating into idealism'.[9] Having regard to the special meaning of these terms, this seems a fair characterization of Bekhterev's views. Lenin had devoted a scathing criticism to Ostwald's 'energetics' and its Russian derivatives as early as 1909 and had used very similar terms in denying the validity of these views from the point of view of Marxism.

(c) *Pavlov's 'conditional reflex' school*
The third school given consideration at this time as a possible Marxist foundation for psychology was that of Pavlov. Pavlov was not guilty of Bekhterev's 'impetuous generalizations', and was careful always to leave some room for a new kind of psychology which should be based firmly on objective techniques and the laws of higher nervous activity. It is true that, by virtue of its recognized deficiencies in the matter of objective techniques in the period when he was active (1904–1935), psychology necessarily occupied a place of secondary importance in his thoughts. It may seem to be too much to say this, in view of the image of Pavlov current in Western psychology. In his Wednesday seminars he expressed nothing but scorn for the psychological explanations of Yerkes, Guthrie, Lashley, Köhler, Claparède, Freud, Janet, Kretschmer. He declared himself to be at war with Köhler and

Gestalt psychology in general. But it should be noted that many physiologists, such as Sherrington, Bethe, and others are also often under attack. And the reason is always the same:

> Dualism still makes itself felt in their midst; dualism is manifested in the form of animism which admits the existence of a peculiar substance opposed to the rest of nature and therefore requiring special treatment on the part of researchers compared with material phenomena.[10]

Some of his associates were not even prepared to allow that it might be possible for psychology to change. In the words of Borovski they 'attempted to overstep the legitimate boundaries in the field set apart for them'.[11] In other words, they wanted to swallow psychology into physiology, without remainder.

The immense prestige of Pavlov as *princeps physiologorum mundi,* coupled with the scientific clarity of all his work, conspired to produce a general uncritical attitude to the physiological laboratory and to the opinions of physiologists. Pavlov's theoretical views which had received considerable elaboration after the Revolution will be dealt with in detail below. At present, the important point is that he himself did not attempt to reduce all psychological processes to physiological laws. He visualized the possibility of a monistic, associationist psychology, basing its explanations on the laws of brain functioning, and not accepting the need for a special set of assumptions contrary to those of scientific method in general.

(i) Pavlov's Fourth Phase (1916–1919): Marking Time

During this period when the whole country was in a continuing state of grave emergency due to the war and revolution, Pavlov continued to work with diminished resources under almost impossible conditions. An assistant recalls those times:

> No difficulties or barriers could exist for Professor Pavlov which were able to force him to leave off any investigation begun: he could therefore be seen working on cold days in the laboratory in a winter coat, fur cap and snow boots. When the whole city was immersed in darkness on the short winter days by the absence of electric light, and no candles or paraffin could be had, Professor Pavlov used to continue his experiments in the laboratory by the light of wood torches . . . Notwithstanding the worst conditions of life and under nearly impossible conditions

for scientific work, both this and the lectures on physiology at the Military Medical Academy continued without a break. If there was no electric light, the demonstrations were carried out before an auditorium of 200 people by the light of one kerosene lamp, and we had to hurry in the big vivisectional experiments because the immobilized animals froze rapidly in the low temperature.[12]

In view of these conditions, it is not surprising that no new great advances were made in the understanding of cortical functions. Pavlov delivered a number of addresses however, in which he suggested that instinctive behaviour could be identified with reflex activity. He had shown how various reflexes could be associated through time, and suggested that an instinct could be thought of as a chain of reflexes. This led to the belief that certain kinds of activity, such as the 'guarding reflex' in the dog, were inborn. At this point he began to talk about the classification of reflexes, recognizing not only the self-preservative, the food, and the sexual reflexes as inborn but also the reflex of 'purpose', the reflex of 'freedom' and the reflex of 'slavery'. He preferred to call these 'reflexes' rather than 'instincts' since the former word conveys a clearer idea of determinism in their operation.

(ii) Pavlov's Fifth Phase (1919–1935): Application to Man

In 1919, laboratory work was revived and soon reached its former scale. Pavlov adopted a new style of work. Previously he had been very actively involved in one or two investigations, spending nearly the whole time with his collaborators. Now he supervised many investigations at once, where facts obtained from one research were used to explain those obtained in another, with Pavlov knowing the interactionships between the various pieces of research. For this reason, beginning in 1921, Pavlov held a Wednesday seminar where he acquainted his collaborators with the results of experiments carried out in the three laboratories under his control – at the Academy of Sciences, the Institute of Experimental Medicine, and the Military Medical Academy. These seminars continued until his death in 1935.

During the whole of this period, the most remarkable additions were made to Pavlov's conception of the regulation of behaviour in the cortex. He turned his attention to other experimental subjects – fish, anthropoids, and finally, man himself. The psychological clinic provided him with the opportunity of using a different kind of method, of making a new kind of observation. His mind was prepared for this operation by his elaboration of a new theory of types.

In a number of places Pavlov had made a few, rather random references to the fact that different kinds of reactions were sometimes to be found with different kinds of dogs. For example, two dogs out of thousands had exhibited the reflex of 'freedom' to an extremely marked degree. Petrova had observed in 1915 that certain types of animal easily passed into a drowsy, hypnotic state on the experimental stand. Pavlov had observed that inhibition travelled at different speeds over the cortex in different dogs, but remaining uniform for each individual as a kind of natural constant. In 1925 he began to approach the question systematically, with the recognition that there were considerable and striking differences in the individual qualities of dogs. These differences could be related to different kinds of nervous system to which he gave the names of the Hippocratic classification – sanguine, melancholic, phlegmatic, and choleric. The sanguine and phlegmatic types are stable, central types; the choleric and melancholic are unstable, extreme types. In the choleric and sanguine, excitation predominates over inhibition; in the phlegmatic and melancholic the reverse is true.

Fig. 2   Pavlov's four types (1928)

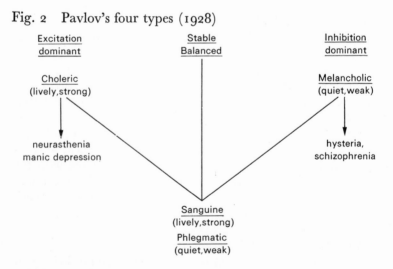

Using the three concepts: types of nervous system (labile, stable, unbalanced, strong, weak); excitation-inhibition; traumatic factors (floods, desertion, stress situations), Pavlov sought to throw fresh light on neuroses and psychoses in man, interpreting them from a purely physiological standpoint. He first studied schizophrenia – those forms where manifest symptoms of apathy, immobility, and stereotyped movements are found. The conclusion he came to was that the symptoms expressed a chronic state similar to the hypnotic trance, resulting from a weakness in the cortical cells. It is a kind of cerebral exhaustion. Likewise, hysteria is accounted for in terms of a weak nervous system by virtue of which the patient lives an unreasoned and emotional life which is directed by the sub-cortical rather than by the cortical centres. Hysterical analgesia and paralyses are produced by localized inhibition. The feelings of 'possession' (*les sentiments d'emprise*) which some hysterics experience are related to a peculiar condition of the nervous system which Pavlov called the ultra-paradoxical phase.

The interest in abnormal psychology arose from the fact that Pavlov had succeeded unintentionally in creating an experimental 'neurosis' in his dogs as a result of setting them a problem in discrimination which (in psychological terms) proved too 'difficult' for them. Pavlov's interpretation was to the effect that, having succeeded in establishing excitation as a response to the stimulus (a circle) and inhibition to a second (an ellipse), by then presenting stimuli in the form of circles which became more and more like ellipses, at a particular stage he succeeded in bringing about a 'clash' between excitation and inhibition at a particular point on the cortex. As a result, the animal had a serious 'breakdown'. This is expressed in the loss of all elaborated conditional reflexes, as well as other behavioural patterns such as barking, attacking the experimenter, refusing to enter the experimental chamber etc.

In an observation made during the Petersburg flood of 1924 when the River Neva overflowed its banks and the animals had to be rescued under dangerous conditions, he noted that dogs with a 'weak' nervous system succumbed to a traumatic neurosis. This was shown by very disturbed behaviour – barking, biting at the harness, loss of conditional responses etc. Pavlov remembered that the attempt to induce excitation and inhibition simultaneously (1921) produced a similar effect. This is how he was launched on the study of experimental neuroses. In 1925 he reported on these studies, recognizing that neurosis could be produced in a number of ways: (i) by conditioning the food reaction to a destructive stimulus (powerful electric shock), (ii) establishing differentation

between two stimuli which are then successively brought towards
equality (as in the circle and ellipse experiment), (iii) presenting
a previously differentiated excitatory stimulus and an inhibitory
stimulus to the same spot on the skin in very close succession without any interval, (iv) a very strong inhibitory stimulus (such as
the unusual flood of 1924, (v) post-operative scarrings in the
cortex (producing quasi epileptiform convulsions), and (vi) some
trauma which subjected the animal to considerable stress, such as
castration. Summarizing a massive series of experiments and observations, Pavlov provides the physiological explanation of these
extremely remarkable phenomena:

> All the foregoing facts allow us, it seems to me, to systematize
> the states to which the cortex is subjected under different in-
> fluences in a definitive, consecutive order. At one pole there is
> the state of excitation, an exceptional increase of the tonus of
> excitation, when an inhibitory process becomes impossible or
> is greatly impeded. Next comes the normal, wakeful state, the
> state of equilibrium between the excitatory and inhibitory pro-
> cesses. This is followed by a long, but also consecutive, series
> of states transitory to inhibition; the most typical of these are:
> the equalization state when, in contrast to the wakeful state,
> all stimuli, irrespective of their intensity, act with an absolutely
> equal force; the paradoxical state, when only the weak stimuli
> act, or when the strong stimuli act too, but produce a barely
> noticeable effect; and finally, the ultra-paradoxical state when
> only the previously elaborated inhibitory agents produce a posi-
> tive effect – a state followed by complete inhibition.[13]

The second development of the theory in its application to
human beings was the recognition of what Pavlov called 'the
second signalling system'. The distinction between man and the
rest of the animal kingdom is that *Homo sapiens* is conscious of
self, can think in terms of abstract concepts, and has the power
of speech. The higher animals, such as the dog or the chimpanzee,
function as complex systems, adjusting to the environment in terms
of given changes which they receive as signals. They are tied to
responding to the here-and-now situation, to concrete reality. Man,
on the other hand, has developed the ability to respond to *words*
which can refer to things physically absent, or to complete abstractions. These represent signals of signals. Language, which includes
the possibility of communicating abstract ideas, constitutes the
complex, second signalling system:

In the animal, reality is signalized almost exclusively by stimu-
lations and the traces they leave in the cerebral hemispheres . . .
This is the first system of signals of reality common to man and
animals. But speech constitutes a second signalling system of
reality which is peculiarly ours, being the signal of the first
signals. . . . It is precisely speech that has made us human.[14]

The main point, which distinguishes Pavlov from virtually
every other independent worker in the area of higher nervous
activity at this time, is his declared materialistic standpoint in
relation to speech and thought. This reveals itself at this juncture
in his expressed belief that the fundamental laws which govern
the activity of the first signalling system must also govern the
operations of the second. This is because we are dealing with
activity of the same nervous tissue. Of course, Pavlov does not
rule out the possibility that there may also be special laws which
operate at this highest level. Indeed this is the point at which the
'legitimate marriage of psychology and physiology', which Pavlov
always advocated, should be consummated. According to Pavlov,
the second signalling system is the most important area common
to psychology and physiology: certainly human psychology
presents its most urgent and central problems here. Pavlov consistently advocated that at this level, as at all lower levels, we
must work in terms of objectively determined relations between
phenomena. In other words, we should not begin the study of
the peculiar qualities of human behaviour, summed up in the
concept of the second signalling system, by assuming such a
uniqueness for man and his psychic life that the normal laws of
causality, of the interdependence of human behaviour and its
material substratum (the central nervous system) can be denied or
ignored. The special laws – *which no doubt exist* – must be discovered by objective investigation and related in their special
forms to the general laws of nature. We do not need an absolutely
new method or new *assumptions* when we approach the subject
of man and his psychic life. Thus Pavlov himself sums up his life-
work in two sentences:

Yes, I am glad that, together with Ivan Mikhailovich
(Sechenov), I and my group of dear colleagues, have won for
the mighty realm of physiological research, the animal organism,
complete and undivided, instead of a vague half. And this,
indisputably, is our Russian contribution to world science and
generally to human thought.[15]

It should be clear from the above that those who seek to explain the vast complex of human behaviour in terms of a simple-minded, conditional reflex arc in the name of Pavlov grossly distort his views. The error involved is the refusal to see, or the inability to appreciate, the specific peculiarities of complex phenomena. The main reason for the rejection of Pavlovianism in the 1929 discussions was the fact that his fully developed viewpoint was not clearly understood. The concept of the second signalling system was put forward first in 1932, after the crucial discussions were over. From Pavlov's earlier writings, a case could be made out that he was guilty of the same error as the mechanical materialists Büchner, Vogt, and Moleschott. It appeared as though he sought to reduce all psychological problems to terms of physiology, even perhaps to chemistry and physics, in the crudest possible way.

In terms of general theory, Lenin, following Marx and Engels, looked on the three categories of inorganic nature, animal life, and human society as three different stages or levels of evolutionary development. Each stage has its own specific laws which operate only at that particular level whilst also obeying the more general laws which operate at a cosmic level. In each of the higher levels 'the lower laws, although they continue to act, are relegated to the background', according to Engels. Again, with almost prophetic reference to this particular controversy the same author asks: 'No doubt we will reduce thinking by experiments to molecular and chemical motions taking place in the brain, but is the essence of thinking completely explained by this?'[16] There is no doubt that Pavlov often expressed himself in a thoroughly mechanistic way, especially in conversation. He was given to talking to himself, and in states of excitement and anger (to which he was prone) he often used unguarded expressions. There is no doubt that he consistently condemned psychological methods, including introspection, as it was then used, not as a supplement to objectively based experimental techniques, but as a substitute for them.

This assertion by the 'impetuous physiologists' that introspection must be abandoned was emphatically rejected by Soviet thinkers, as it continues to be rejected at the present time. Borovski said in 1929: 'The psychologist cannot do without introspection altogether (if only) for the reason that he comes upon many of his most important problems by the way of introspection'.[17] The fact that the physiological laws used to explain human behaviour were established by animal experimentation was singled out as

another reason for rejecting Pavlovianism, being an illustration
of the methodological error of 'reduction'. The causal laws discovered by Pavlov at the 'canine' level were, in principle, thought
to be irrelevant in the study of the human psyche or consciousness.

The content and the conclusions of this particular discussion
were summed up as follows:

> The dialectical materialist is constrained to prove to the non-
> dialecticians and the anti-dialecticians that human behaviour
> in all its specific complexity, conditioned as it is by social
> factors, cannot be mastered by physiology alone. He has to
> prove that all the qualitative peculiarities of human behaviour
> would be lost through an attempt to resolve it into reflexes;
> that physiology and reflexology both have to deal with the
> human being as a representative of the species *Homo sapiens*
> with 'man in general', whereas psychology deals with men
> having certain habits and traditions, the ideology of their class,
> profession, level, etc., and last of all, that it is for this very
> reason that this subject has to be studied by methods, perhaps
> similar, but still somewhat specific and peculiar'.[18]

(d) *Vygotski's 'cultural–historical' school*

The last of the schools prominent in this period was that of Lev
Semyonovich Vygotski. Vygotski's mode of expressing his views
was closely akin to his contemporaries in academic psychology
outside the Soviet Union. This is as far as his style is concerned,
content is a different matter. In his emphasis on the importance
of the cultural environment in the development of human traits
and types (an emphasis which has since found its way into non-
Soviet psychology from anthropology), Vygotski demonstrated
his dependence on Marxism. But, in comparison with Kornilov
or Bekhterev, he made few direct references to the Marxist
'classics', and a superficial reader could imagine that he differed
hardly at all from the leading bourgeois psychologists of Western
Europe and America. The error which lost him the favour of the
official party at this stage of Soviet psychology was described as
his devotion to foreign fashions in psychology. He was certainly
associated with the mental testing movement ('pedology') which
was strongly disapproved in Party circles. But, in fact, the error
he made was more likely to be the fact that he did not interlard
his writings with quotations from Marx, Engels, and Lenin. This
was becoming a fashionable device with those who wanted to

have the name of being Marxists without the trouble of thinking through their materials in relation to Marxist materialism. Even Chelpanov was claiming to be, if not exactly a Marxist, at least better in this respect than Bekhterev. It was claimed against Vygotski that he believed it possible to dissociate the 'facts' of bourgeois psychology from the 'theories' used to explain these 'facts'. The belief that the theoretical presuppositions of the investigator are totally irrelevant is anti-Marxist, which means 'anti-scientific' in this context. The view that an 'open-minded' investigator is capable of collecting objective data is considered to be a basic fallacy. Marxism teaches that objectivity demands commitment. The nature of one's commitment alters the whole picture of the data, even at the observational level. It was for this reason – a supposed lack of 'militant materialism' or 'lack of partisanship' – that Vygotski's attempt (apparently) to construct general laws from his own specialized researches in concept formation in children, logical memory, and speech was regarded as indefensible. His procedures were castigated as illustrating the twin errors of empiricism and eclecticism. In reality, Vygotski and his associates Luria and Leontiev laid the foundation in this period of the Marxist approach to the psyche as a historical, developmental product. They laid emphasis on the social roots of man's consciousness. The whole mode of argument is derived from Marx and Engels and can most correctly be designated as the dialectical mode of thought. The origin of man's psychic qualities, especially the genesis of speech as arising in the process of cooperative labour, is taken directly from Engels. The use of the word, and more obviously, the *concept* of 'reflection' shows the influence of Lenin. Although Vygotski adopts a genetic approach similar to that of Piaget, he relates the mental development of the child directly to the educational process, quite unlike Piaget and in accord with the Russian school of thought on this matter. In all his work he demonstrates a concern for *wholeness* and a systems approach which is clearly Marxist.

Unfortunately, due to his early death from tuberculosis, Vygotski only had ten years in which to complete his work in psychology (he died, aged thirty-eight). From 1921 he developed the theory of the sociohistorical origin of the higher mental functions, logical memory, voluntary attention, conceptual thought, language. According to Vygotski, these mental processes arise in relation to, and on the analogy of, the labour process. Man uses tools, in contrast to animals: in particular, he uses the tools of language. These tools are symbols of social origin, arising from cooperative action for common purposes. They are internalized by the individual who uses them for his own individual psychological purposes.

Vygotski was engaged with the 'second signalling system' of Pavlov, but was not so interested in the *signal* quality of words as in their symbolic character, or meaning. Word meanings are generalized images of reality: these change over time as the concepts associated with particular words change. The relationships between different mental processes, for example, perception and thinking, are different in childhood from what they are in adolescence and adulthood.

Vygotski carried out a number of ingenious investigations on the way in which children's concepts develop. He took the Bolshevik view of the importance and leading role of instruction in the development of the child, emphasizing that this did not only operate to develop understanding and knowledge of specific matters but also went towards the formation of psychic processes themselves. He put forward the interesting conception that each child had a 'zone of proximal development'. This was the difference between actual performance and what the child was capable of doing with adult assistance. School instruction should operate in this area, taxing the child's abilities so as to further their growth most effectively.

Vygotski also worked in the field of mental abnormalities and made significant contributions to our understanding of the thought-processes in schizophrenia devising a block test which is still in use as a diagnostic tool. He was extremely critical of the West European schools – Gestalt psychology (Köhler), personalism (Stern), the Würzburg school (Ach), Jean Piaget, and others. Although relatively free of direct quotations, these criticisms are invariably from the point of view of dialectical materialism.

Empiricism and its dangers were described by Engels:

> Exclusive empiricism . . imagines that it operates only with undeniable facts. In reality, however, it operates predominantly with out-of-date notions, with the largely obsolete products of thought of its predecessors . . . For it, the experimentally established facts have gradually become inseparable from the traditional interpretation associated with them; the simplest phenomenon is presented falsely . . . This empiricism *cannot* any longer describe the facts correctly, because the traditional interpretation is woven into the description.[19]

Vygotski was believed to be engaged in smuggling in ideas from Western psychology which were basically hostile to the aims of collectivization and communization of the new generation. His criticisms of Western psychologists such as Piaget, Bühler, and Stern were not enough to offset his involvement with pedology and other trends of opinion imported especially from America and Germany. It was for reasons such as these that the 'cultural historical' school of Vygotski was found wanting, and condemned. It is now recognized, belatedly perhaps, that Vygotski emphasized aspects of psychology which have since become part of the pattern of Soviet psychology. For example, his emphasis on the principle of evolutionary development and of the influence of the social–cultural–historical environment, his emphasis on the significance of the higher mental processes in behaviour, his emphasis on the distinctiveness of different levels of psychic process in the development of human beings – these are characteristic talking points in Soviet psychology today. But it must be said that these current emphases are derived from Marx and only secondarily from Vygotski's associates.

With his co-workers Luria and Leontiev, Vygotski elaborated important techniques in the fields of concept formation, memory, and affective reactions. The questions he raised in the area of the psychology of cognition have remained a central interest and influence in Soviet psychology up to the present. Although treated cavalierly in some texts, Vygotski is honoured by the important *kollektiv* of Moscow psychologists not only as their teacher, but for laying the foundations of their current research on thinking and speech.

References

1. V. I. Lenin, The Significance of Militant Materialism, in *On Religion* London: Lawrence and Wishart. 1922: 40.
2. P. P. Blonski 1964: 109.
3. Karl Marx: in F. Engels *Ludwig Feuerbach* (n.d.): 74 ff.
4. B. M. Teplov *Thirty years of Soviet Psychology* 1947: 5. Teplov, Shmaryan, Petrovsky all take the same 'line' on this issue.
5. Shmaryan cf. Grashchenkov and Shmaryan 1947.
6. Yudin, Sokolova cf. Petrovsky *Istoriya Sovetskoi Psikhologii*. Moscow: Prosveshcheniye Publishers 1967: 59.

7. V. M. Borovski *Journal of General Psychology* 1929, **2**: 177–186.
8. V. M. Bekhterev *General Principles of Human Reflexology* 1918: 33.
9. B. M. Teplov *Thirty years of Soviet Psychology* 1947.
10. *Pavlov's Wednesdays* 1949: cf. Pavlov *Selected Works* 1955: 601 ff.
11. V. M. Borovski 1929: 177–186.
12. Editorial note in I. P. Pavlov *Lectures on Conditioned Reflexes*. 1928: 25.
13. I. P. Pavlov *Psychopathology and Psychiatry: Selected Works* 1961, **2**: 83.
14. I. P. Pavlov *Selected Works* 1961, **2**: 262.
15. I. P. Pavlov.
16. F. Engels *Dialectics of Nature* 1955: 72.
17. V. M. Borovski 1929: 177–186.
18. V. M. Borovski 1929: 186.
19. F. Engels, *ibid.*

Reading List

Books in English
Carr, E. H. (1951–2) *The Bolshevik Revolution, 1917–1923* New York and London: Macmillan (2 vols.).
Johnson, W. H. E. (1950) *Russia's Educational Heritage* Pittsburgh: Carnegie Inst. of Technology.
Lenin, V. I. (n.d.) *Materialism and Empirio-Criticism* Moscow: Foreign Languages Pub. House.
London, I. D. (1949) A Historical Survey of Psychology in the Soviet Union. *Psych. Bull.* **46**: 241–277.
Murchison, C. (1930) (ed.) *Psychologies of 1930.* Worcester, Mass.: Clark Univ. Press.
Stalin, J. (1953) *Problems of Leninism* (11th ed.) Moscow: Foreign Languages Pub. House.

Books in Other Languages
Blonski, P. P. (1964) *Izbranniye psikholgicheskie proizvedenie* Moscow: Prosveshcheniye.
Tomaszewski, T. (1947) O psychologii w Z.S.S.R. *Kwart. Psycholog.* **13**: 267–315.
Wetter, G. (1952) *Der dialektische Materialismus, seine Geschichte und sein System in der Sowjetunion* Wien: Herder.

Chapter 5 *Influence of Five-Year Plans: 1929–1936*

The discussion of the proper foundation essential for a science of psychology was exacerbated during this period. The Communist Party waged a general offensive against all 'capitalist elements' remaining after the Revolution. Battle was joined on the 'intellectual front'. In psychology this took the form of the disapproval of a group of anti-Marxist conceptions, regarded as survivals of 'idealistic' ways of thinking. 'Criticism and self-criticism' were enjoined on Party and non-Party intellectuals. The directives proposed for this stage of the discussion were to liquidate idealistic trends still surviving and to exploit the 'philosophical heritage' of Lenin.

This involved the categorization of six basic types of error which could be taken as defining, negatively, a Marxist psychology. These 'errors' are discussed.

In this period foreign as well as Russian psychology was subject to considerable criticism and official condemnation. Industrial psychology ('psychotechnic') was liquidated in 1931; intelligence testing ('pedology') which was being used in wholesale fashion in schools for the purpose of 'streaming' and 'screening' children was severely criticized on theoretical and practical grounds. By a decree of the Central Committee, mental testing was abolished in the school system in 1936.

(i) Social and Intellectual Background

In a standard Party history of the USSR, now discredited, the period 1929–1930 is described as follows:

> Now that the backwardness of the country was becoming a
> thing of the past, now that the peasants' fight for the elimina-

tion of the kulak class had taken clear shape, and the Party had adopted the policy of eliminating the kulak class, the offensive against the capitalist elements assumed a general character, the partial offensive developed into an offensive along the whole front. By the time the Sixteenth Party Congress was convened (June 26, 1930), the general offensive against the capitalist elements was proceeding along the whole line.[1]

The year 1929 marks a turning point in the history of the Soviet Union, and no less in the history of Soviet psychology. It is the 'year of the great divide'. The capitalist elements and influences fostered by Lenin's New Economic Policy were to be destroyed, and even their memory eliminated from the minds of men. The internecine battles between the Stalinist control apparatus and the various oppositions, both right and left, had been conclusively settled in favour of Stalin's policies. The Trotskyist opposition had been destroyed and Trotsky himself physically transported beyond the Soviet frontier, never to return. The Bukharinite faction on the right wing, which favoured the continuation of those policies which fostered the reintroduction of capitalism, had demonstrated the poverty of their political ideas. The trade unions had been effectively taken over as an administrative organ of the Soviet government. Stalin felt free to approach the task publicly of wiping out tendencies opposed to the drive towards 'Socialism in One Country' – that is, industrialization under Marxist Social- ist forms and collectivization of all the means of production, dis- tribution, and exchange. The intellectual wing of these various political tendencies had perforce now to be confronted. As part of 'the general offensive along the whole line' crucial importance was attributed to the fight on the ideological or philosophical 'front'.

This 'front' had been described by Lenin in 1922 in his article *On the Significance of Militant Materialism* as follows:

No natural science, no materialism whatever, can hold out in the struggle against the onslaught of bourgeois ideas and the restoration of bourgeois philosophy without a solid philosophi- cal basis. In order to give aid to this struggle and help to carry it to its successful conclusion, the natural scientist must be a *modern* materialist – a conscious adherent of that materialism which Marx represents; that is, he must be a dialectical materialist.[2]

In the period 1929–31 there was widespread discussion amongst all groups of Soviet intellectuals, especially workers in philosophical and related fields. According to the Party directives these discussions had two aims: the liquidation of the Anti-Marxist trends of idealism and 'vulgar mechanism', and the exploitation of the 'philosophical heritage' of Lenin. Of considerable importance in these discussions was the publication, posthumously, of Lenin's *Philosophical Notebooks* in 1929–1930, this being part of the 'heritage' of ideas left behind at his death in 1924. On 25 January 1931 the Central Committee of the Communist Party passed a decree condemning 'menshevizing idealism' and mechanism in philosophy.

The importance of these discussions for psychology was twofold. Firstly, there was a summing-up of the criticisms of the various psychological schools previously discussed. This involved public recognition and acceptance by the psychologists involved of the fact and nature of their methodological errors. Secondly, the direction in which psychology was to develop in the succeeding period was laid down on the basis of the reorientation resulting from these discussions.

The method of 'criticism and self-criticism' had become a traditional technique in the Soviet Communist Party. To discuss its development and significance fully would divert us from our central themes. It is perhaps sufficient to indicate that, theoretically, it originates from Marx's polemical and educational-propagandist activities. At the very outset of his political work, in 1845, he wrote that a party leader 'must on no account be judged by his *system* but rather by his polemical writings'.[3] He early referred to the need for constant criticism and used it as his main method of education and propaganda. The word 'criticism' occurs again and again in the titles of his writings – an early work in fact is sub-titled 'a critique of critical criticism'.

Great importance is attached to *theory* in the Marxist system, and for the need constantly to evaluate this in the light of practice. Engels, for example, suggested as a motto suitable for the American working-class movement in 1886 – '*Durch Schaden klug werden*' ('through mistakes to become clever' – a German folk-saying).[4] This considerable theoretical emphasis on argument with oneself and one's opponents is not a personal foible based on extreme aggression, directed inwards on occasion and outwards on others (Marx's carbuncles have often been cited as a direct source of his irascibility in controversy). It springs from the basic belief in the 'dialectic' – that truth is obtained not by compromise and accommodation but by confrontation and conflict (Greek: polemos) between opposed and contradictory aspects of experience.

The Russian Orthodox conception of *sobornost'*, as developed by Khomyakov, by which is meant the union in fellowship with all Orthodox Believers, which is maintained or regained by frankly and publicly confessing one's sins, provides a religious analogy and indicates that there is something congenial to the spirit of Russian collectivism in these techniques.

Lenin's conception of a serious political party is perhaps the most crucial influence, however – a concept he drew from Marx and from his own experience of Russian conditions. He laid it down that:

> The attitude of a political party towards its own mistakes is one of the most important and surest ways of judging how earnest the party is and how it in practice fulfils its obligations towards its class and the toiling masses. Frankly admitting a mistake, ascertaining the reasons for it, analysing the conditions which led to it, and thoroughly discussing the means for correcting it – that is the earmark of a serious party; that is the way it should perform its duties, that is the way it should educate and train the class, and then the masses.[5]

'Under Stalin this method of public analysis of error was given central significance in his management of Party affairs. In 1938 he writes, 'A party is invincible if it does not fear criticism and self-criticism'.[6] Zhdanov, as Party spokesman in the philosophical controversy of 1947, said, 'In our Soviet society . . . criticism and self-criticism . . is the real motive force of our development, a powerful instrument in the hands of the Party . . . a new form of movement, a new type of development, a new dialectical law.'[7]

The significance of criticism in group organization is clear from its effects. It would be anticipated that 'comradely criticism' and 'self-criticism' would operate to overcome forces of conservatism. It should play a major role in reversing the tendency inherent in elaborately worked-out conceptions (such as Marxism) to ossify into a dogma. In an atheistic institution like the Communist Party of the Soviet Union it could have a similar cathartic effect to that of the extension of the conception of brotherly love resulting from mutual forgiveness in the course of, and as the result of, the formal reconciliation procedures used in certain Christian monastic orders.

Of course, this derivation would hardly be acceptable to Communists. The political and ideological significance of criticism and self-criticism is that those who have taken what is adjudged by the majority to be the wrong path are given the opportunity to admit their mistakes and to rejoin the majority, without prejudice. However, in the heyday of Zhdanov and Lysenko 'criticism and self-criticism' degenerated into an unsubtle form of 'thought-control' which was used to suppress dissident or potentially dissident viewpoints, later admitted to be correct. During this period (now described as the era of the 'cult of personality') the recognized rules, or rituals, in the procedure of criticism, devised to protect the minority from persecution, and the majority from insincere and false avowals by the minority, failed to prevent the degeneration of an excellent principle of critical analysis of errors into a purely formal ritual, often lacking any inner content of conviction. This is an indication that group opinion can be coercive by virtue of its strength rather than by virtue of its validity, and that machinery required to maintain the existence of a political party in a hostile environment is hardly appropriate for the discovery of scientific truth.

In the 1929–1931 discussions, it must be remembered that the ideas of the Communist Party had at this time successfully permeated all levels of Soviet society. Its trained personnel could be found in all scholastic institutions, often in controlling positions. Since the majority of these cadres were dedicated and able people, speaking with the authority of the ruling group, and accustomed to working together in a regular and systematic way to ensure that their common viewpoint should prevail, it was inevitable that control of these institutions should pass to them. Where opposition to the ideas of the ruling power was rife, the institute would sooner or later be closed down altogether, or key personnel moved to other posts.

Whether these processes are regarded as sinister or otherwise must be decided in the light of the preceding history of war and revolution which left in its train a social and economic desolation with which only the Bolsheviks seemed prepared to deal effectively. A fact which tells against the interpretation that Communist views were tyrannously forced on a resisting majority is that considerable public discussion took place in the form of a reasoned examination of the various contending theories. It is true that the discussions were organized by the Communist Party with general Marxist principles as a frame of reference. The directives of the

Central Committee are binding on Party members but, *by them-selves*, do not have the force of law. The demands of everyday life constituted the other base-line to which the discussion of theoretical systems had to be constantly referred. But at no stage were either of these criteria called in question, even by those whose views were *subsequently* held to be theoretically inadequate. The outcome of discussions was accepted by all but a very small minority.

On the other hand, stress should be given to the fact that the discussions were initiated by the CPSU with the twofold demand: for an accentuation of Bolshevik partisanship, and for the develop-ment of a psychological theory which could serve the needs of socialist construction. In the preceding years 'unreliable' or counter-revolutionary elements had been excluded from the universities and higher institutions; leading idealist philosophers, economists, theologians, and other intellectuals had been expelled or forced to emigrate in the period succeeding the Civil War; former entrepreneurs, their sons and daughters, the children of active White Army men, the sons of priests, etc., were excluded from higher education by decree. Many more, in these and similar categories, had disappeared from the scene in the van of the defeated White Armies.

More important for our purpose than a decision on the question of political controls are the details of errors which were defined in the course of these discussions, and the new direction of Soviet psychology after 1931. A difficulty exists here for the Western reader in the fact that a special terminology is used in categorizing anti-Marxist viewpoints. This terminology employs what appears to be a common philosophical vocabulary. But words have acquired a technical, or special meaning, in the course of Marxist polemics over a century of disputation. This terminology can be described as a conceptual shorthand, or restricted code, used in controversy. To the Western ear it often sounds remarkably like personal abuse. But the objective content of this shorthand, and of Soviet discussions, can be elucidated by a close scrutiny of the works of Marx, Engels, and Lenin, as well as the views of their opponents. Lacking this background, the content of Soviet dis-cussions and the points at issue become extremely difficult for the Western reader to understand. Quite apart from the fact that he normally sees only a tiny fragment of such discussions, selected usually to support a particular interpretation of them, the Western reader is, in the normal case, without an over-all perspective which would enable him to assess Russian and Communist viewpoints. It is a formidable undertaking to attempt to penetrate the barriers which the Russian language and Marxist terminology erect in the way of a clear understanding of the points at issue between Soviet protagonists. When combined with the further difficulties which ignorance of the specific social context imposes, it becomes clear why the slick journalist commentators on Soviet affairs continue to flourish.

In connection with the general theory of psychology, six major errors were stigmatized in these discussions. These errors may be taken as a negative way of working towards the definition of a Marxist psychology: that is, they specify the rules which should not be broken. The technique used by the disputants is to assimilate the views they are discussing, by a process of reduction, to a particular category of anti-Marxist theory. This is done by contrasting the disputed viewpoint with some explicit statement by the accepted founders of Communist theory. These statements or declarations are taken as defining directly or by implication the error which the disputed view is said to exhibit. The basic tenets of dialectical materialism are not open to scrutiny at any point in these discussions. Marxism is assumed, on the basis of conviction, and of past experience, to give the only correct scientific methodology. The principles of method have been extracted by analysis as universal, fundamental principles of all development. It was a basic assumption, not open to scrutiny or debate, that those general principles had been declared by Marx and Engels, and confirmed within a Russian and Soviet context by Lenin and Stalin.

This technique of argument creates difficulties for those whose experience and presuppositions are radically different from those participating in the discussion. It is easy for such a person to decide that the argument is *alogical*, unless he is previously convinced of the truth of Marxism and prepared on this basis to concede the primary authority of Marx, Engels, Lenin, and Stalin on questions of scientific method. There is a fundamental difference of approach to the construction of scientific theory, a difference which is fruitful of misunderstandings.

Logically speaking, the central question in the evaluation of Soviet psychology at this level is non-psychological, consisting in deciding the question of the essential truth or falsity of Marxism.

(ii) The Basic Categories of Error in Scientific Method

(A) 'IDEALISM'

As previously indicated, the most important error categorized in the course of these discussions is 'idealism'. It is difficult to discuss exhaustively all the subtle varieties of idealism which have been recognized. Basically they all derive from considering that 'spirit' is prior to or is in some other sense a superior category to 'matter'. But, in effect, *all* philosophy, whether it is of a systematic kind or simply a vague, undeclared set of contradictory beliefs, falls into this category. These views all share this common characteristic: that at some point in the detailed working out of their basic principles non-Marxist thinkers abstract relatively inert categories and set these over against the real dynamic and dialectical development of nature, society, and the individual.

This may seem to be unfair, because too sweeping a characterization of the Marxist view of non-Marxist philosophy. But it is the only possible interpretation of repeated statements, of which the following by Engels is typical:

> This (Marxist historical materialist) conception however put an end to philosophy in the realm of history just as the dialectical conception of nature made all natural philosophy both unnecessary and impossible. It is no longer a question anywhere of inventing inter-connections from out of our brains but of discovering them in the facts. For philosophy, which has been expelled from nature and history, there remains only the realm of pure thought (so far as it is left); the theory of the laws of the thought process itself, logic and dialectics.[8]

This surely means that any past, present, or future philosophy which is not dialectical and materialist is necessarily, and by definition, false. Marxists do not deny that other philosophies may have specific insights into the real interconnections in nature, society, and the individual. This, in fact, is the 'real content' of non-Marxist philosophy which must 'be assimilated by' dialectical materialism. In this process philosophy is at once abolished and preserved. It is abolished as an artificial conceptual system set over against nature and its laws; it is preserved in the form of *science,* that is, the most generalized system of scientific laws abstracted from nature and society. The (Marxist) 'negation' of metaphysics is thus different from that of logical positivism. 'Negation in

dialectics does not mean simply saying no, or declaring that something does not exist, or destroying it in any way one likes.'[9]

In the heat of Soviet controversy the term 'idealism' easily
takes on a blanket connotation, and tends to become meaningless.
It is possible however to illustrate some of the psychological views
which are unacceptable, and which can properly be described as
'idealistic'.

One of the basic questions around which discussion centred is
that of the relation between brain, thought, and the external
world. This question was not considered for its own sake, as of
purely academic interest: on the contrary, discussion was based
on the assumption that a correct solution, when found, would
point in an unequivocal way to the methodology appropriate in
the investigation of psychological problems. This tremendous
emphasis on *the importance of theory*, and on the correct manner
of conducting scientific or practical activities, is alien to empiricism.
The latter proceeds inductively from what is regarded as the safe
ground of experience.

The general view of psychologists outside the USSR is that the
relationship of thought to the brain, and that existing between
each of these and the external world is basically a metaphysical
question which is completely irrelevant to psychological research
and teaching. It is believed that psychological knowledge develops on a pragmatic, empirical basis, research being modelled
on the methods of the exact sciences, often directly derived from
them. Controversies about psychophysical parallelism, interac-
tionism, epiphenomenalism, and the rest, which were at one time
central questions in psychology, are regarded as having been a
complete waste of time and energy and to have added nothing to
the clarification of methodological problems. They belong to a
past era, best forgotten, when psychology was still in thrall to
philosophy and religion.

However, it cannot be simply taken for granted that empiricism,
which has developed in close association with the free enterprise society, must necessarily apply universally, even in conditions where all science (including psychological investigation) is
planned as an activity in which all citizens have a direct vested
interest. Under such conditions clarity about the proper content,
methods, and aims of each of the sciences and, especially about
their demarcation lines, must be effectively considered prior to
scientific experimentation. It is a question no longer of a single
genius working in a backroom, but of society, i.e. the State, assign-

ing responsibilities for research programmes, practical applications, teaching and so on. The desired end-result would be reached less efficiently as the outcome of continuing wars waged for territory and resources between different groups of scientific specialists.

It would be arrogance to assert that a distrust of theory (arrived at by processes other than induction), a distrust characteristic of Anglo-Saxon psychologists in the main, is the only appropriate human attitude; it would be doctrinaire to assume (if only implicitly) that the empirical approach is necessarily, and in all circumstances, the best.

To return to the question of the relation between brain and thought: the most extreme anti-Marxist statement is that of Richard Avenarius. Writing in 1891, he said:

> The brain is not the habitation, the seat, the creator, it is not the instrument or organ, the supporter or substratum, etc., of thought. Thought is not the indweller, or commander or the other half, or side, etc., nor is it a product or even a physiological function, or a state in general of the brain.[10]

The thinking brain, for Avenarius, is a 'fetish of natural science'.[11]

This 'brainless philosophy' was castigated by Lenin. He contraposed to it the materialist view of Engels:

> The material, sensuously perceptible world to which we ourselves belong is the only reality . . . our consciousness and thinking, however supra-sensuous they may seem, are the product of a material, bodily organ, the brain. Matter is not a product of mind, but mind itself is merely the highest product of matter.[12]

A second, less vulnerable and, for Marxists, more dangerous form of idealism was that of Chelpanov. While he did not deny that man thinks with the help of the brain, he suggested that the brain is, in reality, the instrument by which the spirit becomes manifest. Spirit, working through the brain, gives rise to mental phenomena. It is the spirit which experiences, which links, which wishes, etc., through the instrumentality of the brain. This view is in direct opposition to the Leninist conception of 'reflection'. The theory of reflection was a basic assumption, taken for granted by Marx and Engels and referred to only in passing in their published works. The conception was developed by Lenin in more striking fashion in his *Philosophical Notebooks,* published posthumously in connection with these discussions. It regards the various psychic processes as a 'reflection' of external matter, of material processes. The crucial reference is Marx's *Capital* where, contrasting his method with Hegel's, he says, 'The ideal is nothing else than the material world reflected by the human mind and translated into forms of thought.'[13] This view links up in an interesting fashion with the thought of Sechenov, justifying the coupling of Pavlov (who adopted his views as the basis of his objective programme) with Lenin as the two main foundations of contemporary Soviet psychology. In his *Reflexes of the Brain* (1863) Sechenov, supporting the idea of a causal determinism in mental, as in physical and organic processes, said:

> Thought is usually regarded as the cause of action. And if the external influence, that is, sensory excitation, remains unnoticed, as is very often the case, then of course, thought is even regarded as the initial cause of the action. This however is an utter fallacy. The initial cause of every act always lies in an external sensory excitation, because without it no thought is possible.[14]

This 'reflection' is not a passive, mirror-like image of reality. The main difference between Marxist epistemology and other materialist views is that Marx stresses the *active* side of perception and knowledge. In his *Philosophical Notebooks,* Lenin also stresses this aspect: 'The reflection of nature in human thought must be envisaged, not as "dead", or "abstract", or static, or free from contradiction, but as an eternal process of movement, in which contradictions are forever emerging and being resolved'.[15]

The contrary notion, that there is some entity (whether designated mind, sense, spirit, or soul) which stands above or is in some sense outside of mental processes (the locus of which is the functioning of the brain), this mind, spirit, or soul being independent of nervous physiology and directing or interfering with mental processes, is an idealistic notion. It is a dualism which is in essence destructive of Marxism.

It was largely because of his inadequate formulation of this psychological problem (that is, the relation of brain to thought and reality) as well as his solution of it which led to Kornilov's 'reactology' being condemned. He had accepted the formula from Plekhanov, that 'every psychological state is only one side of the process of which a physiological phenomenon composes the other side,'[16] and the crisper formulation by Bukharin: 'The psyche is the introspective expression of physiological processes.'[17]

Both these statements were rejected as being incompatible with Lenin's theory of reflection and partaking of psychophysical parallelism.

For similar reasons Freud's views were, and continue to be, rejected by Soviet psychologists. The rejection of psychoanalysis had taken place almost imperceptibly, being virtually complete by 1930. No formal discussion of psychoanalysis took place. But even before 1917 Freudianism had experienced considerable difficulties in the form of unfriendly scepticism in Russia. In spite of this, two small groups of analysts continued to function up to about ten years after the Revolution.

There were a number of grounds on which Freudianism was criticized. In connection with the error of 'idealism' it was especially his splitting of the ego into a primordial portion which Freud believed developed in virtual isolation from the real world, which was regarded as vulnerable. The psychoanalytic conception of neurosis as the outcome of incompatible tendencies or processes within the individual personality, or as the effect of the narrow familial relationships existing between the infant and his parents (the Oedipus Complex), contradicts the materialist theory of reflection. The supporters of Lenin's theory would say that psychological conflicts result from the failure to resolve the contradictions in the reflection of the real objective conflicts of the external world, especially the class conflicts of a class-divided society. This points to another reason for rejecting Freud: he fails absolutely to observe the real basis of human personality, he seems oblivious to the effects of social institutions (other than the monogamous family) on individual qualities. His idea of the unconscious, as some kind of entity which remains detached from reality, uninfluenced by the external environment, is an abstract construction typical of idealistic thinking.

Freud totally misconceives the nature of the relations between thought and reality. Thoughts do not exist as separate entities, living a free life. They are derivative functions of matter, reflections of external reality, dependent on brain functioning. The idea that unconscious ideas are inherited from prototypal humanity is a scientific fiction deriving from a basic error, namely, psychophysical dualism. Similarly, in therapy, Freud attempts to change people's ideas directly by the magic of 'the word', without reference to the material basis of these ideas. Psychoanalysis, as an abstract reordering of one's thoughts, divorced from any social context, except that provided by the dyadic group, therapist and patient, represents a system of thought which consistently ruptures theory and practice.

In the concepts of unconscious mind, instincts, sexual complexes, we have the notion that it is possible for large sections of the mental life to be shut off from other sections and from interaction with external reality. This kind of thinking is the most characteristic feature of idealism in psychology.

In the same way, psychoanalysis completely ignores the division of society into classes. In particular, the scale of values, the culture of the progressive working class do not enter into, or appear at all, in either the theoretical construction or the therapeutic resources of the psychoanalyst. Freud's 'biologism', that is, his reduction of all phenomena to instincts and their vicissitudes, leads him to a denial of social influences except as negative forces which suppress man's basic animal urges. He ignores the fact that it is society which makes specifically human qualities possible.

Engels, in a famous letter to Mehring discusses the nature of 'ideology,' defining it as a type of idealism in which the ideologist 'works with the mere thought material, which he accepts without examination as the product of thought; he does not investigate further for a more remote process independent of thought.'[18] Freud can be brought within this category of 'ideologist' not only because of the way he ignores totally the effects of the social, political, and economic system on the development of individual neuroses but in his view of *unconscious* mental processes which are believed to function in isolation from reality. The letter to Mehring refers to one fundamental point on which Marxism and Freudianism do agree: that is, the existence of a 'false consciousness.' But the two thought systems, Marxism and psychoanalysis, disagree fundamentally about how this 'false consciousness' comes about, what its nature is, and how it should be brought into line with reality.

(B) MECHANICAL MATERIALISM

The second major error is 'mechanical materialism.' The original meaning of this term can be found in Engels' statement of the differences between Marxism and other types of materialism, especially that of Holbach, Vogt, and Moleschott. Speaking of the materialism of the eighteenth century, he points out that it has three specific limitations: it applies the standards of mechanics to processes of a chemical and organic nature (an example of the 'reduction' fallacy); it is unable to comprehend the universe as a process, that is, as matter developing through time in terms of a determined historical sequence; it remains idealistic in the social sciences inasmuch as it has no rational insight into the interconnections of history.

Mechanical materialism makes an initial assumption that thought, consciousness, and sensation have merely a subjective, or even a fictitious, existence. It divests matter of all those qualities which have some subjective or mental content. As a result, it lands itself in a contradiction. It creates the necessity for a realm of nonmaterial reality. Consciousness, which is arbitrarily excluded from its material foundation, is not thereby exorcised but simply returns to plague the theoretician as an experiential ghost. This process, by which mechanical materialism develops towards spiritualism, can be seen clearly worked out in the development of Bekhterev's reflexology. Consciousness, which is denied at the outset in the construction of 'the system,' reappears in the form of 'energy' which is thought of as being spread throughout the universe. Bekhterev's views, which started by having the appearance of being of an extreme materialistic type, by an inner logic developed to the point where they were in fact an exaggerated form of *panpsychism,* with obvious relationships with pantheism. According to Marxism, this is the fate reserved for all varieties of mechanical materialism. By reducing matter and the psyche to 'energy' as the basic category, Bekhterev committed the error of extending the special laws of physics not only to *psychic* phenomena, but to *social* phenomena as well.

Engels had already condemned this reductive procedure as being a characteristic error of the mechanical materialists:

> The exclusive application of the standards of mechanics to processes of a chemical and organic nature – in which processes, it is true, the laws of mechanics are also valid, but which are pushed into the background by other and higher laws – constitutes a specific but at that time inevitable limitation of classical French materialism.[19]

At this period, and for essentially similar reasons, Watsonian behaviourism was condemned. By its denial of the existence or even the possibility of studying human consciousness, American behaviourism removed an essential element of the subject matter from the sphere of investigation. When Lenin defined the psyche as a reflection of external reality he did nothing to reduce the importance of thinking, or of human volition. There is no intention in Marxism to denigrate thought to the point of unimportance, let alone to vanishing point. On the other hand, this is precisely what behaviourism was taken as doing. In contrast, dialectical philosophy assigns high status to ratiocination. It accords supreme importance to the processes of selection and association, to the logical reordering or enlarging of concepts so that they more faithfully reflect external reality. But, as we have seen, Marxism refuses to grant an independent, autonomous role to thought. To do so would suggest that thought is capable of existing and developing out of contact with matter and of social relations – in a word, 'abstractly'. Thought cannot be divorced from matter; it is matter at a particular level of organization which thinks. The common characteristic of idealism, and of the varieties of materialism which refuse to adopt the dialectical standpoint, lies in the attempt to do just that. Freud, founder of psychoanalysis, and Watson, founder of behaviourism, start from opposite ends but meet eventually on the common ground of the same fundamental error. They misunderstand the nature of the psyche. The former overemphasizes its *independence,* the latter attempts to ignore it altogether. Mechanical materialism (Bekhterev, Watson) is taken as inevitably degenerating into the same kind of idealism as those who emphasize psyche as independent of somatic processes (Freud, *Gestalt* psychology). Both tendencies artificially and erroneously isolate processes, mechanisms, and entities from the actual conditions of life and development.

On the other hand dialectics as the 'science of interconnections' seeks to overcome the specific limitations of mechanical materialism by recognizing the existence, and the need to discover, the *specific* laws of mental functioning. It is not a matter of reducing these to the lower levels of physics, chemistry, physiology, or biology. Dialectical psychology must accept as its task the elucidation of the development of human consciousness in history. It aims to describe this development in the individual case and in the race.

(c) 'REDUCTIONISM'
The third anti-dialectical conception of this period was 'physiologism', or 'biologism'. This can be defined as the attempt to reduce psychological processes on the human level to physiological or biological functioning, failing to recognize that new laws, principles, and explanatory concepts must be posited as we move from lower to higher levels. As an instance of this, Kornilov's definition

of the subject matter of psychology may be quoted: 'The psyche or consciousness is the subjective reflection of physiological processes.'[20] Another approach condemned was the attempt to use the conditional reflex schematism (in contrast to the more elaborate views which Pavlov developed later) as a complete explanation of human behaviour. This formula was a basic principle underlying the various versions of behaviourism elaborated by American psychologists and their Russian imitators. Reflexology, as well as its American counterpart, Watsonian behaviourism, were regarded as totally inadequate substitutes for psychology. Freudianism was rejected for this reason also in that this system, too, blurs the necessary distinction between biological and psychological processes. MacDougall's instinct theory is another example of the same methodological error. On the question of instincts, 'innate psychophysical predispositions', it is to be observed that Soviet psychology has always admitted that both physical and mental characteristics are inherited, but only in the form of anatomical or physiological peculiarities of the organism. It is emphasized that any specific human characteristic or quality, whether it be an emotion, an attitude, or an intellectual ability, develops through activity. There is a dynamic interaction with the environment which changes not only the individual but the environment as well. Our specifically human qualities (language, self-awareness, consciousness) arise through the use of language and within a social environment in which we co-operate with others, and learn. In all this there is presumed to be no conflict between the 'vile instincts' or 'drives', (which are perceived as neutral in character) and rational processes. In fact, these categories of instinct and reason can be separated only in thought, conceptually. In a given human act we have the concrete actuality of behaviour, nothing more. It is the observer who artificially isolates the reason from the passions, the better to study them.

Psychological conflicts are, of course, possible on this view. But they do not arise from any inherent conflict alleged to exist between man's biological nature and civilization – rather they reflect the contemporary class divisions and class conflicts of capitalist society. Neuroses and psychoses involve both psychogenic (that is, social) and somatogenic (central nervous) factors in causation and in treatment. These are a few random illustrations of 'biologism', or 'physiologism', themselves examples of the idealistic, 'reductionist' fallacy.

(D) 'ABSTRACT HUMAN ESSENCE'

The fourth error is closely related to the preceding. It is the attempt to provide a generalized psychology descriptive of man in all times and places. This error is said to be typical of 'bourgeois' ideologists. According to Lenin such individuals characteristically 'overlook' the class struggle in society – that is, the necessary opposition of interest between capitalists and workers which leads to basic differences in the structure of attitudes, character, basic philosophy, and psychological processes generally. Because of their idealistic, 'metaphysical' outlook they attempt to abstract some 'human essence' from each individual, and refuse to see real, concrete human beings in their social-productive relations.

In a sense, this is the central theme of Marxism. In one form or another it appears as a basic theme in all the polemical writings of Marx and Engels. Marxists claim they alone recognize the way in which real personalities, individually differentiated, develop in the context of a real historical and social environment. Other schools of thought construct an abstract scheme through analysis, artificially isolating some abstract 'human essence', out of time and out of history – a 'dumb internal generality', undifferentiated, and therefore unreal.

In that super-polemic *Capital* Marx dealt at some length with this question. Writing of the effects of division of labour, he says:

> It converts the labourer into a crippled monstrosity, by forcing (i.e. 'cultivating') his detailed dexterity at the expense of a world of productive capabilities and instincts . . . The life-long speciality of handling one and the same tool, now becomes the life-long speciality of serving one and the same machine.[21]

Engels adds:

> And not only the labourers, but also the classes directly or indirectly exploiting the labourers are made subject, through the division of labour, to the tool of their function; the empty-minded bourgeois to his own capital and his own thirst for profits; the lawyer to his fossilised legal conceptions which dominate him as a power independent of him; the 'educated classes' in general to their manifold local limitations and one-sidedness, to their own physical and mental short-sightedness, to their stunted specialized education, and the fact that they are chained for life to this specialized activity itself – even when this specialized activity is merely to do nothing.[22]

This must seem irrelevant to the Western psychologist. He would assert that, even if we grant these propositions of Marx and Engels – and common observation of the limitations involved in specialization support their views – the labourer, the 'empty-minded bourgeois', the lawyer with his fossilized legal conceptions, as well as other members of the educated classes, are still *human* and can be studied as members of one single general species or category. The counter-argument, put forward during these discussions, may be paraphrased as follows: it is agreed that different groups of humans belong to a single species and can be placed in one category for certain purposes. But a few questions remain. For example, what is the nature of this classification which places them together? What do these different classes have in common which leads us to place them in the category *Man*? And what *method* is appropriate for studying them within this category?

The answers given by Soviet psychologists are as follows: it is only as biological organisms that these different types of humans can properly be classified as belonging to the species *Homo sapiens*. Only physiology or biology has the right to deal with a 'generalized human nature', with 'man in general'. Psychology must distinguish between different types and classes of men, their different cultures, their habits and traditions, their class ideologies and so on. This, in fact, is what Marx did in his work on *Capital* and, to a lesser degree, Engels in his *Condition of the Working-Class in England in 1844*. Marx provided, in a masterly fashion, not only an economic and social history of the formation of the working class, but with Engels gave an unrivalled analysis of the genesis of attitudes, beliefs, ideology, and psychological qualities of the English worker, male and female.

By ignoring different *levels* of functioning (in this case differentiation by class), and by trying to formulate psychological laws which will cut across all levels, the bourgeois psychologist and the unthinking Marxist psychologists who imitate him are guilty of another type of 'reduction' error. It is the *specific task* of psychology to study individual differences, to show the relationship between social class and concepts of morality, between occupational skills and cognitive functioning, between political consciousness and motivation. Psychology must not seek to establish general laws which unite in a single group individuals from different social classes, or from different cultures, or from different periods of time. It is true that these individuals do belong to the same human type: certain general laws can indeed be stated. But these laws are in the fields of biology and physiology, they can be established only by the specific methods of physiology or biology. As far as psychology is concerned the category MAN is merely a class-name with no definable psychological content. No 'abstract human essence' exists: this is merely an empty sound lacking real, concrete content. To quote Marx on Feuerbach's 'anthropologism':

> Feuerbach resolves the religious essence into the human. But the human essence is no abstraction inherent in each single individual. In its reality it is the *ensemble* of the social relations . . . Feuerbach, consequently, does not see that the 'religious sentiment' is itself a *social product,* and that the abstract individual whom he analyses belongs in reality to a particular form of society.[23]

(E) 'DUALISM'

The fifth error is dualism. This can be defined as any attempt to consider mind as capable of some form of existence separate from matter. In particular, it is the attempt to dissociate mental processes from the functioning of the central nervous system. Dualism appears in many forms, some of these are very subtle and can persist in thinking unrecognized by the scientific investigator, – even when he declares an allegiance to the Marxist position of psychophysical monism. This latter position maintains that the psyche is a product, or derivative, or property of matter at its highest level of organization, namely the human brain.

Commonly, and more crudely, dualism appears in the form of the denial that psychic functions are open to investigation by objective methods. In a more refined form it grants an equivalent status to objective methods and to self-observation (introspection; the subjective method). Or it may suggest that the former must be corrected by the latter. Pavlov's views, as developed during this period, are now regarded as compatible with Lenin's theory of reflection. Thus Pavlovianism is accepted as a special version of psychophysical monism of central significance for psychology.

(F) 'ECLECTICISM'

The sixth methodological error recognized, and defined, in this period was eclecticism. This appeared in the large-scale borrowing of theoretical systems as well as of factual data from foreign psychologists. Neither system nor data are acceptable. The former are regarded as inimical to the Soviet way of life and thought: the latter are assumed to be contaminated at the source. By virtue of their mode of collection, influenced as it must inevitably be by the theoretical viewpoints underlying the decision to attend to these data rather than other so-called 'factual materials,' 'facts' are considered to be far from the 'neutral data' they are claimed to be. According to the Marxist theory of objectivity, data can never be 'neutral', neither can the investigator.

In connection with 'eclecticism' two important developments have to be recorded. The first was in the field of industrial psychology. In 1931 Soviet psychologists turned away from the methods and concepts developed under the capitalist market economy and attempted to strike out on a new path. The second was the decree on the primary and secondary schools. This decree attempted to give a completely new orientation to psychology. Psychologists were now invited to concern themselves with the generalization of the experience of the teachers and practical workers in the schools. In the past, psychology had been concerned with investigating problems which essentially were problems of general psychology. These were studied in laboratories or in other places remote from the actual teaching situation, the results could throw little light on practical questions – learning in the classroom, training illiterate workers to become engineers etc.

The sharp reversals of previous policies, represented by the virtual abolition of industrial psychology and the reorientation of general psychology, were not arbitrary decisions of the Soviet Communist Party. These changes represented the crystallization into action of long-continued criticism of 'psychotechnic' (industrial psychology) and of 'pedology' (the Russian form of the mental testing movement). This criticism centred on the remoteness of psychotechnic from the practical problems of industrialization in a predominantly peasant economy, and on the antidemocratic pre-suppositions on which both movements seemed to be based.

In the first case, the decision to give a new orientation to Russian psychotechnic became widely known outside the Soviet Union. Discussions were held and decisions made at the First All-Union Conference of Psychotechnic and the Psychophysiology of Work, held in Leningrad in May 1931. In pursuit of these decisions the Russian delegation at the Seventh International Conference on Psychotechnics, Moscow 1931, attacked bourgeois industrial psychology. This astonished and dismayed their international colleagues at the Conference since they had had no prior warning anything of the sort was likely to happen. Spielrein, a prominent Soviet industrial psychologist, writing on *The Theory of Psychotechnic,* explained that:

> The task of science in serving the workers of the USSR is to share in the revolutionary struggle of building the socialist state. This is a particularly important function of such a science as industrial psychology which operates to create those new work patterns, in making effective those new drives to work, which distinguish labour under socialism from labour in a capitalist regime.[24]

Before dismissing these statements as nothing more than a political dogma alien to the proper purposes of scientific investigation (which is how they were regarded by the 'time-and-motion' efficiency engineers of the period) we need to remember the actual circumstances confronting the Soviet Union in the sphere of production. We have to remember the overriding demands of the Soviet economic situation and the plan to industrialize the country (without which it was expected by the leading group, the Russian State and people could not possibly survive). The demand by certain scientists in an expanding capitalist economy that their activities are to be regarded as autonomous and not subject to any kind of control is by the nature of the case not one that can be honoured under all circumstances – even if it can be honoured at all. The Soviet Communist Party has never recognized such a right, even in principle. On the contrary, the harnessing of scientists and of scientific knowledge to the plan for transforming nature and society has always been implicit in their conception of society. It represents the elaboration of views on the nature of society and of human knowledge expressed more than a century ago by Marx and Engels.

It must also be recalled that the techniques and theories of 'psychotechnic' had been tested out in factories and institutes devoted to industrial research and to the training of workers. Methods of selection and training of workers (or 'peasants to be transformed into workers') that were developed in countries with a large reserve army of labour, an established system of apprenticeship, and a reservoir of skilled and disciplined workers were found by actual trial to be quite unsuitable for a country consisting predominantly of illiterate and unskilled peasants leaving their villages and hopefully setting out on the path of industrialization. A great number of experiments and improvisations (some of an extremely crude, even laughable character) had been carried out before decisions of this far-reaching character were taken. Far from being the doctrinaire political decision it was made out to be, the decision on psychotechnic was a long overdue one facing up to social realities.

The 1931 decree on the primary and secondary schools intended to, but did not succeed in making such a sharp break with Western methods and theories in the field of educational psychology. 'Pedology', officially frowned upon, and widely criticized by the general public as well as by professional psychologists, continued to live a charmed life until 1936. In that year it was officially proscribed by the decree *On Pedological Distortions in the Soviet School Administration*.

The recognition of the anti-Marxist and anti-scientific tendency of these errors was regarded as a preparatory stage in establishing the foundations for the development of a general theory of psychology which would be at once compatible with Marxism and meet the needs of a socialist society. In the recognition of these errors Soviet psychologists attempted to meet the demands of the Party and Government for Bolshevik partisanship and for the exploitation of the 'philosophical heritage' of Lenin. These discussions gave psychology a new orientation and made possible the development of a positive Marxist science.

But although there was a formal recognition of errors and anti-Marxist tendencies in Soviet psychology, the position did not change overnight. The ideas of the 'pedologist' intelligence testers continued to dominate the Soviet school system: the people's Commissariat of Education continued to harbour 'bourgeois' psychologists who propagated erroneous views about child development. This was shown by the fact that 'pedologists' (mental testers), appointed by the Commissariat of Education, continued to control admission to classes and the grouping of children into streams on the basis of intelligence tests. They recorded the child's progress in class independently of the teacher who found her views constantly disregarded. It was the 'pedologists' who decided the pupil's profession on leaving school. They assigned 'difficult' and backward children to special schools and classes where standards of discipline and teaching were much lower than in the ordinary schools. They also exercised control over the political education of the pupils. The 1931 decree on the schools had little effect.

When we remember that these so-called 'pedologists' were without practical teaching experience or any special knowledge of teaching problems, being specialists with a two years' post-secondary training in the theory and application of intelligence tests and questionnaires, it is clear that they could only work harm in the school system. By virtue of the fact that they controlled the work of the teacher, introducing the methods of 'streaming' as well as the deterministic theories of the tester current at this time into the practice of Soviet education, they were in a position to create havoc in the schools. In this situation, with large numbers of children being certified as mentally backward, where children were being 'streamed' on entering school in such a way as to create an impression of socioeconomic bias in the tests (children of proletarian and peasant origin being penalized) and where the theories of the pedologists directly contradicted the basic assumptions of the new society, there was considerable criticism in Party circles and also by parents and those interested in education. Makarenko, now honoured as one of the founders of the Soviet theory of education, has recorded in various books his brushes with the 'pedologists' and his unflattering opinion of them:

> I have always loathed them and have never made any secret of the fact. They were afraid to meet me. Once they wanted to inspect the way our colony was run and started asking the children such questions as: 'Imagine that you have a boat and it sinks, what would you do?'[25]

Not only did the pedologists assign mentally backward, or allegedly mentally backward children to special schools, but 'difficult' children, often highly gifted, were sent to the same schools. Under the influence of American ideas of 'free discipline' little attempt was made to maintain proper standards either of teaching or of discipline in the normal classrooms. Since the pupils in the special schools were regarded as 'ineducable' the least-qualified teachers were assigned to them. As a result, the children became almost totally demoralized. They fell into bad habits and became more and more difficult to control.

Finally on July 4, 1936, the Central Committee of the Communist Party issued the decree which, once and for all, put an end to this system. The decree abolished the use of intelligence tests in schools altogether. 'Streaming' of children, one of the major causes of educational backwardness when coupled with the deterministic theory of 'innate ability', was also ended. Most of the children in special schools were returned to the normal schools. In Moscow, for example, before the decree there were fifteen thousand children in special schools. After the decree there were six thousand.

Both the theory and practice of pedology were condemned as violating Marxism and common sense. The basic theory of the mental testing movement – namely, that the abilities of children are determined by two factors, the influence of an unchangeable inheritance and of an unchanging environment – was condemned as anti-scientific. Contemporary Soviet psychologists take this decree as being a historical turning-point in the history of Soviet psychology. In 1936 Soviet psychology effected a crucial break with bourgeois psychology: this made possible the development of a psychology which would describe and influence Soviet realities. The abolition of mental testing and the rejection of the 'two-factor theory' made possible a positive theory of human abilities and of child development.

In concluding this section, it may be said that psychology in the Soviet Union is very closely related to basic philosophical positions in a way not obvious with other schools. Soviet psychologists refuse to accept the assumption normally agreed to, without discussion, outside the Soviet orbit: that an inductive science such as psychology can use observations made even on the most atypical group to build up a science of man. In criticizing this approach Soviet psychologists operate on the basis of a logical procedure which can best be defined as 'reduction'. This consists in analysing the assumptions involved in quasi-empirical statements and, by a deductive process, reducing them to one or more of some two dozen categories. These categories are not open to debate or discussion, being accepted as true or false on an axiomatic basis. If it can be demonstrated by this method of reduction that a particular theory or observation is based on a philosophy or a scientific tendency hostile to Marxism, and to science, it must be rejected. For example, MacDougall's theory of instincts is bracketed with Weismann's theory of germ-plasm, Soviet thinkers perceiving a logical and philosophical connection between them. The general conceptual framework of Weismannism is defined on Marxist principles as 'idealistic' and therefore anti-scientific. Consequently MacDougall's theory is rejected without further discussion. It is irrelevant that MacDougall actually quarrelled with the main tenet of Weismannism (the transmission of acquired characters). The essential identity between MacDougall and Weismann consists, according to Soviet logic, in their 'idealistic' conception that a certain something – in one case, a group of 'psychophysical predispositions', in the other, a material substance transmitting hereditary characters – can exist unchanged over time, non-reactive and unaffected by the enveloping material environment. This is the essence of the anti-dialectical mode of thought.

In Soviet psychology there is an antipathy to eclecticism. Data collected by a method which derives from a false view of the relation between psyche and soma is *ipso facto* contaminated by idealism. Any desire to use such data in building a science of behaviour is perceived to be an attempt to reconcile the irreconcilable, science with anti-science. The theory of Marxism is the ultimate criterion of the truth or falsehood of psychological investigations. Empirical laboratory studies cannot be used to construct a general theory of the nature of man and of psychic processes. In this context, it appears that non-Marxist theories and even the experimental data of non-Soviet psychology are tendentious and ultimately and in essence hostile to Marxism and the Soviet system.

These differences arise because of the most fundamental conflict over the nature of truth, of the method of inquiry, and the nature of ultimate reality which divides Marxism from all kinds of liberal thought. There is a unitary, single truth which correctly reflects existing reality. The nature of this reality is contradiction and conflict. Truth about reality is obtained by posing one side against the other, without any attempt to dampen down the opposition. From this conflict truth will emerge. There are rules of dialectical logic which operate, and which can be used to test the validity of this new truth – these rules differ from Aristotelian logic in fundamental ways, most significantly in recognizing that change is of the essence of reality and of truth itself.

(iii) The Basic Theory of a Positive Marxist Psychology

On July 4, 1936, the Communist Party called for a 'Marxist science about children' which 'should rehabilitate pedagogy as a science.' The foundations of this materialist science had in fact already been well established by the great Russian investigator who died only four months previously, on February 26. Ivan Pavlov is universally recognized as one of the great figures of world science. Russian writers compare his achievements to those of Newton and Darwin. As these revolutionized human thinking about physical and organic nature respectively, so Pavlov revolutionized our way of conceptualizing human behaviour. Although he disagreed violently and vocally at times with the policy of the Bolshevik government (specifically on the question of excluding sons of priests from higher education, he himself being in this category), his work was supported very extensively by the Bolshevik government, dating from a special decree of January 24, 1921, signed by Lenin. It was clear to Lenin, although this was not understood by others, that Pavlov's ideas and discoveries were the empirical counterpart of the Marxist theory of cognition and perception, especially in the form developed by Lenin. Pavlovianism could be described as the detailed working out in a laboratory context of Lenin's epistemology. The significance of Pavlov's theories and discoveries in the field of brain physiology transcends the limits of physiology proper. Apart from his influence on the development of an objective psychology, freed from the Procrustean framework of introspection and theology which trammelled it in his day, especially in Russia, Pavlovianism provides the essential basis for the monistic view of the organism. This is of central significance, not for psychology alone, but for physiology and all the other sciences which are concerned with human and animal behaviour.

The importance of Pavlov's work was not understood at this time, the reasons being clear from the foregoing analysis of the discussions of 1929–31. Conflicting schools each had their committed adherents: much time and energy had perforce to be expended in arguing the inner contradictions and scientific sterility of particular schools, as well as their incompatibility with Marxism. The fact that Pavlov was a physiologist, using a physiological technique to study the laws of action of the cerebral cortex, obscured the real nature of his contribution. It was even then not accepted that it was possible, or even desirable, to study the brain in the same way as other organs of the body were studied. Pavlov had investigated the system of blood circulation (1878–88) and the digestive system (1888–1904), using the same basic assumptions and similar physiological techniques as he now used to throw light on problems of the 'higher nervous activity'. This phrase is a synonym for animal and human behaviour. It was in 1903 that he decided to extend these methods to the study of brain function but the importance of Pavlov for the theory of Soviet general psychology only became apparent in 1950.

Similarly with Vygotski. The beginning of his active career in psychology was signalized by his defence of consciousness against Marxists of mechanical materialist persuasion who wished to exclude it as a subject of study. This struggle against Russian forms of behaviorism on the one hand, and the dualists on the other, determined the direction of his ideas and work. His critical analysis of all the psychological schools and tendencies of his time persuaded him that their cardinal mistake lay in attempting to study psychological function (such as thought and speech) without any reference to *development*. It was Vygotski who introduced the principle of historicism into Russian experimental psychology. His studies of psychological processes always took account of their development in time:

> Once we acknowledge the historical character of verbal thought, we must consider it subject to all the premises of historical materialism, which are valid for any historical phenomenon in human society. It is only to be expected that on this level the development of behaviour will be governed essentially by the general laws of the historical development of human society.[26]

Thus, long before Piaget he had worked out a scheme of development of the thought-process through childhood to adulthood. Using the 'method of double stimulation' invented by his colleague Sakharov, a procedure in which two sets of stimuli are presented to the subject, one as objects of his activity, the other as signs which can serve to organize that activity, he studied the process of concept formation in children. Using 'Vygotski blocks' as experimental material, he concluded that concept formation can be divided into three phases, each made up of several stages. These can be shown schematically, as follows:

TABLE 2. *Phases in Concept Formation (Vygotski)*

Phase I	*Unorganized Congeries as classifications: incoherence*
(i)	trial-and-error, random groups
(ii)	syncretic organization based on simple contiguity in space or time
(iii)	syncretic, but elements from different groups
Phase II	*Thinking in 'complexes', not concepts*
(iv)	simple associative complexes
(v)	collection complexes; objects complement each other: contrast
(vi)	chain complexes, consecutive joining of links
(vii)	diffuse complexes: fluidity of linking attributes
(viii)	pseudo-concepts, based on perceptual similarities

Phase III *Conceptual thinking*
   (ix)   grouping of maximally similar objects – abstraction begins
   (x)   grouping on the basis of a single attribute
   (xi)   true conceptual thinking: abstraction, analysis, synthesis

---

In his investigations of the higher mental processes Vygotski demonstrates two kinds of emphasis which mark him out as a Bolshevik thinker. One is his concern for the totality of phenomena. As an illustration, consider his views on the origin of thought in history and in everyday affairs:

> Thought itself is engendered by motivation, i.e. by our desires and needs, our interests and emotions. Behind every thought there is an affective-volitional tendency, which holds the answer to the last 'why' in the analysis of thinking. A true and full understanding of another's thought is possible only when we understand its affective-volitional basis.[27]

The other is his view of the influence of education on the development of the higher mental functions, especially the effects of studying science. This was the crux of his disagreement with Piaget:

> He assumes that development and instruction are entirely separate, incommensurable processes, that the function of instruction is merely to introduce adult ways of thinking, which conflict with the child's own and eventually supplant them . . . (this) bars the researcher from posing the question of the interaction of development and instruction peculiar to each age level. Our own approach focuses on this interaction . . . It could be shown that all the peculiarities of child thought described by Piaget . . . stem from an absence of a system in the child's spontaneous concepts . . . (this) is the cardinal psychological difference distinguishing spontaneous from scientific concepts.[28]

This emphasis on the significance of instruction and the motivational matrix of thinking is to be found in another leading figure in psychology who came to prominence during this period – Anton Semyonovich Makarenko (1888–1939). Makarenko was not a professional psychologist, he was a Bolshevik teacher whose views were extremely hostile to the prevailing psychological doctrines and methods. His influence, on Soviet educational psychology in particular, has been profound. This is due to the fact that he was a leading exponent of the defects of the 'pedological' movement – its theories and practices. Since his books, written for the masses in a popular style, expressed the viewpoint of a dedicated Bolshevik, he was instrumental in forming public opinion about tests which led to the decree of 1936.

The problem which Makarenko faced was the regeneration of a group of young criminals – thieves, murderers, and bandits – rendered homeless and initiated into a life of crime by the First World War, the Russian Revolution and the succeeding Civil War. In 1920 he was entrusted with the task of organizing a colony for homeless children, later named the Maxim Gorki Labour Colony, near Poltava. There he spent eight years, working out his distinctive methods and rehabilitating hundreds of children brutalized by the conditions of war, famine, and revolution. In 1928 he took over a similar colony, the Dzerzhinsky Labour Commune, on the outskirts of Kharkov. In these two situations Makarenko worked out the implications of Marx's expressed ideas on education – three ideas in particular: combining productive labour with book-learning, the principle of the union of mental training, physical, and aesthetic instruction, and the idea of polytechnical instruction, that is, a general education in science centred on learning the basic principles of *all* the sciences and technology. But the most important contribution made by Makarenko was in the field of character education.

On the basis of the Marxist theory of human nature and his own experience of life, he developed a particular régime in the juvenile collectives under his charge. This he described in a personalized narrative in his classic work *The Road to Life* (1935). From his description of situations and his practical procedures we can elicit certain general principles which underlie his work.

As part of his Bolshevik faith he believed in the infinite power of correct education. According to the Communist theory of education there are no limits to human development which a correct orientation and organization of the educational environment cannot overcome. The problem is to bring to bear the whole limitless power of the collective, the totality of its educational, social, and political influence, on to the indivdual. With correct leadership and example and the placing of the most exacting demands on the pupil, while maintaining the utmost respect for his personality, it is possible to transform the individual psychology of the antisocial individualist no less than that of the weak, easily led character. A régime of work is essential. Work is the basis of human life and morals: it provides the context in which a man's sense of duty develops. Competitive group labour with differentiated praise and blame, the use of incentives and appeals to collective duty and group honour – these are the foundations of moral training in Makarenko's system. The idea of predetermined human types, the belief in human goodness or badness as inherent traits of human nature or of individual psychology are, according to Makarenko, unrealistic. He believes on the contrary in mass educability based on adult influence. Discipline and punishment, which does not harm the integrity or personality of the child, are essential components of his educational and reformative system.

These views are basic elements of the Soviet theory of education. Makarenko in his work with juvenile criminals confronted the same problems as did the rulers of Soviet Russia at the end of the Civil War. In essence the problem was how to regenerate a society corrupted for centuries by the brutality, exploitation, and narrow-mindedness of the Tsarist régime. Their task was to transform a basically peasant community of a very backward type socially, educationally, and economically, into an efficient modern, industrial community. Only a limited time was available for this transformation: they had to be able to withstand an anticipated onslaught from the encircling capitalist powers, united only in their expressed hatred of the Communist régime. Makarenko consciously envisaged his work as the creation of 'new men', intelligent and disciplined fighters for the Soviet way of life.

The Bolshevik régime conceived its educational task in the same way and adopted Makarenko's methods, suitably modifying them in accordance with the age and condition of the pupils as compared to Makarenko's adolescent criminals. In this new stage of Soviet development when socialism has been established as an economic system if not as a new political order, the problem is still conceived in the same way, namely to continue to produce disciplined and patriotic citizens, new people suited to operating an advanced economic and social system created by the achievements of communism. The means adopted are suited to the desired end.

Makarenko wrote a number of books and articles – over 100 works, in fact. Included in these are his *Book for Parents* (1937), *Learning to Live* (in Russian *Flags on the Battlements* 1938) and his most famous work, *The Road to Life* (1935). These are all written in a lively, personalized style, the only references to psychological principles being in the form of highly individual attacks on the reigning school of pedologists and 'free' educators in the People's Commissariat of Education.

One other school must be mentioned. Throughout the Soviet period, from the 1920s, the Georgian school of psychology has flourished under the guidance of Dmitri Nikolaevich Uznadze (1886–1950). With his disciples Prangishvili, Natadze, and others, he has carried out a detailed investigation of 'Set' (*Einstellung, Ustanovka*), the phenomenon by which prior events or activity affect the response of the subject so that he reacts to a stimulus in a particular way. The concept developed out of the work of Marbe, Ach, and Watt at Würzburg. The Georgian School has carried on in the same tradition of exact experimentation, rather divorced from life. There seems to be nothing specifically Soviet in the way they have developed this work (except an attempt, spasmodically, to link it to some or other quotation from Lenin). The claim is made, however, that Uznadze's theory of 'Set', based on concrete experimental work over a long period of time, is central to the Marxist theory of human personality.

References

1. Stalin (1939) Chapter 10 on 1929–30 in *History of the Communist Party of the Soviet Union* cf. his *Problems of Leninism* Moscow. 1953: 374 ff.
2. V. I. Lenin Significance of Militant Materialism, in *On Religion* 1922: 40.
3. Karl Marx *The Poverty of Philosophy* 1845.
4. Marx and Engels *Selected Correspondence* 1886.
5. Lenin *What is to be done?*
6. Stalin *On Organization* 1938.
7. A. A. Zhdanov *On Literature, Music and Philosophy*. London: Lawrence and Wishart 1950.
8. F. Engels *Anti-Dühring* 1962.
9. F. Engels *Anti-Dühring* 1962.
10. Avenarius, 1891: quoted by V. I. Lenin *Collected Works* (Russian ed.) **14**: 1941–50.
11. Lenin, op. cit.
12. V. I. Lenin *Materialism and Empirio-Criticism*.
13. Karl Marx, Preface to *Capital* **1**.
14. I. M. Sechenov, Reflexes of the Brain, in *Selected Works* 1952: 119, 136, 116–117.

15. V. I. Lenin *Philosophical Notebooks* 1938.
16. K. N. Kornilov 1930: 243–278.
17. Kornilov, *op. cit.*
18. K. Marx and F. Engels *Selected Correspondence* 1886.
19. F. Engels *Ludwig Feuerbach.*
20. Kornilov *op. cit.*
21. Marx *Capital.*
22. Engels *Anti-Dühring* 1962.
23. F. Engels *Ludwig Feuerbach* (n.d.): 74–75.
24. I. N. Spielrein 1930, quoted in *J. Nat. Inst. Ind. Psych.* **5**: 221.
25. A. S. Makarenko 1954.
26. Vygotski 1962: 124.
27. Vygotski 1962: 150.
28. Vygotski 1962: 116–117; cf. J. Piaget 1962 for rejoinder.

Reading List

Books in English
Emery, A. (1935) Dialectics vs. Mechanics: A Communist Debate on Scientific Method. *Philosophy of Science* **2**: 9–38.
Engels, F. (1962) *Anti-Dühring* Moscow: Foreign Languages Pub. House.
Konorski, J. (1948) *Conditioned Reflexes and Neuron Organisation* (trans. Stephen Garry) Cambridge Univ. Press.
Makarenko, A. S. (1951) *The Road to Life* (2nd ed.) Moscow: Foreign Languages Pub. House.
Vigotski, L. S. *Thought and Language* (edited and translated by Eugenia Hanfmann and Gertrude Vakar 1962) Cambridge, Mass.: M.I.T. Press and New York: Wiley.
Wortis, J. (1950) *Soviet Psychiatry* Baltimore: Williams and Wilkins.

Books in Other Languages
Lenin, V. I. (1938) *Filosofiskie Tetradi* (3rd ed., **38**) Moscow: Sochineniya.
Smirnov, A. A. (1957) Sovetskaya psikhologiya za 40 let. *Voprosy Psikhologii* **3** (5): 9–56.
Volpicelli, L. (1954) *L'évolution de la pédagogie sovietique* Neuchâtel: Delachaux et Niestlé.

Chapter 6 *Soviet Psychology in the Stalin Era: I (1935–1947)*

As a result of the discussions reported in the previous chapter, the basic principles of an acceptable Communist science of behaviour had been stated. However, the action moved away from theoretical discussion during the period leading up to the Great Fatherland War of 1941–5: psychology continued to be taught in universities and other institutions, and research was carried on. But little was actually published and, at least until the outbreak of war, psychology seemed to play little part in the life of the nation. This was because many areas of psychology (social, industrial, forensic, attitude research, testing, etc.) were either forbidden or had been taken over by the political movements associated with Stakhanovitism and other forms of political activism.

The psychological research caried on until 1940 was confined to particular centres of interest – psychophysiology, neurology, thinking and speech. Animal psychology was also a major field of interest. Problems and methods tend to be seen from a single point of view. In clinical psychology treatments based on Pavlov's theories were developed and certain active methods of dealing with psychoses were devised.

During the war period, psychologists were involved in rehabilitation – training of war-injured (especially brain-injured soldiers) and on other military problems.

On August 31, 1935, Alexei Stakhanov, a coal-hewer in the Central Irmino Colliery, Donetz Basin, cut 102 tons of coal in one shift – thus fulfilling the standard output fourteen times over. This inaugurated a new mass movement of workers and collective farmers for raising technical standards and especially for increasing the productivity of labour. Stakhanovitism had been

SOVIET PSYCHOLOGY IN STALIN ERA: I (1935–47) 159

born. Busygin in the automobile industry, Smetanin in the shoe industry, Krivonos on the railways, Musinsky in timber, Evdokia and Maria Vinogradova in textiles, Maria Demchenko, Maria Gnatenko, Pasha Angelino, Polagutin, Kolesov, Borin, and Kovardak in agriculture – these were the pioneers in the Stakhanovite movement. The significance for psychology and related branches of learning – for the intelligentsia in general, but especially for the 'experts' – was formidable. Notice had been served on them that the Soviet Government had transferred the initiative, for good or ill, to the political activists. Stalin had said in May 1935 to the graduates from the Red Army Academies:

> Emphasis must now be laid on people, on cadres, on workers who have mastered technique. That is why the old slogan 'technique decides everything', which is a reflection of a period already past, a period in which we suffered from a dearth of technique, must now be replaced by a new slogan 'cadres decide everything'. That is the main thing now.[1]

The Communist Party cell of the Moscow Institute of Psychology had taken the initiative, on the publication of Lenin's *Philosophical Notebooks* in 1929, to begin the critical assessment of all the existing schools of psychological thought in Russia. By the time of publication of the decree of the Central Committee, *On the Pedological Distortions in the Soviet School System*, on 4 July 1936 *all* the prevailing schools of psychology – reactology, reflexology, Pavlovianism, Gestalt psychology, behaviourism, psychotechnic, pedology, social psychology, forensic psychology – had been discredited. All the technical journals devoted to psychology as an independent brand of knowledge, established in 1928, had been closed down – *Psychology* in 1932; *Pedology* in 1932; *Psychology of Work and Psychotechnics* renamed *Soviet Psychotechnics* in 1934. Until 1955, psychological studies could appear only if they conformed to the requirements of the physiological or educational journals. Psychology, as a professional activity, was in a decline during this whole period when the Soviet Union was preparing, by collectivization of agriculture and accelerated socialist industrialization, to meet the supreme challenge of the Great Fatherland War of 1941–1945.

This does not mean that psychological research ceased during this period – on the contrary. The main difficulty under which research psychologists laboured was that there was no outlet, in published form, for their findings and theories. Many research institutes had been closed down, but psychology continued to be taught in universities and teacher training institutes. But basic research became a backroom activity: in its publicized form psychology tended to become more and more an applied science and less concerned with general laws of behaviour. This can clearly be linked to the disappointing outcome of the theoretical discussions of the early 30s and the growing need after the triumph of Hitler in Germany in 1933 for nation-wide mobilization to meet the threat from the West. Trotsky, Bukharin, Lunacharsky, and Krupskaya had all displayed an active interest in the theory and practice of psychology – but they had subsequently found themselves outside the main stream of party life. According to Teplov, the basic error of the early Marxist psychologists was that they attempted to create their own, new brand of psychology.

In reality, as a common feature, every 'school' in psychology in the Soviet Union up to this time was contaminated with the same basic methodological error – to some degree or other they pictured the reacting subject as essentially a *passive* agent. The decree of 1936 had attacked the 'two-factor' theory which, in this context, means the idea that human behaviour is the resultant of a fixed hereditary factor coupled with a relatively unchanging environment. But Marxism sees man as an active, revolutionary agent, adapting the environment to his needs and, in the process, changing not the environment only but also himself. In the social context of Russia during this period this meant the most radical intervention to change existing conditions and existing people. The successful completion of the First Five Year Plan in four years provided not only an economic basis for the new advance, it also gave the leaders of the State the necessary confidence in their abilities to change the attitudes and skills of the population. As Stalin said:

Are we really going to worship our backwardness and turn it into an icon, a fetish? What is to be done if the working men and women have already managed to grow and to gain technical knowledge? What is to be done if the old technical standards no longer correspond to reality and our working men and women have already managed in practice to exceed them five or tenfold? Have we ever taken an oath of loyalty to our backwardness? It seems to me we have not, have we comrades? (*General laughter.*) Did we ever assume that our working men and women would remain backward forever? We never did, did we? (*General laughter.*)[2]

The theme of the 'New Man', free to act because he has the necessary will to do so as well as the understanding of the laws of his own nature, of nature and society essential to act in accordance with necessity, began to be heard more and more. The 'cult of personality' inherent in the Soviet educational system based on Makarenko, where rewards are given not only for collective but for individual excellence, began to take shape. The New Constitution, adopted by the Soviet Republics in 1936, declared that socialism had been achieved: this provided the rationale for the development of the concept of the 'New Man'. If men are products of circumstances and upbringing, says Marx, then changed men are products of other circumstances and changed upbringing. But neither must we forget that circumstances are changed precisely by man.

(i) The Concept of the 'New Man'

For perspective and comparison, it is useful to contrast other views of the nature of man with the 'anthropology' of Bolshevism. We have previously outlined the Orthodox concept, but at this point it seems of more interest to compare the Soviet view with that prevailing in Western Europe. We are speaking all the time in terms of *ideal* persons, not asserting that these are the reality.

As is well known, the Roman Catholic view of this question is that the essence of man lies in his spirituality; his specific end is the contemplation of the Divine Essence throughout eternity in the Beatific Vision. The ideal man, on this view, is the saint – the method of sanctity being the imitation of Christ who is the norm or sum-total of human perfection. The material goods of this world are useful only in so far as they can be used for the glorification of God. Temporal happiness and pleasure are not ends in themselves, but are means towards man's last end. Civil society, the State, is insufficient for fulfilling the needs of man; sanctifying grace mediated through the sacraments of the Church is necessary to counteract that radical and inexpungeable defect which lies at the very centre of man's being – namely in his will.

In an important sense, historically, the Protestant view represents the secularization of this conception. There exists an organic, historical connection, demonstrated by Tawney for example, between the doctrine of 'the priesthood of all believers' and the theory of 'enlightened self-interest'. In place of a living organism, with every part serving every other, the Protestant revolution formulated the picture of society as a machine, a mere mechanism for the distribution of material goods; these are the real basis of individual happiness and enjoyment. In the completely secularized form of this belief – Utilitarianism – the function of life, the end of man, is the development of individuality. The test of the good society is the extent to which liberty is distributed amongst its members – at least amongst that section of society capable because of maturity and sagacity of benefiting from it. The normal way in which this test is applied is the prosperity of individuals. On this view, society has no spiritual purpose; it is not an organism but a mechanism like a clock. The eternal laws of the market, by a complicated system of checks and balances, keep the mechanism in a fine state of adjustment and good running order.

The Marxist view, especially in its Soviet form, represents a synthesis of these conflicting views of man and of society. On the one hand, going a stage further than Protestantism, the Marxist, as an absolute atheist, claims that the material world is all that one has to enjoy. Hence, efficiency of creation and distribution of material wealth is the criterion by which societies, which are primarily economic systems which remove the human species from absolute dependence on nature, are judged at the bar of history. But on the other hand, material wealth is only important as the basis of the spiritual life. The idea of *service* which formed the constant theme of Soviet exhortations to the young and to other specialized groups in the community – workers, peasants, and intellectuals – is based on that spiritual conception of society which western Europe lost through the Reformation. The fact that there was no Reformation in Russia – disintegrating the unity of knowledge, of society, and of the individual – but a mere Church reform touching a few points of ritual and Church organization is a basic fact which is one of the master-keys to unlock that 'mystery wrapped in an enigma' which constitutes for most people the Soviet way of life and thought.

As the first society to develop a socialist system on Marxist principles, where all the means of production, distribution, and exchange have been converted into national property, the Soviet Union, by 1936, had reached the stage of bringing to fruition a synoptic view of man. This stands, fully developed, as a challenge to the Christian conceptions. It is a considerable advantage in eliciting and elucidating this new conception of man that the Russians are systematic thinkers, who conceived one of their main tasks to be to develop, on the basis of principle, a logical, coherent, and comprehensive theory of man. This was then disseminated as a blueprint to educationists, party workers, scientists, and all other 'engineers of the human soul' for appropriate action.

Perhaps the most interesting question for the psychologist is the extent to which the description of the New Soviet Man, now to be discussed, is a product of Russian tradition, and how far it derives from classical Marxism. The question, posed in this way, is partly at least an artificial one. As we have seen, the development of the Russian outlook is the result of a development taking place along parallel lines which meet in the new concept of man. On the one hand there were the borrowings from Western culture and from indigenous peasant and Orthodox beliefs and customs by the native Russian school of thinkers, Marxists in everything but name and origin. On the other hand, there was the deliberate assimilation by Lenin of West European Marxism to Russian conditions. The importance of the school of native thinkers – represented especially by Belinsky, Chernishevski, and Dobrolyubov – as forerunners of the Revolution and of Soviet ways of thought has been made clear. It is a fact of life that the pattern of thought in the Soviet Union owes at least as much to Dobrolyubov, for example, as it does to Marx himself. The Revolution would not have come to pass had Lenin not been a self-conscious and extremely active Marxist. But with the success of the Revolution and the building up of a new social and economic order, traditional ways of thinking continued to assert their vitality and relevance.

Let us look at the New Soviet Man first, before considering how much he contains of the Old Russian Man. . . .

There is no difficulty in eliciting the Soviet view of what man is, and what man ought to be. As a monolithic society, all the organs of government and opinion were committed to the dissemination by education and propaganda of the picture of the new person. All citizens were enjoined to develop the positive aspects of the New Soviet Man and to extirpate from their psychological make-up the negative features of old capitalist man. It became the duty of teachers, novelists, scientists, and philosophers, to preach and, if capable of it, to practise the new virtues, and to chasten by criticism any backsliding by colleagues.

What are these virtues? And how do they differ from what 'capitalist man' regards as virtues?

The broad, strong lineaments of the positive Russian man were drawn in the 1840s; the picture becomes gradually stronger and more detailed in the 1860s as changing circumstances demand new responses; finally it appears, in Polevoi's words, as a 'Real Man'. To put it otherwise, the various cardinal virtues – of which there are about ten – become organized and organically connected over time, like the fingers on the hands.

The most striking quality of the new ideal man, at least in Western eyes, is his optimism, the confidence in his own strength, the cheerfulness with which he sets out to conquer Nature. The Russians believe that anything is possible to man, that there are no limits to man's power of transforming nature and society. This is not a mere figure of speech, but is to be taken in its most literal meaning. Those scientists who, for example, maintain that the nature of the chromosomes or the mechanism of heredity; the nature of the soil; the operation of sun-spots; the ratio between the surplus of agricultural as compared with industrial products; the descending curve of rates of economic development; or even the condition of the railway rolling-stock, that these or any other factors impose limits to man's conquest of his environment, such scientists are said to exhibit a desertion of principle unworthy of a Bolshevik intellectual.

But on the other hand, this optimism must not degenerate into mere boastfulness. The New Man must beware of the traditional indiscipline and expansiveness. It is *social* man and not individual man for whom all things are – potentially at any rate – possible. As Plekhanov pointed out in 1898: 'Talented people can change only the individual features of events, but not their general trend; were it not for that trend they would never have crossed the threshold that divides the potential from the real.'[3] *Modesty* is the second characteristic feature of the new ideal man.

Thus Soviet Man has nothing in common with the individualism of the man of liberal societies. His characteristic virtue is *collectivism* – that is, he has no purposes which conflict with those of the collective. His particular successes are derived from the good fortune of society, from the success of social, collective work. There is no cleavage within man separating his psychological, individual consciousness from his political or ideological consciousness – in other words, he belongs to the collective without reservations of any kind. Kalinin, speaking at a conference of the best urban and rural teachers in 1938, said:

> The cultural work you do should be linked up with the general work of Socialist construction, so as to ensure that people do not isolate themselves in their thoughts from society. The Philistine is a person whose thoughts set him apart, isolate him, a person who does not bind himself to anybody or anything.[4]

This losing of himself in the community is possible for Soviet Man because of his *socialist humanism*. He loves and cares for people and for the dignity of the human personality, especially for children. Life is better and happier for the Soviet humanist than for the misanthrope individualist of capitalist society. However, this humanism has nothing in common with a sentimental love of all people without exception. Soviet Man cannot love the enemies of the working class, nor anyone who stands across the path to the happy future. It is a virtue to hate the oppressor and to destroy the aggressor.

Patriotism is an essential, outstanding virtue of the ideal New Person. But this patriotism is of a new higher type, and is not to be identified with the exclusive type of imperialist patriotism characteristic of the Black Hundreds and other oppressors of the people. In this new Soviet patriotism, the motherland and the idea of Communism as the ideal of progressive humanity everywhere are inseparably united. Marx said, 'The working man has no country', and this was true in his generation. Now it is no longer so. The Soviet Union, as a multi-national state, is the microcosm of the future of mankind, when all nations shall be united in fraternal co-operation, and the only rivalry between nations relates to the speed at which they build up the new Communist society.

For this is, of course, fundamental. The distinguishing mark of Soviet Man is his *ideological approach* to all questions. In every question it is necessary to adopt frankly the standpoint of a particular social group – the working class. It is only by means of this partisan approach in science and philosophy as in political activity that true objectivity is obtained. Far from being a barrier to truth, political passion, by sharpening the mind of the investigator, may serve as a powerful means of discovering the truth. Unprincipled eclecticism, halfheartedness, objectivism – these are

166 SOVIET PSYCHOLOGY: HISTORY, THEORY, CONTENT

the characteristics of the compromisers, the half-men of liberal society. The true Bolshevik cannot stop half-way, he must go to the end. Science does not tolerate irresolution and unprincipled wavering.

The *sense of duty* of the New Soviet Man is derived from these principles; the duty of the citizen to the motherland, to the Party, to the collective lies at the foundation of the responsible attitude of man to his work and to his mission of constructing communism.

The New Soviet Person has a new *Communist attitude to work*. Kalinin declared, 'In our country work is a matter of honour, glory, valour and heroism; whether it is the work of a brick-layer, scientist, janitor, engineer, carpenter, artist, swineherd, actress, tractor driver, agronomist, shop assistant, and so forth.'[5] Work is not to be regarded as a punishment for sin, but as the very basis of man's life, the centre of his living interests, and the condition of a free, human personality.

The New Soviet Man therefore shows a *readiness to overcome difficulties*. Indeed, it was Lenin himself who taught the Soviet not to fear difficulties, not to close one's eyes to them, but to go towards the approaching difficulties, to struggle with them and overcome them. This was his characteristic attitude to life, never shown more clearly than in April 1917 when he declared that the time had come when the Party must take power in the name of the proletarian revolution. To him alone at this time belonged the courage and the vision. As will is the backbone of character, so it is in the qualities of his will as a *fighter for communism* and a builder of victorious socialism that Soviet Man is sharply distinguished from previous types of men.

It would be a fascinating task to trace the development of the Soviet conception of the New Man at this point, and to disen-tangle traditional elements in it. This has been done perhaps in a sketchy way, in the earlier sections of the book which deal with Radishchev, Belinsky, Chernishevski, and Dobrolyubov. However, it seems more important at this time to state certain principles of interpretation of Soviet society, without attempting to answer the question how far this description of the ideal Soviet person corresponds with the reality. Only through an application of these principles can one approach an interpretation of Soviet life and thought which does not rest on the momentary ideological requirements of the 'cold war', or on personal hopes and fears or prejudices.

Most of the admirers of Soviet society, and most of its critics too, seem to be united in making one cardinal error about the Russian people – they assume, without any prior examination, that in essence the same system of values is to be discovered in the mass of Soviet people, if not in their Soviet institutions, as those with which the critic or admirer is familiar. As subsidiary hypotheses it then becomes necessary to assume that on particular occasions, and for specific Machiavellian purposes, the ruling Party departs from this common norm of custom or value, or (in the case of those who uncritically admire Soviet society) to deny that such departure has been made, or if this is admitted, to justify it from particular historical fortuities. This problem became acute in 1931 and again in 1936, when psychology, as understood and practised in the West, seemed to fall a victim to Communist Machiavellianism. The change of direction in these crucial years was due to certain calculations based on the fundamental principle that the first duty of society owes its members is to survive. Man does not live by bread alone, but he lives primarily by bread. This is the first principle in interpreting the decision to divert certain resources from psychology and concentrate on the task of mobilizing the population – since the logic of circumstances demanded a more radical intervention in the area of political and social consciousness than the professional schools of psychology were capable of. The decision to turn to political leaders like Kalinin to formulate some general principles of Marxist psychology for immediate propagation; the decision to play up the successes of socialist rationalization of industral production by the most public recognition of the value of Stakhanovitism; the continuing mass campaign against illiteracy – this was clearly the official policy. The decision to discredit the opposition group by the mass trials of leading political figures in 1936 and 1937 belongs to the same thought-pattern.

As a second principle, corrective of the fallacy of easy identification with what are seen as 'good' aspects and a rather hysterical rejection of what are seen as totally unrelated 'bad' features of the Soviet system and ideal, it must be recognized that there are very fundamental differences between Soviet civilization and Western civilization, based on differences in their histories. The fact that Russia was influenced, not to say moulded, by the Byzantine form of Christianity rather than by the Roman form; the influence of the Tatar invasion, illustrated in the nineteenth century by the servility to superiors and the subjection of women; by the knout and the almost universal physical violence; the absence of any Reformation in the Western sense of the term; the fact that the ideology of laissez-faire had no roots in Russian life or Russian science; the absence of large-scale industrial enterprise; the rigidity of the social hierarchy under the Tsarist despotism – these are some of the important influences which give to Russian institutions and viewpoints their unique character.

But it goes without saying that it would be equally fatal to truth to assume that these characteristic features have remained unchanged since the Revolution, as they tended to do for long periods under the Tsars. The persistent theme of Russian folktales and of classical Russian literature of the sleeping giant who suddenly awakens and with a tremendous flood of energy completely transforms his environment enshrines a valuable insight into Russian history and character. The New Man is the product of a period of contemplation, of 'gathering strength', lasting about half a century, followed by a tremendous burst of revolutionary energy which has persisted for about the same time. The New Soviet Man is not, as we tend to assume, the invention of an alien propaganda, but represents an organic development of a particular aspect of Russian tradition. If we wish to understand this new concept of man, it is necessary to take account of this history and this tradition and come to some kind of terms with it. One thing is certain that we shall continue to see through a glass darkly so long as we seek only our own image, and refuse to take seriously anything else that may be found on the other side.

(ii) A Survey of Empirical Research: 1936–1947

One of the widespread misconceptions about Soviet psychology is that it is simply an elaboration of the technique of the conditional reflex used by Pavlov as the preferred method of research in the field of cortical functioning.

Because of the fact that Pavlov's ideas were misunderstood by the American behaviourists and other psychologists, a certain mythology had grown up in Western psychology which elaborately dismissed Pavlov's work as a major irrelevancy unrelated to the problems of human behaviour in real life. Pavlovianism was erroneously identified with the particular technique of establishing the conditional reflex, whereas his views about the nature of the organism and its relations with the environment, as well as his laws of cortical activity, were simply ignored. This misconception about Pavlov's work and its application has now been rebutted explicitly and nothing more need be said about it. Because we have been concerned so far only with the development of the general theory of psychology, it has not been possible to say very much in a connected way about actual empirical research carried out by Soviet psychologists since the Revolution. Some attempt will now be made to remedy this omission: a more detailed account of later work will be given in the next chapter.

Sufficient materials have been indicated to suggest that Soviet psychology had an empirical content even in the formative period before, during, and immediately after the First Five Year Plan when questions of basic theory were preoccupying the minds of psychologists. The Soviet discussions of 1929–1931, not to speak of later discussions, clearly recognized the existence of psychology as an autonomous branch of science, distinct from physiology. The principal problem of psychology, that is, the nature and causation of psychic processes, had been solved by the leading school of Russian physiology. Pavlov has shown how psychic processes were inseparately linked with the brain functions and bound up with the adjustment of the organism to the ever-changing aspects of the environment. As a subject having its own problems and specialized techniques of investigation distinct from those of physiology, psychology had been taught for a considerable period in universities, teacher training institutions, military academies (and also in Soviet schools since 1947). A network of institutes and university departments in the USSR had grown up, carrying out research on specific psychological questions. For example, perception, learning, personality differences, and many other fields were studied throughout the whole period from 1917.

Professor Ananiev was an important figure in the development of Soviet psychology, with interests in neurological psychology and the history of psychology. In 1947 he delivered a lecture on *The Achievements of Soviet Psychology* giving a detailed account of psychological research in many different fields. He concludes by discussing the general principles of method which should inform all contributions to this science in the USSR. It is in the field of general methodology rather than in empirical research that the difference between Soviet and non-Soviet psychology is illustrated most abundantly. Professor Ananiev states that the Marxist philosophy of dialectical materialism is the foundation of psychological research, and that the Soviet system created psychology anew, transforming it into a real science. The psychological aspects of dialectical materialism are formulated in six principles of method which define positively the general principles of Soviet psychology.

These positive principles or axioms, which are derived from the Russian materialist tradition as well as from Marxism, were enunciated during the Soviet period, especially between 1930–1941. These six axioms which underlie psychological thinking and research in the USSR are those already discussed: (i) psychophysical monism, (ii) the theory of reflection, (iii) the materialist determination of consciousness and activity, (iv) the principle of contradiction in development, (v) the unity of consciousness and activity, and (vi) the class and historical character of psychic processes.

It should be said that, in isolating the six basic presuppositions of Marxist psychology, one does violence to the coherence and integrality of the Soviet view: this is, of course, probably the most characteristic feature of Soviet psychology. In addition to discussing the six basic principles of materialist psychology, Ananiev gives a valuable summary of Soviet work in various fields.

As will be clear from the preceding discussion, one of the main centres of Soviet psychological research has been in nervous physiology, regarded as the material basis (*substrat*) of mental activity. The advanced state of Russian physiology due to the influence of Sechenov and the important schools based on his materialist views – not only Pavlov, but Bekhterev, Vvedenski, Orbeli, and Beritov were powerfully influenced by Sechenov's programme – made it possible to attack the two most difficult problems of psychology. These are the questions of the origin of individual differences in temperament and character,[6] and that relating to the material basis of psychic activity.

The work of Bekhterev and Pavlov provides a clear picture of the localization of mental processes in the brain. The extreme fluidity and variableness of localization, the very considerable possibilities that exist for the replacement and transfer of functions from one area to another of the cortex, as well as the formation of new centralized functions were put to practical use during the war of 1941–45 in the work of Ananiev, Leontiev, Luria, Zankov, Kogan, and others. Tremendous experience was gained in the diagnosis of neuropsychic shock resulting from wounding of the cerebral cortex and the cerebellum. In addition, an immense amount of work was done on the restoration of nervous and psychic functions destroyed by head wounds. Many thousands of cases of soldiers, who had lost speech, sight, hearing, memory, and other functions as a result of head wounds, were successfully treated so that they could return to the front or to ordinary life. This psychological rehabilitation (which was paralleled on a smaller scale by American psychologists) demonstrated the possibility of forming new dynamic centres in the cortex as a result of the activity of the individual himself, and was believed to demonstrate the correctness of Pavlov's theses on localization of function in the brain.

Another central question of Soviet psychology, arising from the Darwinian orientation of Soviet natural science, is the history of mental development in animals. The origin and early development of human consciousness is of interest from the standpoint of a materialist theory of cognition. Based on the conceptions of Severtsev, an important school of animal psychologists has arisen in the Soviet Union. It must be said that the scope and scale of this work is very restricted when compared with Britain or the USA. But prior to Köhler and Yerkes, the Russian biologist Ladygina-Kohts had studied the mental development of anthropoid apes. She pointed to the similar features, as well as to the differences, in psychic development as between the child and the chimpanzee. (She had adopted a baby chimpanzee and brought it up at the same time as her own child.) Voitonis more recently has made studies of the animal intellect. Wagner and Roginski have also worked in this field. Active research work on birds and fish in a natural setting is carried out in accordance with the theoretical concepts of Pavlov.

Closely linked with this question is that of the psychical development of the child. The work of Rubinstein, Menchinskaya, Lublinskaya, and many others has produced a clear picture of the way in which the psyche develops through individual activity during the life of the child. This work is based on Pavlov's principle of the unity of internal and external conditions. In other words, education is not an external force in relation to the unchanging psyche of the child: it is a dynamic force which becomes internalized and incorporated in new psychic systems. In particular, training and education are the creative motive forces in the moral and intellectual development of the child. The sequential development of sensation, perception, and cognition has been worked out in detail.

Many other problems, including especially those dealing with the way speech develops, the formation of parts of speech and phrases, the development of syntax and so on, have been investigated by these and other Soviet psychologists. The psychology of the pre-school child and of the child in school has been worked out in great detail by such workers as Leontiev, Smirnov, Rubinstein, and others. The central theme of this work has been the importance of activity and individual experience in the development of different psychic qualities. This is in contrast to the views of many Western psychologists who stress the conditioning of development by heredity and environment (conceived as unchanging) and who take up fatalistic attitudes on the question of the transformative effect of education and training.

A fourth field of work which Soviet psychologists have cultivated in a unique fashion is that of perception. The older type of physiological psychology ('psychophysics') concerned itself with the study of thresholds, that is the limiting value of a stimulus which could be perceived by the subject. This was conceived as a study of constant, unchanging, fixed levels or changes of level, unaffected by other conditions. The 'idealistic' schools of psychophysics had no understanding of the lability of thresholds under the influence of training and experience, or of the role of sensation as the origin of all psychic processes. On the other hand, these are the main centres of interest of Soviet psychologists.

The problem as conceived by Soviet psychologists is how to change the apparently invariant thresholds of perception. The question of the objectivity of different perceptions, such as smell, taste, pain, etc., as reflecting the qualities of the stimulus are also of central importance in this period. These problems were seen to be of significance in the light of Lenin's theory of cognition. Kravkov, Kekcheyev, and others studied these problems with interesting results. The question of the way in which one type of perception influences others, the mutual interaction of modalities, became of great significance especially since this could be used as a means of heightening sensitivity.

Another central field of work was that of thought and speech. Indeed, Soviet psychologists regard this as *the* central problem in psychology. Thought is not a mere association of ideas in the mind of an individual thinker. The forms of thought are socially determined, hence a historical approach is essential. Vygotski, Blonski, Sokolov, Menchinskaya, and many others have tackled this question. The conception on which this work is based is that thought and speech represent the highest form of mental activity, principally distinguishing man from the animal kingdom. Of course, this view is common amongst Western animal psychologists also. The origin of speech on the basis of activities and the way in which understanding arises is not only a psychological question (that is, a problem of studying the individual development of the child) but it is also a historical problem. As Engels has pointed out, understanding is a historical product. The development of understanding can be conceived of as a process of the accumulation of the material of thought. It is not, therefore, a product of individual psychical development but rather of social historical development. In the thirties and forties the work of the philologist Marr had a considerable influence, since he drew up a historical scheme of the different stages of human thinking which was coherent, logical, and seemed to be based on empirical material. This has now been discredited by Stalin's critique.

These constitute only a few of the research fields which Ananiev surveys. In addition to this record of progress in experimental investigation he cites the remarkable growth of institutions for research or teaching in psychology. Before 1917 there were no professorial chairs in psychology. There was only one specialist institute. By 1947 there were many psychology institutes, for example, in Moscow, Leningrad, Kiev, Tiflis, Riga, and so on. There were more than thirty chairs of psychology in universities. In addition, psychology had been introduced into the middle schools, so that boys and girls of seventeen to eighteen years were studying the subject, along with logic.

These are, of course, remarkable achievements, especially when we consider the vast social changes and disruption of academic life produced by the Revolution. The relative scarcity of trained personnel who were also acceptable to the régime constituted what many must have regarded as an inseparable obstacle to the development of the Bolshevik programme in this field. During this period it must be said that the distinctive features of Soviet psychological research were not too much in evidence, either in the nature of the problems investigated or in the methods used. The work done was more clearly related to a general organizing framework. Very similar work was being carried out in America and Britain. The main difference appears to be that large areas of psychology studied in the West by rather questionable methods, and certain kinds of anti-scientific theories, do not appear at all in Soviet work. For example, the analytic schools of Freud and Jung and their numerous derivatives are not represented in Soviet psychological literature. Gestalt psychology is not represented. Questionnaire studies and investigations using standardized tests on relatively small and biased populations are not carried out. From the point of view of objective psychology these can be considered positive gains. They leave personnel, materials, and financial resources available to cultivate areas of psychology by methods which are capable of yielding results of value in developing a positive psychological science.

It must be emphasized, however, that a considerable quantity of published Soviet research is not of the first rank. Many articles of this period are merely verbose illustrations of already well-known general principles, or a formal statement of commonplace and generally accepted data on the development of speech or of voluntary activities. These excesses however are the negative features of what seems to be a healthy preoccupation with general theory. There is, relatively speaking, less of the really worthless material often published in non-Soviet journals, the only justification for which seems to be that it has earned the investigator an academic degree. There is none of the fantastic speculation along Freudian or Jungian lines to which numerous non-Soviet journals devote a large percentage of their space. The particular kind of worthless material which sees the light in Soviet journals during this period is the hack article in which some Party nonentity rehashes the basic quotations from Marx, Lenin, Pavlov, and Sechenov within a formal framework of devotional obsequiousness.

The tradition of free choice which runs in democratically organized societies; the proclaimed dichotomy between the individual and the State; the dualism of mind and body and related beliefs are peripheral to the main stream of thought in Soviet society. There is a different tradition, and different presuppositions underlie thought and action. Here we confront the challenge of a society which functions on very different assumptions. The development of mental stereotypes on the basis of social pressures, and the specific experience of living within particular social institutions, must be recognized to be a common factor in both types of society. When individuals in one attempt to discuss the concepts of the other we see clearly revealed the ways in which these processes operate.

(iii) Abnormal Psychology

Russian psychiatry, like its European counterpart, was rooted in materialism. The tradition was established by Sechenov and nourished by his disciples Pavlov, Bekhterev, Tarkhanov, Korsakov, Serbsky and many others. Botkin's principle of 'nervism', that all the functions of the body are under the control of the cerebral hemispheres, operated in such a way as to emphasize the basic rationality of the patient, contrary to the tradition established by Freud. Thus, in a person who is mentally ill, we are confronted by a complicated system that has broken down in some of its parts or relations of its part. This is in contrast to the Freudian model of a machine that, even in the 'normal' case, is under the control of malignant and uncontrollable forces derived from a primordial nature which is basically hostile to man.

The theory of reflection suggests that abnormal behaviour is basically due to some kind of faulty reflection of reality. If in essence, the nature of our views, convictions, strivings, tastes, habits is *not* biological, as Freud suggests, but social as Lenin declares them to be, then changes in the external environment, or in the nature of the learned reactions we have built up, should alter the nature of response. According to Marxism, mental conflicts are not inherent in man's nature: they arise as the reflection of real conflicts of objective reality. It is not the clash of the feelings with the reason, nor the collision of what comes from within with what comes from the outside which causes neurosis. The conflict in man, the contradictions of our thoughts, desires, and feelings, reflect the real contradictions existing in nature and in our social life. In particular, conflicts can arise due to 'survivals' of capitalist ways of thinking and attitudes, still active in the minds of Soviet citizens. Thus the emphasis of the pre-revolutionary psychiatrists, Merzheyevsky, Korsakov, and others, on the influence of social and economic factors in the development of mental disorder, together with the views of Pavlov, are the important elements in the theory of aetiology and therapy of neuroses and psychoses at this period. The mechanisms that produce experimental neurosis in animals are believed to be the same as those which produce neuroses in human beings.

The scientific study of behavioural pathology began in 1885 when Bekhterev opened the first experimental psychological laboratory at the University of Kazan; a year later Korsakov opened a similar laboratory in Moscow. In the 1930s and 1940s the two leading scientific investigators of abnormal behaviour, after Pavlov's death, were Vygotski and Zeigarnik. They both studied the psychopathology of thought, Vygotski being the first person to characterize the nature of the thought-process in

schizophrenia on the basis of systematic experimental investigation. He demonstrated that the special state of the cortex in this
disorder disrupts the system of connections underlying words,
causing a disintegration of the system of concepts. The patient
thinks in terms of 'complexes', not true concepts. This semantic
disorganization is accompanied by various kinds of affective alter-
ations. Zeigarnik used drawings, where Vygotski used blocks, as
materials to study thought-disturbances in 300 patients. She found
distortion of the process of generalization to be the rule in schizophrenia, as well as a lowering of the general level possible to the
individual.

In view of the importance of the cortex in behaviour, and of
the theory of 'nervism' in the basic view of the organism, it is not
surprising to find a tremendous emphasis being placed on *education* in the prevention and treatment of psychiatric conditions.
Rational insight into the nature of the mental illness (a description in Pavlovian terms may be given to the patient), combined
with suggestion techniques, and support from external social
agencies may constitute the total therapeutic régime. The essence
of rational therapy is that the patient must understand the nature
of his illness, that it is curable, and completely subject to scientific
laws. In some cases, for example hysteria, rational therapy does
not always achieve its aim: in such a case recourse may be made to
indirect suggestion. Group therapy, but *not* analytically oriented,
may be used. The second, typically Soviet, emphasis in therapy
is the stress laid on *work*, and the development of a proper attitude
to it. Since it is through co-operative labour that man attains his
highest level of development, work can be used as a therapeutic
agency. Through the work-process in a collective, the patient can
organize his life and his attitudes to the community. Makarenko
had shown this to work with young delinquents. Political education, in the sense of indoctrinating the deviant with the ideal of
the New Soviet Man is part of the treatment. This may be provided in the patient's ordinary environment, using neighbour-
hood groups, trade union, and other agencies as a source of personnel and influence.

Hospitalized patients may be subjected to a more active therapeutic régime. For example, in cases of psychosis insulin shock
treatments, electroshock, sulphur therapy, and colloidoclastic
shock (small quantities of incompatible blood are injected into the
bloodstream) have been practised for many years. Prefrontal
leucotomy was also employed between 1947 and 1950 when it

was abolished by decree. The major difference between Soviet and non-Soviet therapeutics is that these active treatments are based on a general theory of the organism, derived from Pavlov and the physiologists. The behaviour of the patient is comprehended under the general rubric of 'higher nervous activity'.

In this period, considerable attention was paid to the inter-relationships of the first and second signal systems as a source of breakdown in behaviour-patterns; the relations between the cortex and lower level centres also came under close scrutiny. Prolonged sleep therapy was also used as a Pavlovian treatment. It was Asratyan, following the lead given by Petrova, who used this technique on animals who were suffering from an experimental neurosis: it seems to have come into general use about the mid-40s. By a combination of hypnosis and sedation certain types of patient are maintained in a comatose condition for months on end. Between 1943 and 1949 Andreyev had treated over 240 patients using this method. According to Davidenkov, who used prolonged sleep as a therapy in cases of acute neurosis, it is essential to use the method in conjunction with other treatments. Its main function appears to be to improve cortical 'tone'. In catatonic schizophrenia, itself being regarded as a state of protective inhibition, Ivanov-Smolensky has used this technique to strengthen still further the inhibitory condition. Inhibition is used in other ways as a curative agency. For example, by mutual induction, excitation in another area of the cortex may be used to inhibit the point of pathological excitation. Thus, 'diseased points' in the second signalling system (obsessional thoughts) or in the first (obsessive concepts and fears) may be treated by inducing inhibition by applying a very powerful stimulus. The creation of a new living interest of an emotionally coloured and conscious character, one which links the patient with the community and work, has exactly the same effect.

With regard to mental deficiency, the Soviet abandonment of 'pedology' involved not only the disuse of tests but also the abandonment of the conception of normal distribution of traits, such as intelligence, in human beings. Thus, the concept of 'gradualness', of the artificiality of boundary-lines between normal and abnormal, balanced and insane, defective and normal range, etc., is replaced by the assumption of dialectical leaps. Thus, for example, the schizophrenic is *qualitatively* different from the normal person: insanity is *not* just a matter of degree. Similarly, the 'oligophrenic' child is not to be regarded as one who falls below a certain arbitrary point on the normal curve. Mental deficiency is a matter of certain structural and functional handicaps and weaknesses in mental functioning requiring *medical* ascertainment. School backwardness is a different matter entirely. There may be specific disabilities here, such as number weakness, inability to sing in time, etc. These will normally be the result of certain conditional connections which failed to be established at the appropriate point in the child's educational process. This may lead to faulty methods of work, negative attitudes, lack of foundation for later intellectual work. These all result in poor performance, but there is no irreversible intellectual impairment. Missing, or damaged, or incorrectly formed links can be established or restored; at least in principle this is so, however difficult it may be in practice. The 'backward child', with no organically determined deficiency, can be educated. The oligophrenic child is a different case. Here we are dealing with a system that has stabilized at a different level due to constitutional or other inborn factors of development. There is the strong possibility of anatomic and physiological peculiarities in the nervous system. Special schools only take in children with such defects, on the basis of a precise diagnosis: this is essentially a medical question. Considerable research on the psychology of such children was carried out in this period.

(iv) Marxist Methodology in Psychology

The principle of reflection was formulated by Lenin, following Marx and Engels. In brief, it is the conviction that the mind, or psyche, is a 'reflection' of the objective, external world. According to this view, the mental and spiritual life of man is ultimately the product of social influences. Of these, the economic structure and class relations of society constitute by far the most important part. The emotions, the will, the intellect, are conceived to be processes which arise, develop, and change in their manifold ways as a consequence of particular material and social environments. The subjective life of man is not something 'locked away', something personal, or unique, or individual, and developing in isolation from reality, with a special history of its own, out of contact with the real changing world of physical and social relations. Soviet psychologists cannot conceive of man as a contemplative being: human qualities presuppose a world of interaction and human relations. At the same time, it is no contradiction for the Soviet psychologist to say that each individual has his own specific history – to the contrary, this an essential principle of Marxism. Man is himself a necessary element of the social situation; he is involved in changing it, and in doing so he changes the situation certainly, but more important, he changes himself. It is clear from this that genetic psychology cannot be studied in isolation from the historical forms of man's social existence – as non-Soviet psychology seeks to do. On the other hand, the study of a given social situation which attempts to explain the response of the human agents abstractly, that is, apart from their individual history must be completely fallacious.

This leads up to a statement of the second assumption of Soviet psychology. If psychic processes are to be explained by a peculiar interactional relationship between man and his environment, then it follows that the search for universal psychological laws is misconceived. There can be no such thing as a generalized human nature, except in the most platitudinous sense. This is the theory of the historical and *class* determination of psychic processes. The preceding argument leads logically to the conclusion that there must be essential and characteristic differences in the psychology of members of different classes in a class-divided society, and between men of different cultures and periods. In particular, according to this view *Soviet* man must be fundamentally different from non-Soviet man. This is because the economic basis and social relations of Soviet society are basically different from other societies. Production, distribution, and exchange are organized in a new way – this has a determining influence on the forms of social consciousness. It is claimed that the socialist system, by abolishing private property in the means of production, opens up new possibilities of human development and creates new forms of consciousness, new people. The new Soviet man is claimed to be different from the old Russian man. It is obvious, of course, that there must be differences in mental content. But it is implied that there are qualitative differences also in the nature of the *psychic processes* in Soviet and non-Soviet man. These differences do not relate so much to the elementary processes of memory, perception, modes of emotional expression, etc.; they are centred in the area of the higher qualities of personality, will, and morality, and in the relationship between mental-functioning-as-a-whole and the social environment.

The view that Soviet man is different from other kinds of humanity in fundamental ways was the theme of psychological texts from the highest level down to the materials of the daily newspaper during this period. Since the death of Stalin in 1953, and the revelations of the Twentieth Party Congress, less has been heard of the 'New Man'. But the principle of historicity, first introduced into Russian psychology by Vygotski, remains one of the most basic assumptions.

The third basic assumption is that of psychological monism. According to Marxism, there is only one substance, matter. This has a number of properties all of which are based on differences in the way matter is organized. At the atomic level, for example, it is the number and disposition of protons, electrons, and other particles which determine the nature of the element or compound. The difference between living matter (free movement, growth, reproduction) and inorganic matter is based on the way a particular arrangement of carbon, oxygen, nitrogen, and hydrogen becomes possible, yielding protein-like substances that possess these qualities. At the highest level of complexity, the human brain, we have the possibility, given by this most complex arrangement of material, of consciousness and other psychic processes emerging. We do not know the exact relationship between the mind (or consciousness) and the brain, except that one is dependent on the other. Mind is inseparable from matter. The human brain is, relatively speaking, a new form of matter. It is made up of exactly the same elements as the crust of the earth, but these are organized in new forms of movement, therefore new qualities appear. The subjective world of man's mind comes into being, and disappears again when this particular structure disappears. Consciousness, the psychic sphere, has its own laws. But these can only be discovered by treating the phenomena of mind in exactly the same way as we deal with other phenomena – as an *object*. Any idea that there is something else apart from matter and its properties, independent and subsisting separate from matter, is a misconception.

The fact that other philosophies and other psychologies exist can be explained in terms of the fourth basic assumption. This is to the effect that forms of consciousness are the product of the material forces of production. The different conceptions of man, society, and nature arise as a by-product of the differences between social systems – at this particular period the socialist and capitalist. The difference between these systems is essentially the difference between the economic bases – on the one hand, an economy based on the market and private property in the means of production, on the other a planned economy based on common ownership. These

beget two kinds of superstructure. Capitalism generates empiricism, eclecticism, dualism, objectivism, and religious concepts;
socialism generates dialectical materialism, partisanship, objectivity based on commitment, monism, and atheism. Lenin accounts
for oligopolistic tendencies and Government intervention under
capitalism in terms of an inherent tendency towards monopoly,
imperialist expansion and the ideological corruption of broad
strata of workers and managers in the pursuit of super-profits, as
for example, in the United States. These questions of detailed
analysis of specific developments are not our concern at this point.
'Bourgeois science' is caught up willy-nilly in the categories imposed by the particular type of social organization in which it
develops. Soviet psychologists would concede that they too 'philo-
sophize in a cage'. But they would maintain the superiority of
their cage, Soviet society having overcome the specific limitations
and conditions of capitalism. It is claimed that, under Soviet
socialism, man is consciously aware of the influence of social forces
on his forms of thought, whereas in pre-socialist societies we have
the unconscious generation of ideologies which control men independently of their will. Human freedom consists in making the
decisions and choices open to us in conformity with the determining tendencies and not in opposition to them.

The fifth proposition is that of the unity of consciousness and
activity. The separation of man's internal world and his practical
activity runs through the whole history of philosophy and psychology. It acts to stunt human creativity at all levels.

The conscious mental activity of man is the ultimate level of
functioning of the world of nature. Consciousness is a peculiarly
human attribute, not found in other animals. But at the same time,
in the case of the individual it develops from and rests on a foundation of primitive reflexes and physiological connections. It is
true also that our most abstract concepts are built up on the basis
of activities with objects. The human child develops the powers
of generalization and abstraction from working with concrete
materials in play and in school. Similarly, in the history of the race,
the activities of men, repeated thousands of times, become fixed
in consciousness as number concepts, logical categories, principles
of science. Social relations generate their own abstractions in the
form of conventions, prejudices, axioms, codes. In course of time,
these become transformed into ideologies, religions, myths.

In the beginning is the deed, then the word, then consciousness
– except that sometimes these run together to form a dialectical

182 SOVIET PSYCHOLOGY: HISTORY, THEORY, CONTENT

unity. Mental skills are based on, and are indeed isomorphic with, practical skills. These relations and connections become lost to view in course of time. This is one reason why introspection by itself can never provide objective truth about behaviour. The number systems, logical categories, abstract concepts then appear to be eternal and independent of man's consciousness. The ideologies, religions, and myths also appear to be something given, outside of man, foreign importations. At this point his mental creations take control of his actions – the dead seizes the living. Nevertheless, the *idea* remains nothing more and nothing less than the material world, acted on by man, reflected by consciousness, and translated into forms of thought.

The sixth basic assumption accepted by Soviet psychology as a methodological principle is that of dialectical contradiction. In his philosophical notebooks, Lenin summarizes this principle as follows:

> The division of the One and the knowledge of its contradictory parts is the essence of dialectics. It is one of the essential aspects of being, its fundamental characteristic . . . The identity of opposites is the recognition, or discovery, of the contradictory, mutually exclusive and opposed tendencies in all the phenomena and processes of nature, mind and society.[7]

Dialectics is a method of thinking about scientific problems. It involves working out the basic contradictions underlying psychological processes and demonstrating how the various 'sides' of the process interpenetrate each other to form a new, temporary, conditional unity. Three psychological problems in particular have been the special problem of Soviet psychology – it is claimed that these have been solved in this period. The first is the relationship between matter and consciousness. The second is the transition from perception to thought. The third is the relationship between the individual and the social consciousness.

References

1. J. V. Stalin *Leninism* 1953: 657–662.
2. J. V. Stalin *Leninism* 1953: 672.
3. G. V. Plekhanov *The Role of the Individual in History.*
4. M. I. Kalinin *On Communist Education* 1950.
5. M. I. Kalinin *On Communist Education* 1950: 182.
6. Reference to the question of the origin of individual differ-

ences in temperament and character as seen from a Russian viewpoint is covered in sections dealing with Pavlov and a later section dealing with Teplov (see pages 223–5; 250–3).
7. V. I. Lenin Philosophical Notebooks, in *Collected Works* (Russian ed.) 1938, **38**: 251.

Reading List

Books in English

Bauer, R. A. (1952) *The New Man in Soviet Psychology* Cambridge Mass.: Harvard Univ. Press (2nd ed. 1959).

Natadze, R. S. (1972) Fifty years of psychology in Georgia, in Brožek, J. and Slobin, D. *Psychology in the USSR: A Historical Perspective* New York: IASP.

Rothstein, A. (1948) *Man and Plan in Soviet Economy* London: Muller.

Shore, M. J. (1947) *Soviet Education: Its Psychology and Philosophy* New York: Philosophical Library.

Unadze, D. N. (1966) *The Psychology of Set* (English translation) New York: Consultants Bureau.

Woodworth, R. S. and Mary Sheehan (1964) Chapter 4: Soviet Psychology as a 'School', in *Contemporary Schools of Psychology* (3rd ed.) New York: Ronald Press.

Books in Other Languages

Bekhterev, V. M. (1913) *La Psychologie objective*. Paris: Alcan.

Teplov, B. M. (1947) *Sovetskaya psikhologiya za 30 let*. Moscow: Pravda Publ.

Vygotski, L. S. (1956) *Izbrannive psikhologicheskie issledovaniya* Moscow: Acad. Ped. Sci.

Chapter 7 *Soviet Psychology in the Stalin Era: II (1947–1953)*

In this period, the Communist Party actively intervened to change the direction of Soviet science. Many tendencies had appeared, or continued to exist, in the field of Soviet culture and science which were basically anti-Communist or anti-Russian. The policy of *Zhdanovshchina* (named after A. A. Zhdanov) was put into operation, to recognize these tendencies, to categorize the nature of their unacceptability, to ensure by 'criticism and self-criticism' that they were given up, and to deal with recalcitrant minorities which persisted in holding these views. This critical evaluation of cultural and scientific trends took place in the form of conferences of writers (1946), philosophers (1947), biologists (1948), psychologists and physiologists (1950), physicists ((1948), and many other specialists. The discussions were reported verbatim not only in the specialist journals but in the Party and popular press. The content of these discussions represents a new phase in Soviet thinking which is vital for the understanding of contemporary psychology and of Soviet science in general. Most of the questions discussed are of vital importance for psychology. The nature of the discussions reveals the context or environment within which psychology and psychologists make their contribution. In 1950, in a series of extraordinary interventions Stalin criticized the Georgian philologist N. Y. Marr and inaugurated a period of 'thaw' which persisted until, and after, Stalin's death in 1953.

Arguing *ex post facto,* it would be congenial to say that, as a consequence of being associated as victorious allies in the most devastating war of all time (1941–45), many ideas were shared between the West and East, Soviet and non-Soviet peoples. But this is simply not true. The *'cordon sanitaire'* which the former combatants erected to shield Western Europe from Bolshevik ideas after 1917 was replaced by an *'iron curtain'*, lowered by mutual agreement, to ensure that any ideas which did manage to pass from one side to the other could clearly be branded as 'alien' before being admitted. It is now obvious that the cultural 'exchanges' during the war period represented no meeting of minds, or any real sharing of experience on either side: they partook more of the character of a confrontation between a lion and a bear who agreed to a temporary pact of mutual non-aggression during a forest fire.

(i) Zhdanov on Literature, Music, and Philosophy

In 1946–47, therefore, when A. A. Zhdanov (1896–1948) on behalf of the Central Committee of the Communist Party attacked certain writers and editors of literary journals, one of his charges was that they had shown an 'obsequious and awestruck' attitude towards foreign literature. But this was simply a continuation of the remarks he made in 1934 at the First Congress of Writers:

> The eradication of vestiges of capitalism in people's consciousness means struggle against every vestige of bourgeois influence over the proletariat, against laxity, frivolity or idling, against petty-bourgeois licence and individualism, against graft and dishonesty towards social property.[1]

On the basis of these criteria it is clear that it was not only a political error but also a literary lapse when the journal *Zvezda* published Zoshchenko's *Adventures of a Monkey* and some of the poems of Anna Akhmatova. In his speech to the writers in 1947 he accuses Zoshchenko of 'philistinism, superficiality and lack of political belief (apoliticism)'. Akhmatova, 'half-harlot, half-nun', he identifies with 'preachers of defeatism, pessimism and faith in the hereafter'.[2] He goes on to say:

> Our literature is no private enterprise designed to please the fluctuating tastes of the literary market. We are certainly under no obligation to find a place in our literature for tastes and ways that have nothing in common with the moral qualities and attitudes of the Soviet people.[3]

Calling for 'partisanship' (*partiinost*) in literature, Zhdanov refers the Union of Soviet Writers to Lenin's views published in 1905, where he proclaims that 'literature cannot be an individual matter divorced from the general proletarian cause'.[4] Referring the writers to Stalin, Zhdanov emphasizes the need for Bolshevik criticism and self-criticism. Any organization is liable to degenerate without criticism: this is even more necessary with respect to literature which influences the young than it is in the field of industrial production or planning. 'Spiritual wealth is no less important than material wealth'.[5]

In a similar speech at a conference of Soviet musicians in 1948 Zhdanov pointed out weaknesses in the ideological direction of Soviet music. The situation on 'the musical Olympus' was described as 'alarming' – formalism was drying up the sources of musical development and stagnation was the result. There was an absence of creative discussion, of criticism and self-criticism:

> It is, of course, not only a case of the roof of the Conservatoire leaking (that is, an organisational problem), and needing repair . . . it is a case of a far larger crack appearing in the foundations (that is, the question of the whole direction of Soviet music).[6]

The leaders of the formalist trend in Soviet music, Shostakovich, Prokofiev, Myaskovsky, Khachaturyan, and others had gained a monopoly position to the degree that they themselves were dissatisfied – at least, so they said. Cosiness and stagnation representative of the formalists had ousted the progressive, realist trend based on Russian classicism, folk-music, and folk-song:

> Classical music is marked by its truthfulness and realism, its ability to blend brilliant artistic form with profound content, and to combine the highest technical achievement with simplicity and intelligibility. Formalism and crude naturalism are alien to classical music in general and to Russian classical music in particular. The high level of the idea content in classical music springs from the recognition of the fact that classical music has its sources in the musical creative powers of the people, in a deep respect and love for the people, their music and song.[7]

By implication, the formalist trend does none of these things – indeed it is 'antipopular', estranged from the people, often pathological in its manifestations, decadent.

Zhdanov goes on to raise the theme of national spirit in music (*narodnost'*) as opposed to cosmopolitanism. The latter is an obsequiousness towards anything foreign combined with a denigration of one's own national culture and achievements. 'It is impossible to be an internationalist in music or in anything else unless one loves and respects one's own people'.[8]

In a plea for beautiful and gracious music, Zhdanov attacks atonality, cacophony, naturalistic sounds, assonance: 'These represent not only a violation of the fundamentals of musical sound but also an assault upon the fundamental physiology of normal human hearing'.[9]

In another discussion in 1947 on Alexandrov's *History of West European Philosophy*, Zhdanov spoke in a similar vein. This was the first Marxist textbook on this subject and had been given a great welcome at the highest levels in the State, on publication. Zhdanov, on behalf of the Central Committee, detected a number of gross errors in Alexandrov's approach. For example, he does not emphasize the absolute revolution in philosophy effected by Marx and Engels, their creation of a completely new philosophy, but treats Marxism as being only more consistent and scientific. Unlike the philosophers of the past, Marx and Engels realized that the discovery of absolute truth was a philosophical will-o'-the-wisp, and that the pursuit of relative truths could be attained only along the path of the positive sciences, *and the summation of their results by dialectical thinking*. Thus was philosophy abolished, to be replaced by science and dialectical materialism, that is, by a method of investigation and a method of thinking.

The main defect of the work however lies in the lack of *partiinost'*, party spirit, partisanship. Alexandrov appears in his book as 'a preacher of toothless vegetarianism' in relation to his philosophical opponents: he finds it possible to say something good about almost every philosopher of the past. This leads inevitably to objectivism, to subservience to bourgeois philosophers. Lenin enjoins us, 'Materialism includes, so to speak, partisanship, i.e. the obligation when estimating any event to adopt directly and frankly the viewpoint of a definite social group'.[10]

As in the music discussion, Zhdanov refers to the absence of critical discussion in philosophical circles. The 'philosophical front' resembles a stagnant creek, or a bivouac far from the battlefield. The Central Committee was calling for militant Bolshevik partisanship on ideological questions, for an end to formalistic and apolitical attitudes, to bowing down before foreign influences. It is only through the process of criticism and self-criticism that advances are now possible:

In our Soviet society, where antagonistic classes have been
eliminated, the struggle between the old and the new, and consequently the development from the lower to the higher, proceeds not in the form of struggle between antagonistic classes
and of cataclysms, as is the case under capitalism, but in the
form of criticism and self-criticism which is the real motive-
force of our development, a powerful instrument in the hands
of the Party. This is incontestably a new form of movement, a
new type of development, a new dialectical law.[11]

(ii) The Discussion on Physics (1947)

In dealing with the Russian Machists in 1909, Lenin had used
the argument that, far from the 'new physics' giving the death
blow to Marxism, it was one of its most dazzling verifications.
Mechanical materialism was certainly no longer a viable philosophy in the light of the radioactive disintegration of matter and
the disappearance of Euclidean space. But it was certainly possible
to argue that Engels had foreseen, and forecast, these developments. The publication of the posthumous *Dialectics in Nature*
in 1927 clinched this argument for Marxists.

Then came Einstein and quantum physics. The perennial discussion was reopened in Western Europe with, allegedly, matter
again disappearing and, this time, taking the law of causality with
it. Heisenberg's indeterminacy principle declared that it is impossible, in principle, to measure the velocity and the position of
an electron simultaneously. This arises from the fact that physicists have been forced to accept two mutually exclusive 'models'
of the ultimate particles of matter. Electrons are pictured, for
some purposes, as corpuscular particles, for other purposes as a
wave-motion. Only by combining these two (mutually exclusive)
pictures can we give a complete account of submicroscopic particles. This is Bohr's principle of complementarity: others refer to
it as 'the crisis in physics'.

Einstein had demonstrated that matter and energy are inter-
changeable, according to a rule which includes both laws of conservation (matter and energy). He had also shown that at velocities
approaching the speed of light the ordinary notions of space and
time break down – bodies moving at this speed would have infinite
mass and zero extension!

As a direct consequence of Zhdanov's intervention in the philosophy discussion, a new philosophical journal *Problems of Philo-*

sophy was started in 1947. The first number was filled with the verbatim account of the discussion – the second contained an article by Markov *On the Nature of Physical Knowledge*. He raises the question whether the new physics does not lead to problems in relation to causality, to the nature of physical reality, to the theory of knowledge, especially that of the relationship of the object to the perceiving subject. His whole article seeks to explore the consequences of the fact that we cannot observe submiscroscopic particles directly but must use macro-appliances. The 'difficulties' in quantum physics (Bohr, Heisenberg) arise, according to Markov, because we seek to interpret the micro-world with macro-concepts, such as energy, time, momentum, space etc. We seek to enter the micro-world 'in coat and galoshes', and find that we must take off either our coat or our galoshes, but not both together. In this way he makes the point that quantum physics is anthropomorphic in character. In other words, 'idealist philosophy', masquerading as objective science fails to see that there is, in fact, no 'observer' in the microscopic world, shooting a beam of light at an electron to 'see' its position and momentum. The idealizing physicist forgets that the notions of 'particle', 'waves', 'momentum', and 'position' are transferred by analogy from the universe of macroscopic phenomena to the sub-atomic world. It is precisely the breakdown of the analogy which creates the 'crisis' in physics.

The crux of his explanation of physical knowledge is that the macroscopic instrument *observes* the micro-sphere but translates its observations and *converses* with the physicist in macro-language, this being the only kind of talk he understands. In plain language, the instrument transmutes the micro-phenomena into an analogical model: this is not a working model as are those of classical physics, it is merely illustrative.

This ingenious explanation is, of course, Neo-Kantianism of the purest order. Although Markov was at pains to say that from the point of view of the theory of knowledge quantum theory brought forward nothing new, half a dozen contributors took pains to point out that his views led to agnosticism, if not to idealism. Storchak in a polite way, Maximov in the role of militant materialist, took issue with him. Storchak adapts Lenin to the new situation by saying that the laws of quantum mechanics are, without question, the objective laws of the behaviour of micro-particles. But neither the quantum theory, nor any other theory whatever, can add anything new to the philosophical conception of objective reality, namely that it exists independently of man. The author (Markov) confuses two questions: that of the objective *existence* of matter and the actual *nature* of matter. The former question has been answered for all time. Our conceptions of matter change certainly as our knowledge increases, but any changes in our knowledge cannot possibly alter the reality of matter.

Maximov sought to show Markov's relation to idealism, agnosticism, and the early Russian Machists. His critique of Markov is more traditionally Leninist in structure in that he seeks to demonstate by quotations the similarity of Markov's basic assumptions and conclusions to those of Bogdanov, Bohr, and Heisenberg. It is taken for granted that having done this there is no need for further discussion, as the idealistic nature of their views is already accepted by Soviet physicists and philosophers.

The editorial board of *Voprosy Filosofii* (*Problems of Philosophy*) intervened at this point to say that the publication of Markov's orginal article was a mistake which should not have happened. The problems raised by Markov had, in fact, been explained and decided by Marxist–Leninist philosophy long ago. Markov's error lay in putting forward a discredited view of physical reality as being a system of 'hieroglyphs' (a theory propounded by Plekhanov). This was a retreat from Marxism due to an uncritical acceptance of the physical theories of contemporary bourgeois scientists.

(iii) The Biology Discussion (1948)

The discussion in the Academy of Agricultural Sciences during the first week of August 1948 illustrates the principle of *partisanship:* we then discovered it to be a quality exhibited not only by Soviet scientists but by scientists of other nationalities as well. The discussion was about the practical value for agriculture of the theories of genetics, as these had been developed in the West, based on the work of Mendel, Morgan, and Weismann. Fifty-six distinguished scientists contributed: Forty-eight were hostile to genetics. These included Trofim Denisovich Lysenko (b. 1898), the President of the Academy, who delivered the two main speeches. The problems discussed are of a most complex nature: the history of these problems, as they developed in Russia before and after the Revolution, is even more complex. Only the main issues central to an understanding of Soviet psychology can be lightly touched upon at this point.

The whole discussion centred around the question of two schools of thought about animal and plant breeding and the theory of reproduction. Biology is divided by Lysenko into two schools – one materialist and progressive (Darwin, Michurin, Timiryazev, Williams, Dokuchayev), the other reactionary and idealist (Mendel, Weismann, Morgan, Western geneticists, and their Soviet disciples). Lysenko's immediate forerunner, Ivan Vladimirovich Michurin (1855–1935), was a horticulturist who spent a lifetime producing new species of fruit-trees and vegetables, after 1917 with increasing support from the Soviet government. He was a Marxist and sought to link his practical work with his understanding of dialectics. After Charles Darwin he was the most honoured biologist in the USSR. In 1934 he stated the principle of partisanship as it refers to scientific work:

> Science, and its concrete branch natural science in particular, is inseparably bound up with philosophy; but since man's outlook manifests itself in philosophy, the latter is, therefore, a weapon in the class-struggle. Partisanship in philosophy is the chief orienting factor . . . By its very nature, natural science is materialistic; materialism and its roots lie in nature. Natural science spontaneously gravitates towards dialectics. To understand the problems of natural science properly, one must understand the only true philosophy – the philosophy of dialectical materialism.[12]

Thus Lysenko was not stating any new principle when he referred to the two trends in biology – the great majority of Soviet biologists had given up the idea of a 'single world science of biology' (Julian Huxley)[13] as far back as 1931. Professor Zhebrak, who had written an article in the American journal *Science* in 1945, in which he suggested that he and his fellow-geneticists in the Soviet Union were helping to build up 'a common, world-wide biology' *in opposition to* the Lysenko school, was accused of having committed a treasonable act. Yuri Zhdanov in a letter to Stalin which played a certain role in the discussion said, 'In science, as in politics, principles are not subject to compromise, but gain victory: struggle proceeds, not by damping down but by disclosing contradictions'.[14]

It would be grossly inept, however, to decide that the prevailing school at the Lysenko debate rejected classical genetics because it does not conform to certain, dogmatic presuppositions of a 'philosophical' (meaning 'irrelevant') character. It is important to note that Lysenko does not attack Mendel's work on *Pisum sativum*. What is under attack is the theory of inheritance – the union of

Mendel's autonomous particles, Weismann's 'germplasm', and Morgan's chromosome theories with their implications for practice. The forty-eight agricultural specialists who spoke against genetics all provided evidence of the attempts to apply the concepts of heredity and environment of Mendelism over a period of anything up to twenty years in plant and animal breeding with a total lack of success. In an attempt to improve the quality of sheep, for example, a very large-scale experimental programme was carried out in the vast spaces of Central Asia: it ended up as a total fiasco. The scientists participating decided that the outcome could be explained in terms of the erroneous principles of genetics, as follows: ignoring differences in the environment as a possible factor in determining the quality of the offspring; ignoring the influence of the ewe in determining the quality of the offspring since, according to genetic principles, this cannot be readily assessed, the ewe producing too small a number of offspring for the nature of her genes to be assessed; reliance on chance, the breeder playing a relatively passive role instead of acting on Michurin's maxim: 'We must not wait on favours from nature, we must wrest them from her'.[15]

In other words, the contributors to this discussion were saying that the ultimate criterion of a scientific theory is: does it work? Lenin's aphorism is quoted by a number of speakers – 'practice is superior to theoretical knowledge, because of its universality and concrete actuality'.[16]

Apart from its practical uselessness, the school of classical genetics is criticized theoretically on many grounds. Perhaps the most important, because the most general, is that it operates on the basis of an 'atomistic' approach to nature. The particulate mechanism of Mendelian inheritance assumes the organism to be a mosaic of characters which exist side by side without any effective interaction. Neither is there any interaction of an effective kind between the environment and the reproductive mechanism: the organism may change and the environment may change, but according to genetic theory, this has no effect whatever on the quality of the progeny. This is the notorious problem of the inheritance of acquired characteristics. Following Darwin as well as Lamarck, Lysenko accepts this principle that directed changes in the life of the organism (under certain conditions) are inherited.

This is a special case of the principle of the inseparable relationship between the organism and its environment, a principle sponsored not only by Michurin but by Pavlov and many other progressive Russian scientists. Michurin and Lysenko operate on the organism in its natural environment, they produce changes in the environment to which the organism can respond and, using various techniques such as vegetative hybridization, they interfere with the heredity of the organism so that it is forced to 'assimilate' the change produced in the environment:

> This causes the organism itself or parts of it to change. Now, if the altered section of the body is the starting-point for the next generation, the latter will to some extent or other differ from the earlier generations in its requirements and nature.[17]

This means that its heredity has been changed, according to Lysenko's definition of heredity (1943): 'the property of a living body to require definite conditions for its life and development and to respond in a definite way to various conditions'.[18]

The main message of the Lysenko discussion is not that Soviet biologists, under pressure, accepted an outmoded Lamarckianism but that, in attempting to make a breakthrough on the 'agricultural front', it was believed that *all* the agricultural sciences must be integrally connected around the conceptions of Williams (*travopolye,* or grass rotation system), Dokuchayev (soil-science), Goryachkin (theory of mechanization), and Michurin (vegetative hybridization). The Vice-Chairman of *Gosplan,* Dmitriyev, who spoke, put the discussion into this broad context when he said:

> Some of our scientists at work in various fields, such as soil science, irrigated farming etc. believe that the struggle now being waged against reactionary theories, concerns only biology, or even only genetics, while as for the rest of the sciences, the old state of affairs will remain unchanged. That, in my opinion, must not be permitted.[19]

In reality, the underlying theme of the conference was the implicit demand on the scientists to adopt the attitudes of the 'New Soviet Man' in their scientific work. Soviet science should be distinctive in terms of its dialectical and materialist qualities; equally, Soviet scientists should reflect this distinctive quality by abandoning a contemplative stance. They should confront nature and creatively regulate the development of new species in accordance with the needs of the transition from socialism to communism. In other words, it is not so much 'explanation' that is needed as the practical mastery of nature. The variations of animals and plants must be brought under control. The idea that there is something unknowable, and hence uncontrollable ('mutations'), disarms practice and holds back necessary advances. Similarly, the notion that there are natural limits to variation, limits imposed by the nature of the hereditary process, or of the soil or climate, is anti-Marxist. The idea of the 'germ-plasm' as a special, hereditary substance isolated from the general metabolism, and having an autonomous development in the organism – this is sheerest idealism. Heredity is a property of *every* cell, *even* of the chromosomes, says Lysenko.

Lysenko put forward about ten important points countering the basic assumptions of 'Mendelism–Morganism', or classical genetics, as it is better described. On the first of these, the absence of struggle between members of the same species, he encountered very considerable opposition: it was dropped from the final summary statement which was endorsed by over seven hundred participants. These main points are summarized below:

LYSENKO'S CLAIMS: (1948)

1   Darwin's view, based on Malthus's theory of overpopulation, that there is a struggle between members of the same species is false.

2   The evolution of living nature involves the recognition of the necessity of the hereditary transmission of individual characteristics acquired by the organism under the conditions of its life.

3   Weismann's assertion that there are two categories of living material – the hereditary substance and the nutrient substance – and that the bearers of the hereditary substance (the chromosomes) represent a separate world, a world independent of the organism and its conditions of life, is an 'idealistic' and 'metaphysical' conception, contradictory to Marxism and science.

4   The chromosome theory of heredity contradicts the fact of the inheritance of acquired characters and many other detailed facts of agro-biology and is therefore false.

5   The nature of vegetable and animal organisms can be altered in a direction required for practical purposes by regulating the conditions of life. The idea that mutations are 'indefinite' and cannot, in principle, be predicted raises a barrier to practical foresight thereby disarming practical agriculture.

6   The Michurin trend in biology has been suppressed in an unprincipled way until now by the academic Mendel-

Morganists (that is, the believers in classical genetics), who have pushed 'the Morganist metaphysics, which is, in its entirety, an importation from foreign reactionary biology, hostile to us'.

7 From the point of view of practical application, the Morganist 'metaphysics' is worthless. It has no application to practical agriculture. In the war period the Morganists contributed nothing, and their plans for the post-war development of science and agriculture are abortive, not to say ridiculous.

8 The organism and the conditions required for its life (the environment) are an inseparable unity. *Heredity* is defined as the property of a living body to require definite conditions for its life and development and to respond in a definite way to various conditions.

9 Sexual cells, and many other cells through which organisms propagate, are produced as the result of the development of the whole organism by means of metabolism and transformation. The stages in the evolution of an organism are accumulated, as it were, in the cells from which the new generation originates (the 'phasic theory of development').

10 According to the chromosome theory of heredity, hybrids can only be produced by sexual reproduction (union of zygotes). Michurin and Lysenko have, however, produced many vegetative hybrids, in fact, more than 350.

(iv) Psychology in 1948

A generalizing article of considerable significance in summing up the position reached by Soviet psychology in 1948 was published by Chernakov under the title *Against Idealism and Metaphysics in Psychology*. In form this was a review of a standard textbook, Rubinstein's *Foundations of General Psychology,* published originally in 1940 and awarded a Stalin prize a year later. Under the influence of the Zhdanov and Lysenko discussions it was singled out for particularly critical review. In view of later developments, the bases of the criticisms are specially interesting. Rubinstein is accused of the methodological error which Soviet psychologists regard as characteristic of *bourgeois* psychologists – that is, he seems to be interested in describing some abstract, universal, human personality, instead of devoting attention to the specific features of Soviet man and his activities. Although in words he admits Lenin's basic theses (i) that the psyche is a product or function of the brain, and (ii) that it is a reflection of the conditions of the external world, he makes the mistake of admitting another kind of psychic process of a subjective or internal character. This error lies, not in admitting the existence of subjective processes, but in regarding some part of them as being in some sense 'locked away' from the influences of the external world, as being autonomous in their nature. In other words, he admits of a 'private world' standing over against society, a world which is not a reflection of reality but is generated from some profound depths in the organism. In other words, Rubinstein makes the same mistake as Weismann, in this case distinguishing between two kinds of consciousness, or two parts – experience which is wholly ours and knowledge which arises from reflection of the external world. This suggests the possibility of some kind of division between Soviet man and Soviet society. He removes from psychology its special Marxist character by denying the influence of class on consciousness. Rubinstein recognizes the influence of unconscious forces – he drags into Soviet psychology a so-called science of unconscious mind 'copied entirely from Freud, Lewin, and other no less reactionary bourgeois idealist psychologists'. Chernakov does not, of course, deny the influence of interoceptors which signal the condition of our inner organs to the brain. What he does deny is the impossibility of drawing out volitional or emotional processes from the organic depths of man. The emotions and the will originate as reflections of external reality – any other formulation is vulgar, mechanistic materialism, or idealism.

Chernakov then seeks to demonstrate Rubinstein's debt to the James–Lange theory of emotions, associating this theory with James' attempt to suppress the fact that there were real objective reasons for fear, anger, sorrow, and despair in the conditions of life under capitalism. William James is taken to task for using the groundless fears of insane people as an argument in favour of his theory – Soviet psychologists cannot follow him in ignoring the difference between normal and abnormal people. Nor can they accept the idealistic theory which emphasizes the organic and not the social nature of human feelings. It is impossible to separate our feelings from the external world. We cannot love or hate someone unknown or something unknown. Nor can we be moved by something unknown. Even when we shut ourselves away our thoughts and ideas are necessarily images of the external world. Similarly, our views, convictions, strivings, tastes, and habits are mental images, reflections of the external world.

Rubinstein is indebted to Schopenhauer and to Freud for his conception of the will. He describes it as arising from impulses which are identified with organic needs. Although he balks at accepting Freud's theories of pansexuality and the dominance of unconscious over conscious impulses, Rubinstein's whole treatment of volition is simply copied, or paraphrased, from Freud. This is a complete departure from Marxism. There is no necessity in Marxism to separate will from obligation, morality, aspirations, intelligence, and consciousness. There is no split or conflict in man between primeval instincts inherited from our animal ancestors and the ethical principles we learn in social living. Idealistic psychologists, such as Chelpanov and Freud, can talk freely about impulses proceeding from the depths of the organism in such a manner that will can come forward as the antagonist of consciousness. But this kind of dualism is not acceptable in Soviet psychology. Ideals, as an expression of what one *ought* to do, as distinct from what one wishes in reality, do not exist and are impossible. (So much for Kant's 'categorical imperative'!)

In contrast to Freudianism and Rubinstein's conceptions Chernakov states the Marxist position:

> The activity of man is conscious, i.e. it is directed and controlled by his consciousness, ideals and notions as ideal impelling forces. Genuine materialism consists not in denying or minimising the role of ideas in the activity or conduct of an individual or of society, but in a correct understanding of the origin of ideas as the reflection of economic relations and the acknowledgement of their great part in the life and activity of man.[20]

The error of mechanical materialism lies in ignoring the significance of ideals in the behaviour of people: the error of idealism lies in taking these ideals as primary and refusing to go beyond them to their source in external reality. Marxism recognizes the force of ideals in individual and group behaviour and explains them as the reflection of socially conditioned needs based on reality. At the same time it understands that dialectical contradiction is the basic source of all development. Contradiction exists objectively, but not in the form of any alleged conflict between the animal and the human in man. In his classic article *Leo Tolstoy: Mirror of the Russian Revolution* Lenin gave a completely scientific explanation of the conflicts, contradictions, and ambiguities in Tolstoy's life and teachings. These had nothing to do with any internal bifurcation of his mind or feelings. Tolstoy through his writings, his sufferings, and protests expressed the contradictions in Russian life during the last third of the nineteenth century:

> An artist of genius . . . a landowner wearing the martyr's crown
> . . . direct and sincere protest against social lies and hypocrisies
> . . . a wornout hysterical sniveller . . . publicly beating his
> breast . . . I no longer eat meat, and now live on rice cutlets . . .
> relentless criticism of capitalist exploitation . . . weak-minded
> preaching of 'non-resistance to evil' . . . soberest realism . . .
> propaganda in favour of clericalism of the worst possible
> type . . .[21]

Finally, Rubinstein's prize-winning book which introduced two or three generations of Soviet psychologists to the subject is dismissed as an example of abstract, non-partisan science, of science for science's sake.

Chernakov seems to be creating an opportunity to re-emphasize the positions gained by Soviet psychology over the previous thirty years. His criticisms break no new ground. What is of value is that he presents for the first time a convincing Marxist analysis of the higher mental functions of will and character based on the theory of reflection.

The articles by Chernakov (1948) and Ananiev (1947) raise a number of important questions. On the credit side, Soviet psychologists have succeeded in carrying through the revolution in thinking necessary to overcome the Cartesian dualism. This revolution, which Western psychologists seem incapable of compassing except in words, was made easy for them in that Descartes made little impact on Russian philosophy. The dualistic tradition in Russian thought was more closely linked to the Orthodox religion from which it penetrated philosophy. Soviet psychology contains a much larger proportion of deduction than is expected in an inductive science. One of the major concerns of the Soviet psychologist at this stage appears to consist in making the assumptains a much larfer proportion of deduction than is expected in possible to do. This is done, not on the basis of experimental inquiry, but in terms of Marxist doctrine and of the realities of Soviet life. For other psychologists the historical and political nuances associated with a particular method or theory are largely irrelevant. This means that a characteristic feature of American as well as British psychology is a brash eclecticism.

However, in the Soviet Union the word 'eclectic' is regarded as a term of abuse. It is used to indicate that the person in question is not intellectually competent. In other words, an eclectic is an irresponsible person who has not deliberately examined the assumptions underlying his viewpoint. Were he to do so, he would discover the incompatibility of the sources from which he had borrowed his basic presuppositions. It is assumed by Soviet critics that there is a single, indivisible truth. Therefore, if one borrows from two different philosophical tendencies, it is obvious that one's basic philosophical presuppositions must be mutually contradictory. Further, since truth is indivisible, one's borrowings necessarily partake of the nature of the ultimate political tendency of the systems from which the borrowing is made. *All* concepts, including psychological concepts, are *class* concepts according to Soviet thinkers.

To sum up: general psychology in the Soviet Union in the period 1945–1950 returned to its earlier concern with basic philosophical concepts. It categorically rejected the assumption that an inductive science can use observations made on even the most atypical group to build up a science of man – perhaps after suitable modification in the light of some kind of operational criticism. Soviet psychologists, in discussing other theories, as a principle of methodology, use the method of reduction. This means that the assumptions involved in quasi-empirical statements are first 'teased out' and then reduced to one or other of about two dozen basic categories. These are taken, without further discussion, to be either true or false on the basis of a previous methodological critique. When it can be demonstrated by this process of analysis that a particular scientist is indebted to tendencies which are known to be, or which are considered to be, hostile to Marxism and science, these views are rejected.

In Soviet psychology, throughout this period, there is an antipathy to eclecticism. The theories of Marxism and the needs of the new society give the theoretical and pragmatic criteria of truth which are used to test the truth or falsehood of psychological investigation. Empirical laboratory studies cannot be used to discover or to construct general theories of the nature of man and of psychic processes. Because of the anti-eclectic bias, non-Soviet theories, and even the experimental data of non-Soviet psychologists, are taken to be tendentious and, ultimately, and in essence, hostile to the Soviet system. No compromise involving principle is considered possible. 'The new Socialist Society based on Soviet construction successfully transforms people in the spirit of socialism'. It is the function of psychology to assist in this transformation and to help in the creation of the New Man. Soviet psychologists accepted this as one of their functions: they were not aware of the fact that they were shortly to be placed in the Pavlovian balance. . . .

(v) Stalin on Linguistics (1950)

Nicholai Yakovlevich Marr (1864–1934) came late to Marxism. As a linguist, archaeologist, and philologist whose main area of interest was the Caucasus, he achieved great fame and success in the Soviet Union where from the 1930s his theories dominated Soviet linguistics. He believed in a number of rather strange notions – that the original human language consisted entirely of gestures and hand-signals; that all spoken languages developed, by stages, from four elements *sal*, *ber*, *yon*, and *rosh*; that languages do not evolve so much as come into existence as *explosions* associated with changes in the economic basis of society, each stage being sharply distinguished from the preceding; that language and thought are simple ideologies with a class basis and class differences, in contrast to the higher ideologies, religion, art, ethics, law, politics, science, and philosophy; that language, including grammar, is part of the superstructure, defined by Marx as arising as a fantastic reflection of the basis; that under Communism all languages will disappear to be replaced by a single new form of communication – thought.

In May 1950, a free discussion was opened in *Pravda* on Soviet linguistics. On 25 June 1950, three days before the Pavlov discussion, a letter from Stalin was published, to be followed by four further letters, each in the form of answers to questions about Marr and Soviet linguistics. His attitude, to say the least, was rather negative towards his fellow countryman Marr (half-Scot, half-Georgian), as well as to Soviet linguistics:

> At one time there were 'Marxists' in our country who asserted that the railways left to us after the October Revolution were bourgeois railways, that it would be unseemly for us Marxists to utilize them, that they should be torn up and new 'proletarian' railways built. For this they were nicknamed 'troglodytes'. . . .[22]

Stalin's intervention in the debate had something of the impact of an atomic bomb, not only in linguistics but in every manifestation of Soviet intellectual life. His five letters were received almost as though Karl Marx himself had risen from his last resting-place in Highgate Cemetery with a totally new conception of how the Soviet State should be managed. Even before the last of the letters appeared, the Academy of Sciences Philosophical Institute had organized two conferences to discuss those already published; in the course of a year members of this Institute alone published fifty learned articles and delivered 350 lectures, a large collectively written book had been published, and on the anniversary of the first letter a conference was held attended by over 1,200 scholars.

This is all the more surprising since, at first sight, the letters seem to contain the merest commonplaces about the science of language: what is said about Marxism does not take us much further than Marx's (1859) statement of the materialist conception of history. However, in their Soviet context they appeared to leading intellectuals to be 'a new world-historical contribution to the treasury of Marxism'.[23] In effect, apart from the purely linguistic questions discussed, Stalin's letters implicitly provide a key to the whole intellectual history of the period 1945–1950, and also indicate the beginnings of a 'thaw'. This is signified by the fact that, for example, he quotes mild critical remarks about his first letter and indicates that he is prepared to deal with more and fiercer criticism.

The purely linguistic questions can be soon disposed of since they almost certainly merely provide the occasion for a more important intervention in the social and intellectual arena. Marr is declared to be totally in error in assigning language to the superstructure, neither is it part of the basis. It does not change as the economic basis changes. It is created by the whole of society, and not by a class, as a means of intercourse between people. Russian served capitalism and bourgeois culture before the 1917 Revolution just as well as it now serves the socialist system. Marx and Engels have been misunderstood by Marr in their statements about the bourgeoisie and the proletariat having their own language. There is no process of 'explosion' (*vzryv*) which brings new languages into being: Lafargue is wrong in so describing the situation in France between 1789–1794. It is impossible to imagine a separation between thought and language such as Marr predicts under Communism – 'save us from N. Y. Marr's Marxism!' Marr, according to Stalin, never was a Marxist, but looked more like a Left-Communist-Revolutionary, muddled, boastful, and arrogant. As for the four elements, *rosh, ber, sal,* and *yon,* these simply provide Soviet linguistics experts the excuse to 'loll on the stove, sucking coffee beans and telling fortunes in tea-cups'. As for deaf-mutes:

> The thought of the deaf and dumb arises and can exist only on the basis of the images, sensations, conceptions they form in everyday life with respect to the objects of the outer world and their relations among themselves, thanks to the sense of sight, of touch, taste and smell. Apart from these images, sensations, conceptions, thought is empty, deprived of any content whatever, that is, it does not exist.[24]

Stalin's 'revisions' of Marxism consist more of a change of emphasis than of anything really novel. In letters to Bloch, Mehring, and (especially) to Starkenburg in the 1890s, Engels had modified Marx's original statement of the materialist conception of history by emphasizing that the ideological superstructure of law, theology, science, etc. was not a passive reflection of the economic base but that these 'disciplines' have a certain measure of independence in their development. Stalin takes this very much further:

> The superstructure is a product of the basis, but this does not mean that it merely reflects the basis, that it is passive, neutral, indifferent to the fate of its basis, to the fate of classes, to the character of the system. On the contrary, having come into being it becomes an exceedingly active force, actually assisting its basis to take shape and consolidate itself, and doing everything it can to help the new system finish off and eliminate the old basis and the old classes. It cannot be otherwise . . . The superstructure has only to renounce this role of auxiliary, it has only to pass from a position of active defence of its basis to one of indifference to it, to adopt an equal attitude to all classes and it loses its virtue and ceases to be a superstructure.[25]

This remarkable passage reasserts the Marxist interpretation of history, the active role of human beings in making history, the fact that there is an over-all direction which the class-conscious Marxist can detect, that justifying all the day-to-day sufferings and sacrifices of the masses in a transitional period there is a vast, comprehensive, progressive movement of history. For anyone who had lived through the Stalin era it gave a rational explanation and justification of much that had happened and made sense of the current campaigns against cosmopolitanism, atonality in music,

Western genetics, quantum physics, and the rest. It explained the demand for Soviet patriotism, Bolshevik partisanship, *Zhdanovshchina*. This is the significance of Stalin's letters *Concerning Marxism in Linguistics*.

At the same time, Stalin makes it clear that 'Talmudists' and 'dogmatists' should not be tolerated. The question remains: why was Marr so tolerated? In the field of linguistics his ideas had ruled since the 1930s, although these ideas were prime examples of mechanical materialism. According to Stalin, Marr's disciples had established an *Arakchayev* (reactionary, militarist) régime in linguistics which held back recognition of error: 'It is generally recognized that no science can develop and flourish without a battle of opinions, without freedom of criticism'.[26]

In his first letter Stalin also re-emphasizes the possibility of development, of evolution, through non-antagonistic contradictions, 'by the gradual and prolonged accumulation of the elements of the new quality'. This applies in the evolution of languages as well as to other social phenomena. In a society without hostile social classes this will be the normal way in which change takes place.

(vi) The Pavlov Discussion (1950)

A striking remark from the agrobiology discussion by the Vice-Chairman of *Gosplan* may be quoted to introduce the discussion which took place between June 28 and July 4, 1950, in a joint meeting of the Academies of Sciences and of Medical Sciences. Dmitriyev said at the earlier discussion:

> One of the most important conditions for the further advance of science is that an end be put once and for all to the 'lone-furrow farming' in science that still goes on under the name of scientific schools.[27]

In this conference, devoted to an evaluation of the teachings of Pavlov, 1,200 participants listened to over eighty speeches and considered fifty-one written submissions. The leading physiologists, psychologists, and psychiatrists in the USSR took part in the conference. There were two basic themes: (i) the actual contribution of Pavlov in relation to our understanding of behaviour, and (ii) the need to integrate the medical sciences around his teachings.

As in the case of the Lysenko discussion, two main points of view emerged – 'orthodox Pavlovianism', including Bykov, Ivanov-Smolensky, Asratyan, Ragenkov, and others; in addition there was the 'opposition group', including Orbeli, Beritov (Beritash-vili), Anokhin, Kupalov, and others. The outcome included decisions accepting the necessity to develop Pavlov's basic ideas as the natural-scientific basis of biology and medicine; to silence various opposition groups, such as the schools of Beritov and Stern, who preach various 'metaphysical, pseudoscientific conceptions' with the support of reactionary scientists abroad; to censure certain disciples of Pavlov, especially Orbeli; to promote the ideas of Pavlov in practical medicine; to reconstruct psychology on Pavlovian lines, and to revise higher educational programmes in the light of these proposals.

The factual content of the conference revolved around the following ten methodological principles:

THE PAVLOV CONFERENCE 1950

1 Concepts must not contradict the seven principles of dialectical materialism.

2 Pavlov's conception of the organism as a self-regulating system is basic: his views on physiological process reflect those of dialectical materialism.

3 All the medical sciences, including in particular psychology, psychiatry, and physiology, must be integrated around Pavlov's views.

4 In the case of man, research must concentrate on the problem of speech (the second signalling system): this problem should be dealt with by the objective methods of science and not by introspective methods uncontrolled by objective experiment.

5 Analytic techniques must be supplemented by synthetic (that is, the organism as a whole in its natural setting), and vice-versa. Analysis must always eventuate in syntheses.

6 Western 'facts' and 'theories' are in their tendency, in general, hostile to Marxism (which alone is considered science). Therefore they must be eliminated from Soviet science. The scientific elements, if any, have been assimilated in the past into dialectical materialism. In the future this will happen, but to a lesser extent, since Soviet science is already capable of discovering these elements within a correct context.

7 'Animal psychology' is methodologically unsound, since it attributes analogically man's subjective states to the animal

in a fashion which *necessarily* lacks scientific control. It must be entirely replaced by the cortical dynamics elucidated by conditional reflex techniques or similar objective methods.

8   There is nothing 'spontaneous' in the organism in the sense that things can happen independently of external or internal stimulation. Determinism is basic to science. It is the function of science to elucidate laws of exceptionless validity in *all* phenomena, including psychical phenomena.

9   Mental activity 'reflects' the external world, and is also experienced subjectively. There is a unity of subjective and objective in the higher nervous activity. The concepts arrived at on the basis of the introspective method must be interpreted in terms of data obtained from a strictly objective investigation of the higher mental activity. The main task is to establish the relation and coincidence between that which was formerly described by the subjective psychological method and that which is obtained by objective physiological research.

10   'What we need is not description of phenomena, but disclosure of their laws of development. No science comes from description alone.' (Pavlov.)

At this point, it is not necessary to present a detailed account of Pavlov's views since these have been set out earlier. It must be said, however, that the significance of Pavlov and his integral theory first became plain to many of the participants and to Western psychologists after this conference. The opposition to Pavlov's views had been independently summarized and developed by the Polish physiologist Konorski whilst working in Cambridge. His survey of the writings of Anokhin, Asratyan, Kupalov, and Beritov provide the essential context to the reports of Bykov and Ivanov-Smolensky, the main Pavlovian protagonists. Konorski's two main points are that Pavlov's attempt to develop a theory of higher nervous activity based on the cortex was totally misconceived as Sherrington had already provided this on the basis of spinal reflexes, and that Pavlov's views cannot be reconciled with our knowledge of the micro-structure of the nervous system. According to Konorski, Pavlov became more and more cut off from the broad road of physiological progress which continually verified and made use of Sherrington's general conceptions. This view is very common amongst non-Soviet physiologists – in fact, it could be described as the prevailing viewpoint.

To make matters worse, Pavlov adopted the same terminology to describe his mal-observed phenomena, but introduced new meanings for such basic terms as inhibition, excitation, irradiation, induction, facilitation etc., and in this way has confounded the process of communication. Konorski's chief line of evidence is that there is nothing special about the cortex – the structures and the pattern of neuronic connections are precisely the same throughout the nervous system. Botkin's conception of 'nervism' is a fantasy – at least, Konorski must believe it to be so. Pavlov makes no attempt whatever to explain, or to take account of, the fact that the cerebral cortex, like the entire nervous system, possesses a neuronic structure. This is the *pons asinorum* where the whole theory must eventually founder and come to grief.

Konorski concedes that Pavlov's theory was a mighty instrument in his own hands, greatly stimulating experimental work. But it crystallized more and more until it became a dogma inhibiting the development of this branch of physiology. It is full of intrinsic contradictions and is out of step with contemporary thought about the central nervous system. Konorski sums up this part of his argument against the Pavlovian system, as follows:

> We have this impression that in the course of discussion of the above experiments we have to some extent elucidated the secret of the already-mentioned flexibility of the Pavlov theory and the ease with which it can be applied to explain the most widely different of experimental results. Indeed, once we are provided with the law of irradiation and concentration of excitation and inhibition, and the law of the mutual induction of these two processes, by arbitrarily applying these laws according to the results obtained, we can explain every fact concerning the interaction between stimuli. . . . And whereas in Pavlov's hands the above-mentioned laws were none the less living and rich in content, and he continually attempted (though we think unsuccessfully) to find certain general principles governing the application of these laws, some of his pupils juggle arbitrarily with these concepts and quite mechanically stick corresponding labels on various categories of phenomena.[28]

Soviet physiologists were, of course, very familiar with these criticisms: they had been developed first by Beritov (1927), Anokhin (1933), Asratyan (1934), and Kupalov (1938) in the Soviet Union, and by many non-Soviet scientists.

The attempt to centre the whole of nervous activity around

what happens at the synapse (Sherrington's term for the place where neurons connect with each other), and on Sherrington's concepts in general, was exactly the nub of their quarrel with the Soviet and non-Soviet critics of Pavlov. Simultaneously with the promotion of Pavlov's integral conception of the organism, a war was being waged against Virchow's conception of the cell (1858) which had dominated medicine and physiology for just under a century in the form of an 'atomistic' concept of the body and its functioning. Lepechinskaya was the main protagonist in this particular dispute. The question as between Sherrington and Pavlov in the Soviet view can best be settled *not* by recourse to the microscope, but by consideration of the intact organism functioning in an environment and by clarity about the structure of scientific theory. Konorski ignores the concept of levels of functioning entirely in his discussion – this is his scientific error. Ideologically he is also in error, since by aligning himself with Sherrington against Pavlov he is promoting the dualistic and theological conceptions of *animal* behaviour, to say nothing of human behaviour, sponsored by Sherrington in his Gifford Lectures, *Man on his Nature (1940)*.

Mayorov had replied to the American critics of Pavlov in 1948. He notes Razran's (1937) admission of the 'geographical and linguistic isolation' of the American workers on conditional reflexes. This only partly accounts for their marked ignorance of the work done in this area. The fact is that the research done in the USA is dominated by every sort of psychological conception – the subjective, idealistic, and dualistic explanations of results show a total misunderstanding of Pavlov's ideas. The Americans do not appreciate the significance of the fact that Pavlov was working at a new level of the nervous system, and that new specific laws and new physiological conceptions are necessary to describe the phenomena. Their work is marred by the attempts to introduce statistics as a method of analysing the data, instead of establishing the actual dynamics and mechanisms underlying conditional reflexes. American research workers use large numbers of experimental subjects in an extremely superficial way, seeking to establish the presence or absence of conditional reflexes instead of trying to discover new regularities amongst the phenomena. The interpretations they present oscillate between the two poles of primitive, mechanistic animism and subjective, idealistic, and dualistic anthropomorphism. They use Bekhterev's motor method instead of Pavlov's salivation reflex – this accounts for a great number of 'imaginary discoveries'.

Pavlov, in fact, took account of *all* the behaviour of the experimental animal and taught this method to his students (Mayorov worked with Pavlov on typological problems). The Americans make an issue of this, pretending that Pavlov only counted drops of saliva. Similarly, they allege groundlessly that his conclusions do not refer to animals running free in a natural setting: in fact Pavlov's experiments on the intellectual functioning of anthropoids used exactly this method. Vatsuro has continued this work and Kupalov has studied the behaviour of dogs in exactly the same way, both using Pavlov's conditional reflex and his other conceptions to interpret the phenomena observed in theses cases. The basic error made by American psychologists such as Hilgard and Marquis is that they fail to understand that Pavlov was not working on 'the theory of conditioned reflexes' – after 1927–29 Pavlov reformulated his approach as 'the study of higher nervous activity (behaviour)'. Absolutely no use is made of this concept by the Americans who know only the conditional reflex – they loosely refer to 'reflexology', a term Pavlov never used – they are totally ignorant of the elaborated theory of behaviour.

The Americans multiply terms unnecessarily: this is bound up with their attempts to produce their own individual theories, doctrines, and principles, regardless of the fact that no new enlightenment is produced by this haphazard description of the same data in a variety of ways. Some do positive harm by confusing the essence of the matter, polluting science with a multitude of unsound and unnecessary terms. The work of Gantt in Baltimore and of Liddell at Ithaca NY is commended by Mayorov as producing new facts and new generalizations. But for the rest a great proportion of American work on conditional reflexes to 1948 is dismissed as misconceived, irrelevant, and botched in execution and interpretation. It is a matter of methodological training.

This is all introductory to a discussion of nine criticisms of Pavlovianism current in American works. These objections are: (i) cortical dynamics, as expounded by Pavlov, are hypothetical and inferred, and not based on direct observation of the cortex (but control and prediction are possible); (ii) irradiation of excitation and inhibition over the cortex is not a uniform process over time and space (Pavlov has not so pictured it since 1911); (iii) the concept of processes like irradiation having a spatial character, which accounts for generalization, is of limited value (but this spatial character of irradiation has been confirmed by many American workers); (iv) the idea that irradiation of excitation is the physiological analogue of generalization must be given up (Pavlov thought of irradiation or summation, now one, now the other being the basis of generalization, after 1935–36 – experiments of Abuladze); (v) contrary to Pavlov's views, conditional reflexes can be formed in the absence of the cortex (nowhere is there a categorical statement to the contrary, the claim is that the cortex is the organ of conditional reflexes in the higher mammals); (vi) it is disputed that areas of the cortex remaining after extirpation of other areas can function vicariously, reinstating the original function (the experiments quoted against Pavlov require verification); (vii) Fulton and Liddell dispute the whole theory of conditional reflexes whilst agreeing that the *method* works (this is completely unconvincing); (viii) Pavlov's teachings cannot even explain neuroses in cats let alone human neuroses (Masserman does not begin to understand Pavlov's theories and methods which are actually in use in Soviet clinics); (ix) the whole of Pavlov's work is unacceptable because of its materialistic character (the whole of the American critique is permeated with this ideological approach – time will decide the issue).

(vii) Implications of Zhdanovshchina for Psychology

To understand Soviet science in general, and psychology in particular, as these have developed since 1917, it is important to recognize them as developing from pre-revolutionary foundations which differ in significant ways from Western science. This is seen most clearly in biology and the social sciences. For example, Russian thinkers refused to accept many of the assumptions of Darwinism based as they were on a *laissez-faire* ideology ('this is the doctrine of Malthus, applied to the whole animal and vegetable kingdom' – Darwin).[29] The Russian tradition in science shows a stronger leaning towards *a priori* reasoning than towards reasoning *a posteriori:* in the scientific 'mix' there is a greater proportion of deduction than in the British and American tradition where empiricism, pragmatism, and individualism are very noticeable. This has nothing to do with Communism, except to make it more congenial to Russian scientists since it belongs very much in this same tradition.

As far as the biology discussion is concerned, a number of emphases which are relevant to an understanding of psychology,

and of other sciences, emerged. The atomistic approach to phenomena was censured for creating artificial barriers which do not
exist in nature. A holistic concept (but without the dualistic and
spiritualistic trappings which this word often implies – Smuts, the
Gestalt psychology), is proposed in the form of the conception of
a *system*. The idea of working for oneself in science 'like a private
gentleman', already condemned by Timiryazev, as well as the
'lone-furrow farming' in science must be given up. The artificial
dichotomy of 'explanation' as opposed to the practical mastery of
nature ('varieties are created not for other experts, but for collective farms') must disappear. The gaps and lack of co-ordination
between different areas of scientific work, the isolation of scientific
specialists from each other and from practical activity, the artificial boundaries between closely related areas (soil science, plant-
breeding, field cultivation, theory of heredity etc.) must be
abolished. These tasks can be achieved at the most general level
only with the help of Marxist philosophy. At the level of particular sciences generalizations such as the creative teachings of
Michurin in natural science, of Pavlov in psychology are needed.

Factionalism is to be avoided in scientific work. But the opposite
error of non-partisanship is equally pernicious. The true scientist
does not fence himself off from the people, neither is he a dilet-
tante. As he has something to give, so the people have something
to contribute to science – namely, the test of practical application.
'Practice is superior to theory', says Lenin, 'because of its universality and concrete actuality'.[30]

The idea of 'unknowability' is wrong as a scientific principle;
it also disarms practice. Science gives an exact knowledge of objective reality. The proof of this is the fact that we can creatively
direct the processes of nature, we can restrict the sphere of action
of scientific laws, and use them for social purposes. But we cannot
abolish them. The idea that nature sets limits which cannot be
overcome by man (for example, that salinization of soils cannot
be prevented, that the number of mutations is now small because
of exhaustion of the 'genofund' etc.) is unjustified. Scientists who
propagate such notions do a disservice to humanity.

There is, and can be, no such thing as a single 'world science'
whilst capitalism continues to confront socialism. Reactionary,
idealistic trends, foreign to the world outlook of the Soviet people,
are endemic in Western science. Even Darwinism is contaminated
with elements of Malthusianism (that 'hideous blasphemy against
humanity' – Marx).[31] Russian biologists, such as, Timiryazev,

Berg, Kropotkin criticized this aspect of Darwinism. It is not merely a theoretical question but has all kinds of practical implications – for example, for tree-planting. The reactionary theories of Weismann, and of genetics, as it has established itself since his day, are already recognized even by Western biologists to be faulty and erroneous. But special vigilance must continue to be shown *not* to import such alien ideas which are basically and in essence hostile to the Soviet system.

The positive ideas of the biology discussion specific to biology, but which have a relevance also for other sciences such as Soviet psychology, include such theoretical principles as: that acquired characters are inherited under certain conditions; that the evolutionary process can be directed by man; that one of the easiest ways to effect this is by vegetative hybridization which alters the heredity of plants; that reproductive and somatic cells are not separated from each other as if by some Chinese Wall, they share a common metabolism; that plants undergo a process of phasic development, each phase is determined primarily by a succession of demands the growing plant makes on its environment; that by studying each of these phases we can direct the development of plants as, for example, in the vernalization of seeds.

At a general level, certain ideas directly relevant to other areas, especially to psychological thought, were stated as follows: the dialectical unity of the organism and its environment; the active role of external conditions on the evolution and development of organisms; the functions of human activity in intervening and changing these situations; the test of practice, of application in evaluating theoretical viewpoints.

The discussion on physics concluded by reasserting two basic positions of Leninism. The first is to the effect that the most fundamental characteristic of materialism is the assumption that science gives objective truth about the material world which exists independently of man. Idealism, in one way or another, asserts the dependence of matter on mind, or consciousness, or the psyche. For the materialist the psyche is secondary, derivative; it is the manifestation of a special quality at the highest level of organization – the human brain. The second principle is that the deviation towards reactionary views on this first basic issue by one particular group of scientists in one branch of science (quantum physics) is a temporary defection from the intuitive, healthy materialism manifested by scientists in their actual scientific work. The idealism rampant amongst quantum physicists represents a period of sickness in the history of science. It is diagnosed as a kind of failure of nerve brought on by the extremely abrupt breakdown of old-established concepts in this field. The generalization made by this group from a *description* of matter which is suggested by particular theories to the question of the *existence* of matter is illicit. The supposed contradiction between the answers to these two questions was, in fact, predicted by dialectical materialism and is readily resolved in terms of the principles of this philosophy.

The psychology discussion reopened the whole range of questions which, as we have seen, had been dismissed since Blonski's and Kornilov's interventions of the 1920s. These questions, of course, constitute the whole subject matter of psychology. It is as though there had been a kind of interregnum period from the mid-30s (in psychology since 1936) while the Party, under Stalin's leadership, sought to convert the vast peasant economy of the Russian Empire into a modern, industrialized, and powerful state. Lenin had foreseen in 1917 that 'the dictatorship of the proletariat' must be prepared to stand up to, and counter, hammer blows from East and West. 1936 found psychology in some disarray as a consequence of the decree on 'pedological distortions'. The healthy growth of experimental investigation over a very wide range of topics continued – to this the Pavlov discussion of 1950 testifies. But there were difficulties associated with the relative absence of publication facilities, isolation from 'healthy' influences from the West, and low prestige in the eyes of the ruling Party. The drive for Stakhanovitism, for the 'New Soviet Man', for Makarenko's home-made psychologizing, even Krupskaya's theories about how to teach literacy to adults, owed virtually nothing to psychology as a science – or where they did the fact was just not mentioned.

This explanation probably accounts also for the continued survival of Marrism in linguistics. The development of the Stakhanovite movement, and industrialization, in the 1930s which distracted the Party from its earlier solicitude for the 'ideological front', found Marrism in a highly favourable position, as it found psychology in a relatively unfavourable position. Marr had actually carried out extremely valuable work in the matter of Caucasian languages and dialects – even Stalin admitted this, under pressure. But his disciples, cashing in on his posthumous glory, proceeded to develop Marr's crazier ideas. The work of Vygotski, who also died in 1934, actually presented a thoroughly Marxist and acceptable psychological theory of the relation of thought and speech. But his work was totally ignored during the whole period except by his immediate associates – Leontiev, Zaparozhetz, and others.

Stalin's references to the need to smash 'the *Arakcheyev* régime' in linguistics, his repeated statements about freedom of criticism, and of the need for Marxism itself to develop and improve, presaged the 'thaw' in intellectual matters which set in just before his death in 1953. The setting-up of the new journal *Voprosi Psikhologii* in 1955 was one of the public manifestations of this period when all kinds of adjustments and readjustments were made.

References

1. A. A. Zhdanov, First Congress of Writers, 1934, in *On Literature, Music and Philosophy* 1950: 11.
2. A. A. Zhdanov 1950: 24.
3. A. A. Zhdanov 1950: 26.
4. A. A. Zhdanov 1950: 38.
5. A. A. Zhdanov 1950: 46.
6. A. A. Zhdanov 1950: 55.
7. A. A. Zhdanov 1950:
8. A. A. Zhdanov 1950: 63.
9. A. A. Zhdanov 1950:
10. A. A. Zhdanov 1950:
11. A. A. Zhdanov 1950:
12. I. V. Michurin. Academy of Agricultural Sciences 1948: 486–487.
13. Julian Huxley. Soviet Genetics and World Science in *Pravda*.
14. Yuri Zhdanov's letter to Stalin. *Pravda* (this was published the day before the conclusion of the Lysenko conference in August 1948).
15. I. V. Michurin *Selected Works* 1950.
16. V. I. Lenin *Philosophical Notebooks* 1947: 185.
17. T. D. Lysenko *Heredity and its Variability* 1948: 6.
18. T. D. Lysenko *op. cit.*
19. cf. Academy of Agricultural Sciences *On the Position in Biological Science* 1948: 307.
20. cf. Chernakov 1948.
21. V. I. Lenin *Five Essays on Tolstoy*. New York: Critics Group 1938.
22. J. V. Stalin *Concerning Marxism in Linguistics* London: Lawrence and Wishart. 1950: 13.

23. G. Wetter *Der dialektische Materialismus* Vienna: Herder. 1957: 200.
24. Stalin *op. cit.*
25. ibid.
26. ibid.
27. Academy of Agricultural Sciences *On the Position in Biological Science* 1948: 307.
28. J. Konorski 1948: 48–49.
29. Charles Darwin *Origin of Species*.
30. V. I. Lenin *Sochineniya* 1947: **14**, 185.
31. Marx – Engels *Selected Correspondence*.

Reading List

Books in English
Asratyan, E. A. (1953) *I. P. Pavlov, His Life and Work*. Moscow: Foreign Languages Pub. House.
Bykov, K. M. (1947) *The Role of the Cerebral Cortex in the Activity of the Inner Organs* Moscow: Medgiz. American trans. W. H. Gantt, N.Y. 1947.
Lenin Academy of Agricultural Sciences (1948) *Conference on the situation in biological sciences* Moscow: Acad. Agric. Sciences.
Medvedev, F. A. (1969) *The Rise and Fall of T. D. Lysenko* New York and London: Columbia Univ. Press.
Schlesinger, R. A. C. (1947) *The Spirit of Post-War Russia: Soviet Ideology* London: Dennis Dobson.
Zhdanov, A. A. (1950) *On Literature, Music and Philosophy* London: Lawrence and Wishart.

Books in Other Languages
Academy of Sciences of the USSR (1950) Conference *Nauchnaya sessiya posvyashchennaya . . . Akad. I. P. Pavlova* Moscow: Akad. Nauk.
Okon, W. (1955) Die Bedeutung der Lehre Pawlows für die Didaktik *Pädagogik* **4**: 278–292.
Pavlov, I. P. (1949) *Pavlovskie Sredy* (2 vols.) Moscow: State Publishing House.

Chapter 8 *Half a Decade of Pavlovian Psychology: 1950–1955*

In 1950 there took place a famous conference called by the Soviet Academy of Sciences. At this conference it was decided that future work in psychology should be centred around the development of Pavlov's theories and methods of work. There is no doubt that Pavlovianism provides the materialist context for the psychological study of the organism, as well as establishing the fundamental laws of brain processes which provide the natural-scientific basis for the study of behaviour.

The discussions of 1950, in line with earlier Soviet discussions of the same themes, accepted a system of materialist monism, which is at once consistent, systematic, and potentially fruitful as a basis for the scientific study of human behaviour. This system differs from the earlier mechanistic schemes of (say) LaMettrie or Helmholtz in two ways. It recognizes (i) the existence of levels of function (mechanical, chemical, biological, psychological); and (ii) the need for a relatively independent science of psychology.

Pavlov investigated the general laws of nervous activity. But his own special contribution was to elaborate a science of higher nervous (cortical) activity with its own specific laws. The main content of his life's work was the intensive study of what he called the first signalling system, that is, the relationships which develop as a result of experience and learning between the organism and the material objects and situations of its immediate environment. The second signalling system, by which he means human behaviour based on speech signals (with its own special laws), was mentioned by him as an extremely important extension of his work, and a completion of the study of the higher nervous activity of man. But unfortunately death prevented him from making any special contributions in this field.

The study of the second signalling system (which, of course, is not absolutely distinct from the first system) is especially

within the province of psychological investigation. Pavlov's conception of the second signalling system, which arises on the basis
of, and obeys, in part, the same laws as the first signalling system,
marches with the Leninist conception of reflection. The latter
doctrine states that thought, emotion, volition, and all other
psychological qualities and processes arise out of objective, environmental conditions and not from animality, unconscious
urges, or self-existent 'minds' or souls. It teaches the unity of the
mental and somatic, for which the Pavlov–Botkin conception of
'nervism' (the theory that the cortex is the supreme co-ordinator
of all somatic processes) supplies the scientific foundation.

Thus the discussions of 1950 took Pavlovianism and Leninism
as the twin pillars of Soviet psychology. These two systems provide the tools of conceptual analysis. It remains to be seen what
use has been made of these tools over the succeeding decade.

Those who read the teacups and crystal balls for the Rand Cor-
poration, retrospectively, on behalf of the Pentagon, see a cosmic
significance in the fact that the Pavlovian conference coincided
'almost to the day' with the launching of the Communist invasion
of South Korea. The suggestion is obviously trembling on the lips
that the Russian psychologists, having run out of dogs as experimental subjects, wanted to obtain some American POWs. to try
out their theories about 'brainwashing' – but for some reason this
particular connection is not made explicitly.

The demand that had been made at the 1950 conference was,
in reality, for an all-out drive to recommit psychology to scientific
principles. From description to explanation, to creative control
through education, of the formation of psychic processes and the
psychic qualities of the 'new Man' as builder of the Communist
society – this was the programme outlined by Rubinstein for the
reconstruction of psychology. The theoretical basis of the new
science could be no other than a living unity of the systems of
Leninism and Pavlovianism.

(i) Initial Reactions to the Pavlov Conference, to 1953

The first reaction of many psychologists was confusion – many
had little idea of what Pavlovianism was about; others failed to
see what relevance it had for psychology; many decided to stand
aside and wait it out until the reconstruction had actually taken
place. Teplov believed the task to consist of providing a physiological foundation for each psychic phenomenon investigated
– the psychic content would be studied integrally with its

physiological mechanisms. This, of course, is psycho-physical-parallelism of not too subtle a type. In particular, it preserves the pre-Pavlovian psychic categories. It is not clear how exactly the psychologist is to avoid the error attributed to Kupalov in the 1950 discussion – what Pavlov might call the 'psychological error':

> In his conception and explanation of the factual data of animal behaviour he has investigated Professor Kupalov deviates from the strictly objective method of investigation worked out by Pavlov, and from his basic principles of the physiology of the higher nervous activity, inasmuch as he explains this or that behavioral act of the animals as a result of their internal experiences, as an expression of their subjective world, as an external manifestation of their feelings, emotions, and so on. In other words, Professor Kupalov is departing from the path of strictly-objective physiological investigation onto the old, animal-psychology path which Pavlov repudiated.[1]

The problem is not, as Teplov posed it, to relate the psychological categories to the *substrat* or groundwork of physiological mechanisms (reflex arc, mutual induction, irradiation, etc.) but to *re-categorize* the 'psychic content', and understand it as causally related to higher nervous activity but as an effect, *not as a cause*. To quote Lenin:

> The fundamental distinction between the materialist and the adherent of idealistic philosophy consists in the fact that the sensation, perception, idea, and the consciousness of man generally, is regarded as an image (*obraz* – image, shape, form) of objective reality.[2]

About the same time as Teplov was seeking to redefine the subject matter of psychology, Ananiev attempted to state the basic tasks of Soviet psychological science. Four months after the conference, where he made no contribution either oral or written, he suggests that the most basic tasks of psychology are to explain the dialectical leap from matter to consciousness (which involves an explanation of the relationship of consciousness to matter, and the emergence of mind from the development of the material world); the dialectical transition from feeling to thinking (which must take account of the sensory basis of thought, its relation to language, and its dependence on social-material conditions); the relationships between individual and social consciousness. Some attempt is made to establish links between Pavlovian physiology and Soviet psychology but no integral connection is established. It is not clear that the Conference has made any real difference to Ananiev's thinking about the specific purposes and methods of psychology.

The psychologists met in conference in 1952, in 1953, and again in 1955, seeking to discover the solution to the problem of integrating Marxism – Leninism and Pavlovianism with their day-to-day work as psychologists. The 1952 conference was attended by over 400 psychologists. It was admitted that psychology was still proceeding at an 'intolerably slow' pace in the task of decisive and fundamental reconstruction of the entire content of psychology. By purging the subject of all elements of idealism, subjectivism, and introspectionism, psychology would justify its existence as an independent subject. As Pavlov said:

> Psychology is a formulation of the phenomena of our subjective world – a completely legitimate matter and it would be idle to quarrel with terms. On this basis we act, on this basis is composed the whole of social and personal life, there can be no question about this . . . But psychology, as a study of the reflection of reality, as the subjective world, linked in a well-known manner defined by general formulae – that is, naturally, an unavoidable matter.[3]

Thus it could not be agreed that psychology must be reduced to physiology. The concept of consciousness could not be discarded. On the contrary, all the phenomena of conscious experience must be strictly correlated, on the basis of the reflex principle, with their environmental determinants. This indeed could be defined as the task of psychology. Far from liquidation, psychology was the only science capable, on the basis of Pavlov's conceptions, of opening up the subjective world of man to objective study, and thereby to regulation. It was at this point, in 1952, that an attack was made on Uznadze's concept of the 'set' and the legitimacy of experimentation in this area. This theory emphasized the role of conscious and unconscious expectancies in the determination of behavioural reactions. As we have suggested previously, there is nothing to distinguish this school, its methods, and organizing concepts from non-Soviet psychology, except perhaps a tendency to quote (infrequently) from the works of Marx and Lenin. Like the Marr school in linguistics it survived a number of campaigns to Sovietize the intellectual disciplines – it survived this attack also.

It was realized in the course of these discussion conferences that psychology must come to terms with Stalin's views on linguistics and that Pavlov's 'second signalling system' provided one or two obvious links between a reconstructed Soviet psychology and a reconstructed Soviet linguistics. At the time of Stalin's death in 1953, a number of studies had been made, and publicized at the annual psychological conferences, as attempts to meet the demands of Pavlovianism in substance as well as in declaration – research deeds supplementing ideological words.

As an example of this research we may consider Schwartz's paper on *Raising the Sensitivity of the Visual Analyser*. The visual analyser in Pavlov's scheme is the whole mechanism of visual perception, including the eye and its neurological connection with the brain, the cortical centres, and their connecting fibres. Schwartz measured the sensitivity of the dark-adapted eye, defined as the reciprocal of the measured amount of light needed to recognize the position of the letter E presented in one of four possible positions. Each of these positions corresponds to a different letter of the Russian alphabet: Э, Ш, m, Е = ye, t, sh, e. By practice alone, without being told whether his answer is correct or false, an average subject can increase the sensitivity of vision from an initial level of 100 to 140. Knowledge of results causes his sensitivity to be increased from 140 to 310. With 'punishment', consisting of slight electric shock for wrong responses, visual sensitivity increases from 310 to 470. On being given a 'norm' at each session the subject can increase his visual sensitivity from 470 to 845. Experiments with a second group of subjects who passed directly from the first stage (practice only) to the last (setting of targets with competition against one's previous record) the visual sensitivity increased from 100 to 150 at the end of the practice period to a final level of 1,200! Schwartz concluded that his experiments demonstrate 'the enormous, apparently limitless possibilities in human nature'.[4] This is, of course, one of the basic assumptions of Marxism about human beings.

Schwartz's explanation of his results, which are indeed very noteworthy, is in Pavlovian terms:

> During the whole series as well as in those individual experiments which can be regarded as stages towards the completion of the final task, the problem before the subject brought about intimate interaction of the first and second signalling system. This is attested to by the concrete conceptions of the task which

were developed by the subject. The instructions to the subjects that they should increase their visual sensitivity by a definite amount in a certain time, resulted in an adequate level of excitation. This persisted at corresponding points of the cortical end of the analyser as a result of positive impulses from both signal systems. Of course, the persistence of this excitatory condition of the cortex was due also to strong nervous impulses directed from the sub-cortex to the cortex. This is demonstrated by the heightened emotionality which was observed in the subjects during the experiments. The effect of these processes was the strengthening of the conditioned connection between weakly discriminated stimuli and the required discrimination. This resulted in a heightened sensitivity. This view requires confirmation and needs to be made more precise.[5]

Schwartz also demonstrated that the increase in visual sensitivity was maintained for a long time, and was manifested in the recognition of other similar objects.

A similar piece of research of first-rate quality is Sokolov's *Higher Nervous Activity and the Problem of Perception,* carried out at Moscow University. Using normal adults between twenty and forty years as subjects, Sokolov studies the effects of perception of a stimulus on the whole system. Besides the general organic, vascular, and skin-galvanic reflexes, Sokolov measured physiological changes taking place in the optical system, such as turning of the eyes, changes in the electrical activity of the cortex, changes in visual sensitivity, and so on. As stimuli Sokolov applied strictly regulated auditory, visual, tactile, thermal, and other types in a predetermined order.

The result of these systematic studies of the 'orienting reflex' (Pavlov) was to demonstrate that *the whole organism is involved in response* and not only the particular modality being stimulated. For example, a sound stimulus brings about changes in everything being measured – visual reactions, skin reactions, blood pressure, etc. The biological significance of this total reaction of the organism is, of course, immense. The excitation results in a great reactivity of the particular analysing system required to perceive the stimulus. Maximum efficiency of reception of the signal and response to it is brought about by mutual induction and inhibition in the cortex and other central levels. Sokolov has demonstrated conclusively in relation to the 'orienting reflex' how the human organism functions as a whole, as a system in dynamic equilibrium. His investigation, and the same is true of Schwartz's, is a model in terms of methodology in an area cultivated since the Revolution as a major field of research interest. It is also a model of presentation.

Another major interest of Soviet psychologists is mental and educational backwardness. A leader in this field of research is Professor Leontiev. Basing himself on Pavlov, Leontiev considered that intellectual weakness, where not obviously the consequence of pathological weakness or developmental failure in the brain and nervous system, is due to a system of conditioned brain linkages which is functioning badly. Learning by experience consists in a process of associating qualities and relations through a system of temporary connections. Knowledge, which can be of many kinds, is assimilated by the organism through the establishment of conditioned connections between neurones in the cortical layer of the brain. It is possible, indeed inevitable, that through lack of necessary experience, or because of some failure of the cortical processes of analysis and synthesis, essential links may not be formed. If this happens on a large scale, the individual may give the appearance of deficiency; for example, he may appear to be mentally or educationally sub-normal, he may appear to be tone-deaf or to have some similar deficiency. In principle, all defects which arise out of faulty training or the paucity of the life-experience of the individual are remediable. What needs to be done is to establish which are the missing, or damaged, or incorrectly formed linkages and reform these in the appropriate way.

Leontiev has carried out remedial work of this kind. He works on the basis of establishing or reforming damaged or missing conditioned linkages. For example, his work with subjects suffering from 'kinaesthetic blindness' (an inability to recognize objects by touch) because of war-wounds of the arm or hand, demonstrated that re-education is possible, based on the formation of new touch, kinaesthetic, and visual reflexes. We can substitute new elements for those processes of the perceptual system destroyed as a result of deformation of the musculature and the destruction of tissues caused by the wound. The result of this so-called 'homosystematic compensation' is to reinstitute the damaged function with no appreciable modification of its original perfection.

At another level Leontiev has carried out remedial teaching with children whose teachers thought them to be incapable of benefiting from music teaching. They were unable to reproduce melodic phrases in singing. It was discovered by Leontiev that these children could not even 'accord' their voices to a continuously sounding note. The method used to overcome this deficiency was to show the children visually the pitch of the note, using a cathode-ray oscillograph. The oscillograph also indicated the pitch of the note they were producing themselves. Lessons graded in difficulty were carried out by this means until the subject was able to sing simple melodies. After only eight to ten experimental sessions of this kind of instruction the subjects could be returned to their classrooms and could take part in the ordinary music lessons. Leontiev believes that these children were lacking in that particular ability which develops as a result of experience before any systematic education is given at all. This is the ability to make simple auditory-vocal connections in an organized systematic way. For some environmental reason this system and these particular connections had not been formed in these 'tone-deaf' children.

The study of higher mental processes carried on under Leontiev for many years at Moscow University presents the same picture. The basic theory underlying this work is that internal mental processes develop on a foundation of conceptualization and memory. This foundation arises as a result of operations with material objects in the child's environment. Slavina has shown that children who are backward in arithmetic are actually suffering from the incorrectly formed cortical associations which relate to the elementary arithmetical processes. This condition made it possible for them to make progress in arithmetic. If the child is led to form the links which are missing it is not only their ability but their general attitude to arithmetic which improves. This is so to a degree that they can take their normal place in the classroom. According to this approach, there is no special innate 'arithmetical ability', the absence of which accounts for educational backwardness. In fact, no psychological quality or peculiarity is directly innate. Abilities and personality qualities are always formed in the process of development, especially during the education process.

The same attitudes and programmes of remedial teaching are taken up with children who would here be consigned to a special school as mentally defective. As we have seen, intelligence tests are never used for diagnosis because mental backwardness may be due to a great variety of causes. Such tests simply obscure the true causation. Professor Luria, who during this period was responsible for work on 'defectology' (which includes blindness, deafness, spasticity as well as mental backwardness) at the Institute of Defectology of the Academy of Pedagogical Sciences, Moscow, considers that only those children who have suffered a brain injury at birth or in early childhood are properly classified as feeble-minded. It is only after the most lengthy and detailed examination by teachers, parents, school doctors, and neurologists that a child is certified as mentally defective and sent to a special school. The theoretical orientation of all this work on human abilities and qualities is given in the following quotation from Leontiev:

> The development of human psychic qualities takes place in a series of consecutive stages. In the course of these stages different links are formed. These provide an indispensable foundation for the composition of that final mechanism which underlies the specific trait or quality. Certain of these links may form in the normal case of themselves, in a hidden fashion, and outside the control of the educator. In such cases it follows that, if some link or other which normally antedates the formation of the completed mechanism, either fails to develop, or develops incorrectly, inevitably we get a picture of incapacity. But if the missing connection is discovered and formed, development will proceed normally.[6]

The implications of these views, if valid, for the sum-total of human happiness as well as for the theory and practice of education are boundless. Pavlovianism is the scientific basis of Soviet optimism about the transformative effects of education and a changing environment. It is the theoretical justification of the claims made as to the significance of the Socialist Revolution in changing 'human nature'. In this area, as in many others, there is a direct and very close link between Marx and Pavlov in their thinking.

Soviet psychologists also pushed forward the application of Pavlov's theory of temperament to human beings during this period. As is well known, Pavlov revived the ancient Hippocratic classification of temperament. In place of the Greek emphasis on the bodily humours he interpreted constitution in terms of central nervous processes. In this field the leading Soviet figure was the late Professor Teplov. According to his view the foundation of individual qualities is not heredity but rather the stable systems of conditional reflexes (Pavlov: 'dynamic stereotypes'), built up in the course of life-experience. Even in the field of human temperament Soviet psychologists believe that Pavlov's dictum is borne out:

The chief, strongest, and most permanent impression we get from the study of higher nervous activity by our methods is the extraordinary plasticity of this activity and its immense potentialities. Nothing is immobile or intractable. Everything may always be achieved, changed for the better, provided only that the proper conditions are created.[7]

Our temperament, on this view, in no way corresponds with our 'destiny'. Human types are merely genotypes manifesting the qualities characteristic of the species. The phenotype, or individual character, is an alloy made up of the characteristics of the type and of the changes produced by the external medium.

The main interest of Teplov's work lies in the fact that he has worked out ingenious ways of determining to which temperamental type (sanguine, phlegmatic, choleric, or melancholic) the individual subject belongs. These methods depend on the study of voluntary movement as well as on the mode and speed of formation of conditional reflexes. The Pavlovian typology depends on (i) the intensity, (ii) mobility, and (iii) type of equilibrium of the nervous processes in the individual subject. This branch of Soviet psychological research was still very much in its infancy in 1953. Among other results, it had been shown that temperamental qualities do not determine academic success, they merely influence the individual method of work, the amount of sleep necessary, and so on. This has been established experimentally by Leytes. It has been shown by Rozhdestvenskaya that attempts to alter the basic temperamental type of the individual are not ruled out.

The problems of higher mental processes meet in the great central question of human speech. This was brought within the ambit of objective scientific study by Pavlov, according to Soviet thinkers, in the following formulation:

Speech is first and foremost, special kinaesthetic stimuli, which reach the cortex from the organs of speech; that is, it is made up of secondary signals, signals of signals. These constitute an abstraction of reality and make possible the process of generalization which constitutes our individual, *specifically human, higher thought process* ...[8]

A number of Soviet physiologists and psychologists have studied the phenomenon of speech by conditional reflex methods. In 1927 Ivanov-Smolensky started a long series of investigations. Another well known student of the speech system is Krasnogorsky who also

worked in this field for a large number of years. It has been established by work on children that the laws which govern the first
signalling system apply also to the second system. This is extremely
important. In the Pavlovian scheme the activities of the two signalling systems which function through the medium of various
cortical centres *embrace the entire activity of man as a totality.*
The motor-speech analyser acts in such a way as to generalize the
work of the whole brain. This is done by the formation of verbal
conditional reflexes, because these are formed with all the analysers. The demonstration that Pavlov's laws of irradiation-concentration, mutual induction, and his other laws of cortical action
appertain also to verbal stimuli is of the first importance in veri-
fying Pavlov's claim that the whole human organism was won for
physiological research by the conception of reflex action. It is unfortunately true that relatively little progress could be recorded at
this stage in the establishment of the *special* laws of the second
signalling system. But this problem is incomparably more complicated than those which Pavlov had succeeded in solving. At this
time, great activity was proceeding, not only in Russian, but in
Polish and Rumanian laboratories on this problem, using Ivanov-
Smolensky's multiple-choice apparatus.

Krasnogorsky himself had studied the development of language
in the individual child. Numerous investigations of special topics
had been made, but no integrated body of theory specific to the
second signalling system had appeared. One of the most interesting studies was reported by Volkova in 1951. This was a study of
generalizing words, or 'integrators', as the Pavlovians call them.
If a conditional reflex is formed using the names of other birds,
Volkova demonstrated that words representing a higher level of
generalization also produce the conditional response. The further
the new stimulus happens to be from the original level of generalization the lower is the level of conditional response obtained from
it. For example, the initial stimulus being the word 'crow', eight
drops of saliva are produced to this word after the reflex response
has been established. (The reflex is established by saying the word
'crow' and simultaneously allowing a sweet to drop into the
mouth of the reclining child. This is repeated 10–20 times until
the word 'crow' without the sweet causes salivation). At this stage,
'crow' being equivalent to eight drops of saliva, 'bird' produces
six drops, 'flying' four drops, while 'living' produces only one
drop. The further removed the generalizing word is from the
initial stimulus word the lower is the conditional response. Similar

work had, of course, been done in America by Razran, a long time previously.

(ii) Theoretical Psychology at the End of this Period, 1955

One of the most important outcomes of the various annual conferences, and the empirical work reported at them indicating a solid basis of Pavlovianism in psychological research, was the establishment of the special journal *Problems of Psychology* (*Voprosy Psikhologii*) in 1955. The appearance of this journal makes the task of surveying the development of Soviet psychology much easier than it would otherwise be. Since about 1932, Soviet psychological research was published in a number of specialized university periodicals and monographs which were extremely difficult to obtain. Even the American abstracting journals which aim at global coverage of psychology summarized much less than fifty per cent of Soviet material. Access by Western students of Soviet materials was mainly to philosophical, or physiological, or educational studies. These were seldom oriented in the direction of empirical research which is the main basis for judging the status of psychology as a science. In the first number, pride of place is given to Professor Rubinstein's remarkable theoretical analysis of the problems of psychological study. He tries in this generalizing article to indicate the great advance along the single line of Marxist analysis which Soviet psychologists have made in their approach to theoretical questions. The article is an attempt to reconcile the two demands made on psychology in the Soviet Union: that it should be based on dialectical materialism, and that it should take Pavlov's theories and methods as the model in research and theoretical formulations. Rubinstein indicates the way to a solution of this dual task in relation to such basic questions as the problem of determinism in psychology, the relationship between physiological and psychological investigation, the connection between physiological processes and the psychological properties of the human being as well as the special problems of the psychology of thinking.

On the problem of determinism, Rubinstein says that it is the task of psychology to find a new, specifically psychological statement of this principle. In the conception of the conditional reflex, physiology has found such a statement. But psychology cannot simply accept the physiological statement of determinism as a solution: it would blur the distinction between the two sciences and stand in the way of their 'legitimate marriage' (Pavlov). Rubinstein suggests the formula, '*External causes operate through internal conditions*' as a suitable basis for the science of higher nervous activity which would be the product of this union of psychology and physiology.

These two sciences study the same object and processes but by different methods, according to this leading Soviet psychologist. Psychical activity, the object of psychological investigation, goes on in the human brain. Therefore it is subject to all the laws of cortical neurodynamics discovered by Pavlov (the laws of irradiation-concentration; mutual induction, etc.) Hence it is obvious that psychological investigation cannot be opposed to the physiological study of neurodynamics, or isolated from it. But, similarly, psychology cannot be assimilated to neurodynamics. The psychical phenomena which are its object of study appear in a new, specific form. They are determined by relationships from which physiology has been excluded. Rubinstein proceeds on this basis to criticize certain formulations which had earlier appeared in Soviet journals. The theory that the physiological and the psychological represent co-ordinated sides of one process is rejected. This is because it conceals the fact that we are dealing with a hierarchy of lower and higher, that although neurodynamic processes are at the basis of psychological phenomena they do not determine their form or content. Similarly rejected is the theory that physiological and psychological descriptions are separate 'components' of a complete description of behaviour. This is regarded by Rubinstein as a mechanistic and dualistic view. It presents a false antithesis between physiological and psychological laws. The third view which has been canvassed in Soviet journals is that the neurodynamic process is the material basis on which there is erected a psychological superstructure. This notion breaks the essential link between physiological and psychological phenomena and must be rejected also.

The actual relation to physiology of psychology is described by Rubinstein in terms of the analogy of physiology and biochemistry. The discovery of the biochemical basis of physiological processes did not result in the established physiological laws being abolished. Nor did it reduce them to the laws of chemistry. On the contrary: biochemical laws were found to be a new and original manifestation of physiological laws. They enabled the general laws of physiology to be extended to a more specialized level. In precisely the same way the laws of neurodynamics find a new, unique manifestation in psychological phenomena. This is expressed in psychological laws. Rubinstein says of the relationship between physiology and psychology:

> This is the general law which regulates the interaction between different disciplines in the system of the sciences: The higher levels pose problems to the lower, and the lower furnish the means for their solution: the former delineate the phenomena which require explanation, the latter serve to explain them.[9]

Professor Rubinstein then goes on to discuss the difference between real psychological laws and the behaviourist, stimulus-response approach, taking Pavlov as exemplar of the former. Behaviourism merely establishes connections between stimulus and response. It tells us nothing about the internal regularities which underlie phenomenal appearance. In studying the psychology of thinking, for example, we need to show the particular way in which analysis-synthesis operates in specific cases. We must describe how generalization and abstraction work in different situations, how it is affected by different materials, and the way it operates at different psychic levels. In this way we can formulate a complete description of thinking. On the other hand the behaviourist approach confines itself to noting that transfer of training from one situation to another takes place under such and such conditions. It remains entirely on the superficial level and fails to reach any understanding of psychological laws.

In another generalizing article the Ukrainian psychologist, Kostyuk, compares the dualism of Wundt, Titchener, Sherrington, Adrian, and Eccles to the monistic conceptions of Soviet psychology. Dualism springs from the denial that psychical activity is related to the functioning of the brain. It is higher nervous activity. Denial of this formulation necessarily entails a phenomenological approach to behaviour, which is anti-Marxist, of course. Tolman, the American psychologist, is taken to task for saying that any problem of human psychology can be dealt with on the level of the rat running a maze. This ignores the basic fact about human beings that human consciousness is a historically determined phenomenon, that personality is formed as a result of definite social conditions. We must study what is general in the psychical activity of man. But we must consider also those specific features of personality which are formed in concrete historical conditions of human activity, according to Kostyuk.

Kostyuk's paper, concerned with the nature of psychological laws, covers the same ground as Rubinstein's. But it is much less original. It confines itself to the exposition of generally accepted Soviet theses about the relations between subject and object and the nature of the human psyche.

Both papers show a definite growth by differentation in Soviet psychology since the 1950 discussions. Although no new principles are stated, the implications of Leninism and of Pavlovianism have been clarified in relation to general psychological theory. The contrast with the state of general psychological theory in foreign science is explicitly made by Rubinstein. He notes the fact that there have been no new broadly based, theoretical generalizations in psychology outside the USSR since the 1930s. Psychology is still based on the theoretical ideas of the last generation. These are now outmoded. Psychological theory in foreign countries, according to the Soviet school, is corroded at its foundation by neo-positivism and phenomenalism and by other anti-scientific tendencies. Only the philosophy of Marx and Lenin is regarded as a satisfactory basis for scientific investigation.

As an illustration of the conceptions of this contemporary period which have been discredited and discarded there are the views of the Georgian physiologist Beritashvili (Beritov in its Russian form). For many years he had worked in direct opposition to Pavlovian principles. In 1927, for example, he suggested that there was a discrepancy between Pavlov's theory of cortical dynamics and the general physiology of the central nervous system. As we have seen, this same theme was elaborated more recently by Konorski, the Polish physiologist in great, but rather unconvincing, detail. In 1935, in his *Individually Acquired Activity of the Central Nervous System,* Beritashvili attempted to establish his own theory of higher nervous activity based on the general physiology of the nervous system, in opposition to Pavlov. The most recent form of his views (1951) is the notion that there is a special 'psycho-nervous activity'. This he considers to be a stage higher than Pavlov's 'higher nervous activity'. He also thinks that the reflex principle cannot be extended to this level. Animals possessing a cerebral cortex (for example, all mammals) are believed by him to be directed in their behaviour by 'ideas' which are analogous to those of man. By positing a *'spontaneous activity of nervous elements'* he abandoned the conception of determinism which Pavlov had developed. These ideas are totally unacceptable to the ruling school in Soviet psychology.

References

1. Academy of Agricultural Sciences *O polozhenie* 1948: 68.
2. V. I. Lenin *Philosophical Notebooks* 1947: 180.
3. B. G. Ananiev 1948: 8.
4. Schwartz, Luria and Leontiev. Papers presented at Montreal. *Voprosy Psikhologii* 1955, 1.
5. ibid.
6. A. N. Leontiev 1960: 1–12.
7. I. P. Pavlov *A Physiologist replies to Psychologists* 1961.
8. ibid.
9. cf. S. L. Rubinstein *Voprosy Psikhologii* 1955, 1.

Reading List

Books in English
Brazier, Mary (ed.) (1959, 1960, 1961) *The Central Nervous System and Behaviour* (3 vols.) New York: Josiah Macey Foundation.
Ivanov-Smolensky, A. (1954) *Essays on the Patho-physiology of the Higher Nervous Activity* Moscow: Foreign Languages Pub. House.
Kalinin, M. I. (1950) *On Communist Education* Moscow: Foreign Languages Pub. House.
Leytes, N. S. (1962) *Concerning Mental Ability* Washington: Office Tech. Serv.
Platonov, K. I. (1959) *The Word as a Physiological and Therapeutic Factor* Moscow: Foreign Languages Pub. House.
Simon, B. (1957) *Psychology in the Soviet Union* London: Routledge and Kegan Paul.

Books in Other Languages
Leontiev, A. N. *et al.* (1953) *Dokladi na soveshchanii po voprosam psikhologii 3–8 iyulya 1953* Moscow: Akad. Ped. Sci.
Leontiev, A. N. *et al.* (1954) *Communications au XIV Congrès International de Psychologie* Moscow: Akad. Ped. Sci.
Silow, G. N. (1952) *Die Lehre Pawlows über Organismus and Umwelt* Berlin: Verlag Kultur und Fortschritt.

Chapter 9 *Soviet Psychology: A Survey*

In the brief space of one chapter it is impossible to do justice to the wealth and variety of current Soviet research. The topics chosen for presentation here constitute a mere fraction of the ground covered by empirical research; they represent a sample, about ten per cent of the total, as does the actual work reported under each heading. The intention is, by the particular selection made, to represent certain key principles characteristic of the Soviet way of conceptualizing main issues, such as the psychology of the emotions, of set, or of social psychology.

There is an impression abroad that Soviet research in these, and other areas, is 'coming round' as the result of the 'thaw' to which reference has been made earlier. The appearance of Soviet psychologists at International Conferences (the first being at Montreal in 1954) and the holding of the great International Conference at Moscow in 1966, together with the massive amounts of translated materials that have become available throughout the sixties, contribute to this feeling.

It must be said however that co-operation is at the administrative level and not at the theoretical. Soviet psychology has not abandoned any of its traditional principles, – partisanship, materialist monism, theory of consciousness as the reflection of reality, development as a dialectical process involving conflict and synthesis. Here there is no accommodation. Certain aspects of Lysenko's views have been discredited, because practice has shown him to be wrong about inter-specific struggle. Einstein is acceptable because he was, on balance, found to be on the side of materialism. The emphasis on Pavlovianism as a basis of psychology has been transposed from a major to a minor key but the basic commitment remains and continues to be emphasized. Empirical studies of groups and of crime are no longer taboo as belonging to applied political science. This is because the need for 'hard' data on these questions demands such action.

But the general picture of Soviet psychology presented in previous chapters remains accurate, as of today, and it seems unlikely to change in any major fundamental in the 70s – except that certain loosenesses of expression in relation to particular kinds of bourgeois psychology will almost certainly be brought under Party control, as in 1929, 1947 and 1950. We can be certain that Soviet psychology will continue to make massive strides not only in the central areas of learning, thought, language, perception, but in newer branches such as cybernetics, computer analysis, space psychology, social psychology. These advances will be made on the foundation of the Marxist materialist conception of the psyche.

(i) The Soviet Treatment of Emotions

It is probably in the area of emotions, feelings and affect in general that the theoretical gap between Soviet and non-Soviet psychology is widest. The gap, in fact, here widens to become an abyss, on one side of which we find the psychophysical monists under the banner of Pavlov; on the other side are variegated groups under many flags – Freudian, phenomenological, behaviouristic, hormic. The essential difference consists in the fact that Soviet psychologists displace the main locus or centre of the emotions from the internal organs, associated with the processes of the vegetative life, to the cerebral cortex. This means that the cortex acts as the central co-ordinator, interpreting perceptual signals, monitoring the complex 'reports' from the peripheral and inner organs and sending back signals to the appropriate effector organs. There is no *autonomous* centre or 'seat' of the emotions – it is the whole organism which acts, directed by the central, cortical process. This conception of the emotions is unique to Soviet psychology.

Traditionally, Western psychology has placed the seat of the emotions in the heart or bowels (following the lead of the Semites), taking them to be the source, cause, or impulsion to action (following the Greeks). Plato's metaphor of the charioteer seeking to control the two fiery steeds, the reason and the passions, comes to mind. This is the kind of matrix in which our thinking about the emotions is embedded – three points: (a) they are causative of behaviour, (b) they work generally in opposition to the rational principle, so that behaviour is a kind of resultant of rational and irrational forces, and (c) they are 'located' internally, in general below the neck but with nervous connections to the thalamus and the 'lower' parts of the brain. The latter is appropriate since emotions belong to our 'lower', animal-like nature. As a consequence of the fact that they are regarded as causative factors in behaviour, the emotions have been subjected to a very close scrutiny in Western psychology, beginning with Macdougall. Grandiose experiments and numerous longitudinal studies of children's development have been carried out in this area.

On the other hand, a recent Soviet text defines the emotions as follows:

> Emotions or feelings are a special form of man's relations to objects and phenomena of reality conditioned by their correspondence or non-correspondence to his needs. In addition to perception and thinking, emotions are one of the forms of the world's reflection in the consciousness. But they have their own specificity. Reflecting the real relations of the world, man experiences them as his own subjective relations to it.[1]

Thus, consciousness is a reflection of external reality: the instrument which 'reflects' is the human brain. Some part of this complex reflection is experienced by us as emotion. This experience testifies to the fact that a nervous stimulation has spread not only to the subcortex (which operates to increase or reduce the *intensity* of the emotion) but also to the cortex. Emotions are 'mental acts' and, like all mental acts without exception, are reflexes (Sechenov), or reflections of external reality (Lenin).

According to Sechenov, emotions are psychical (cerebral) reflexes which have an intensified end. They originate in elementary sensual pleasures as smells, sounds, warmth etc. but due to associations of one kind or another they become more complex and more generalized in terms of the stimuli which trigger them off. The strength or depth of an emotion derives from frequent repetition of the reflex: its vividness depends on the mobility of the impression which in turn is associated with the sum of pleasures possible at the given time. Sechenov concludes:

> Absolutely all the properties of the external manifestations of brain activity described as animation, passion, mockery, sorrow, joy, etc., are merely results of a greater or lesser contraction of definite groups of muscles, which, as everyone knows, is a purely mechanical act.[2]

This constitutes Sechenov's monistic materialism, which Turgeniev (who attended some of his lectures), as well as Dostoievsky, Tolstoy, and most other Russian writers of the period, deplored.

Pavlov deals more briefly with the emotions, identifying them with 'complex unconditional reflexes'. He appears to equate emotions and instincts, and to separate both from the 'feelings', on the basis that the first are primitive and innate while the latter belong to a different class altogether. Emotions are caused by such conditions as hunger, sexual attraction, anger etc., whereas feelings refer to 'something agreeable or disagreeable, a feeling of ease, difficulty, happiness, torment, triumph, despair etc.' Emotions and feelings are differentiated physiologically in so far as emotions are due to nervous stimulation which centres in the subcortex (spreading to the cortex in a kind of 'overspill') whereas feelings centre in the cortex (with an 'overspill' to subcortical centres). Processes in the cortex not only generate feelings, they also constitute the basic regulatory principle in the development and expression of these feelings. This is the Botkin–Pavlov principle of 'nervism'.

In the struggle for an independent science of psychology in the Soviet Union, certain methodological principles were, and had to be, established in relation to the emotions and feelings. Obviously, whilst not accepting the dualistic principle that emotions *cause* behaviour, it had to be acknowledged that they were important phenomena of the subjective life which had to be investigated. Their strictly determined character was, of course, a basic assumption without which emotions and feelings could not be considered as material for scientific study. Their nature, as a peculiar reflection of reality, linking man with his environment, had to be worked out and the implications examined. The connection between the emotions and the feelings, as well as the distinction between them, required clarification since the notion of a basic dichotomy between the feelings and the emotions was rejected as dualistic. In investigating the origins, evolution, and development of emotions and feelings, it was essential to approach the problem from the point of view of both individual development and development in the race. This involves study of the evolution and expression of the emotions in our subhuman ancestors. In this endeavour, the experimental and observational work is based on the Sechenov–Pavlov model.

Vygotski, in an article written in 1932 but not published until 1958, surveys the theoretical work done in this area beginning with Darwin. Ribot and William James are criticized. James is taken to task for claiming that whilst emotions are the consequence of visceral changes (a view refuted by Walter Cannon), the higher emotions or feelings are qualitatively different in their origin and manifestation (this assertion stemming from James's dualistic approach). Vygotski proposed to clarify many of the problems by turning to psychopathology as a source of basic data on the emotions. On the other hand, Rubinstein (1946) proposes that the foundations of feelings and emotions should be sought for in the historical forms of man's life. Since human emotions are intimately connected with activity, work constitutes an important area to be investigated as the source of emotions. He suggests three levels in emotional expression: (i) emotions associated with organic needs, (ii) 'object' feelings, such as intellectual, aesthetic, and moral feelings, (iii) generalized feelings connected with a 'world outlook', for example, humour, tragic feeling, etc. Kostyuk (1955) emphasizes that feelings are a special form of a person's attitude to reality. They arise in the course of activity located in an environment: they reflect the course of the individual's vital relationship with this environment. Feelings are universally connected with cognitive processes; they are closely related to motives and interests. Yakobson (1955) similarly, emphasizes that feelings should be studied in the context that they are the product of a complex, social–historical, human development. In a later study (1958) he analyses the changes which may arise in the emotional sphere in the course of performing a purposeful action. Blagonadezhina (1956) emphasizes that, whereas emotions are always linked with situations, feelings may be stabilized as a kind of a generalized emotion, not situation-bound. Kovalev takes a similar line, and argues that stable attitudes of the personality, definitely oriented towards particular objects or subjects, such as love, hate etc., should be classified as feelings. A feeling is a stable formation or attribute of the personality, whereas an emotion is the process by which the feeling is manifested. Feelings are determined not so much by human attitudes towards the external world, as by the objective world itself, which forms or shapes the feelings and the personality.

In addition to these generalizing articles, Soviet psychologists have closely investigated the various indices of emotion, manifested as organic signs as well as in the behaviour of the individual. These studies differ from similar studies in Western psychology in seeking to verify the views of Pavlov on the physiological foundations of emotions and feelings. Investigation of pulse and respiration rates, changes in the electrical resistance of the skin and in blood composition, peculiarities in the motor and verbal reactions

236 SOVIET PSYCHOLOGY: HISTORY, THEORY, CONTENT

of the subjects were used as indices pointing to the nature and quality of the experienced states. The work goes back to 1918 when Kaelas attempted to validate Wundt's tridimensional theory of feeling. This states that feelings vary not only along a dimension of *'pleasantness–unpleasantness'*, but also simultaneously, and independently, along two others, *'strain–relaxation'* and *'excitement–calm'*. Kaelas used the pulse rate, since Wundt claimed this to be a particularly sensitive index of emotionality. Subjecting his subjects to a variety of types of stimulation, Kaelas came to very radical conclusions. These were based on introspective reports. Amongst these conclusions was the view that there is no direct connection between any sensation in general and changes in the organism. Not only the method used by Kaelas but the formulation of the problem, and the conclusion can be regarded as philosophical idealism, in the tradition of Wundt himself. Chuchmarev's investigation (1926), carried out a decade later, refuted Kaelas's conclusions. Here pulse rate and respiration were studied as indices of emotion: Chuchmarev later included also the galvanic reflex for recording reactions to various experiences. The psychogalvanic response, respiration rate, and blood pressure measurements make it possible to recognize the presence or absence of an emotional reaction; but only the pulse-recordings enable us to identify the character of the emotion. It was about this time that Luria and Leontiev (1926) carried out their research on affective states, using the 'combined (reflected) motor method'. Here the subject, in conjunction with a word-association test, is asked to give a free association to the word and, simultaneously, press a bulb with his right hand whilst the experimenter records the tremor in the left hand. Studies were carried out on students before and during an examination period, on a criminal apprehended after an offence, during hypnotic sleep, and in other emotion-generating and control situations. The 'motor method' provided data which threw light on the affective inhibition of central processes, generated by a conflict situation. Not only is it possible to identify the verbal reaction in the word-association test; the method also enables the experimenter to identify an *impulse* towards such a reaction when the action itself is suppressed. The criminal's attempt to conceal a particular emotional response to certain words increases the affective symptoms by creating a secondary effect. Similar studies, using indices such as the proportion of catalase in the blood-stream, blood-sugar, leucocytosis, blood pressure etc., were carried out, sometimes in association with Luria's 'motor method'. These are to be found in the recent literature. The problems investigated centre round the effect of stressful situations on the generation and expression of the emotions. The situations studied included flight instruction on the ground and in the air, examinations, conflicts of set (when a set for one language is established and words from another used), criminal suspects undergoing interrogation, diseases of the nervous system and of the thyroid gland. The psychogalvanic reflex, as a guide to the activity of the vegetative nervous system, has been intensively studied by Myasishchev (1939), Kolodnaya (1938), and Vlasova (1954), using analogous conflict or stressful situations. Platonov (1956), using Luria's 'motor-method' has established a high rate of agreement between laboratory tests of emotional-motor stability on the ground and during flight in individuals undergoing pilot training.

Osipov, in 1924, sought to amalgamate the James–Lange theory of the emotions with Pavlov's conceptions. He said:

An emotion, or an emotional state, regardless of the quality and degree of its development, is a subjective experience. It is associated with a number of objective expressions and conditioned by external and internal stimuli. It excites a reflex influence on the lateral, striated muscles, on the organs of involuntary movement and their reflection in psychic activity in general. These features constitute the essence of the emotional process.[4]

This revision of Pavlov was opposed by Ivanov-Smolensky (1934). An emotional state in his view is a central process located mainly in the cerebral hemispheres and involving the entire organism. The complex muscular-visceral response has its *beginnings* in signals from the cerebral centres; the responses from each locale are *monitored* there; a generalized response is elaborated by the organism on the basis of *synthesis* of all incoming messages by the cortex; return signals to the internal organs and other effectors are *transmitted* from this centre. This is what 'nervism' implies. Anokhin (1949), considering the same problem, adds that an emotional state can, in certain cases, be the only criterion of the successful action of the effector organs (muscles, viscera, etc.). Feofanov (1952) attempts a psychological classification of the emotions, pointing out the significance of Pavlov's distinction between emotions and feelings. The distinction is not an absolute one, for an emotion may be converted into a feeling – for example, fright may be converted into fear. The view that emotions and feelings are associated with the disturbance or breakdown of 'dynamic stereotypes', or the difficulty in forming a new one (Pavlov, 1932), is also explored. This last topic is taken up in depth by Romanyuk (1956). The interaction and interdependence of the cortex and subcortex in relation to the generation of feelings is investigated by the same writer. Emotions (subcortical centres) can be a source of impulses which strengthen or intensify the feelings (cortical centres). An increase in the intensity of the feelings may result in a transformation of the feeling into *affect* where there is a great predominance of the emotional component. These three terms 'emotions', 'feelings', and 'affects' (which tend to be used interchangeably in Western psychology) have each a special meaning in Pavlovian psychology. In fact, Western psychology confounds the language still further by identifying these three subjective states with drives, strivings, motives, needs, affects, tension symptoms, determining tendencies, attitudes, and mental sets (Rapaport, 1948). According to the Soviet definition, *emotions* are the associates of complex unconditional reflexes (lust, fright, hunger sensations); *feelings* are cerebral, more stabilized, more generalized (love, fear, joy); *affects* are feelings which are taken to an extreme, infused with an overwhelming reinforcement of emotion (ecstasy, terror, grief).

(ii) The Soviet Concept of Set

The research on set forms a unique chapter in Soviet psychology – for a number of reasons. In the first place it was carried on mainly in one institution under the direction of a single leader for over twenty-five years, and continues with undiminished vigour to the present day. The work of this school was largely unknown, not only in the West, but in the Soviet Union until comparatively recently. The research reports of the Institute were published in Georgian, a language which hardly anyone not born in that country can read. The school has been almost totally immune from criticism until recently, even from critical appraisal. This was in spite of the fact that the objective of the school was, and remains, to develop a general theory of psychology based on the study of human reactions – this to be done in a prescribed and restricted laboratory situation.

When we recall how other schools of very similar orientation and aspiration – Kornilov's reactology, Bekhterev's reflexology, for example, come to mind – had such a short spell of active life under Soviet conditions, this immunity from criticism, not to say the actual survival of Uznadze's 'psychology of set' for something like forty-five years, is a most remarkable phenomenon. This is especially so in view of the fact that it is not a Marxist school of psychology in the sense that it starts from Marx's aphorisms on behaviour and seeks to work out their empirical consequences. The important fact seems to be that, while there is no close kinship between the notion of set and Soviet Marxism, neither is there any incompatability.

The concept of 'set' (*Einstellung, ustanovka*) arose during the investigations of the thought-process by the Würzburg school. Henry J. Watt devised the method of dividing up the consciousness to be examined by the observer into four parts or stages – (i) the preparatory, (ii) the acceptance of the stimulus word, (iii) the search for its co-ordinate, the reaction word, and (iv) the occurrence of the reaction word. The subject was asked to concentrate on different parts of the process during one period, then another, and so on. The expectation was that the third period would yield most of the data being sought for, but in fact it was specially this period that was found to be lacking in content. The first period turned out to be the most interesting: it was here that the subject was given the task (*Aufgabe*) and developed the appropriate direction, set, or tendency (*Einstellung*). This all happened in 1904.

At about the same time Charpentier published his well known illusion in which on two wooden cylinders of the same weight, but different sizes, being raised by a cord, or by hand, the larger one appears to be lighter. This, as well as the earlier work of Fechner (1860) on the size–weight illusion, was explained in terms of expectancies; the subject expecting ('being set for'), a heavier weight puts forth slightly more energy to deal with the greater volume. The object therefore 'flies upwards' and hence appears to be lighter. This is the basic experiment in the theory of set, as developed by Uznadze, Natadze, Prangishvili, and many other Georgian psychologists.

In justification of its truly Marxist foundations, the Georgian school notes that Marx considered the main defect of pre-dialectical materialism to be that it disregarded the influence exerted by the activity of the human subject on his thought-processes and consciousness in general. This, of course, is precisely the area exploited by set theory: 'living conditions are examined not only in the form of the object, or contemplation, but rather as human sensuous activity'. Through the medium of 'set', Uznadze and his colleagues claim to work with the real man, not a dead abstraction:

> Science is called upon to formulate the question of the laws of human activity. . . . This activity includes the behaviour of the subject as an integral whole, it is the activity of a real individual, a personality . . .[5]

That is to say, the object of study for psychology is not psychic phenomena, or isolated psychic processes, but actual, living human beings who are exhibiting these phenomena. It is the subject himself who enters into an active relationship with reality. By entering into this relationship the reality is changed, but so is the subject – the *active* relationship with reality, in other words, is of a mutual kind. In his activity, whatever it may be, the subject is *aided by* individual psychic processes, such as, cognitive functions, or the feelings, or the will. But it is the whole subject who acts, not his cognition, feelings, or will. The active agent is not reducible to a sum of states of consciousness.[6]

This view of the integral organism responding to cues in an environment is absolutely compatible, not to say isomorphic, with Marxism; it is also isomorphic with Pavlovianism. By stressing the active role of the subject, Uznadze is closer to authentic Marxism than is Pavlov. It is of interest to note that a recent estimate of set theory in relation to reflex theory (Yakushev, 1965), written from a Pavlovian standpoint, concludes that while there is no real connection between the theory and the experimental data both the theory and the data are valuable – the theory because it does not contradict Pavlovianism, the data because they supplement certain aspects of our understanding of behaviour.

What of the experimental data? Following on Fechner's, Müller's and Schumann's studies of the size–weight illusion Uznadze developed his basic experiment. The subject, blindfold, is presented with two spheres (equal weight, different sizes) placed simultaneously and momentarily one in each hand. This is repeated ten times, each time the larger sphere being placed in the same hand, left or right. The subject reports each time which hand has the larger sphere, left or right. This 'fixes' the set. Without warning, the experimenter after about ten trials, switches the spheres using two of equal volume as well as equal weight.

About ninety-eight per cent of subjects perceive the spheres as unequal. There are three possibilities.

TABLE 3. *Nature of the Set Illusion*

Ten presentations, larger sphere in the *left* hand
Critical test, two equal spheres, one in each hand
Subject reports on left hand sphere

'heavier'	'the same'	'lighter'
contrast illusion	adequate perception	assimilative illusion

This represents a set in the haptic modality. It is as easy to establish sets in any other – kinaesthetic, visual, auditory, heat sense, touch, cold sense, etc. Indeed, one of the first findings is that a set *irradiates* so that the set trials having been run through in one modality (for example, as in the experiment described above) the subject will then see two equal circles presented tachistoscopically as unequal. These two facts, of irradiation and universality in terms of modality, prove that we are dealing with a central phenomenon, involving higher mental processes and that 'set' is not confined to the peripheral organs. The set is an integral state, a real modification of the individual. By carrying out the set tests (or trials) on hypnotized subjects, then awakening them for the critical tests, Uznadze, finding the same effects with these subjects as in their normal state, decided that set has nothing to do with 'disappointed expectations' but represents something much more basic. Experimental studies reveal that personality differences affect the kind of set the subject develops – there is a typology in terms of 'set' characteristics. Bzhalava (1957) related set to psychopathology in the neuroses and psychoses.

The different phenomena of set manifest a remarkable similarity to the characteristics of conditional reflexes. Sets are reinforced by repetition of trials; they generalize; they are extinguished in various ways, similar to reflexes. They can be differentiated and they irradiate. They are closely related by Uznadze to the needs of the organism and a situation which can satisfy these needs. This calls to mind the relation between conditional and unconditional reflexes. There is a connection between the way in which extinction occurs in three phases: contrast, assimilation, and adequate perception in each subject, and the individual qualities of his personality. In other words, the speed of formation of 'sets' and their rates of extinction vary from person to person depending on qualities belonging to his psychic make-up. The individual differences in this adaptation to reality enables a typology to be drawn up which has a clear relationship to the type of central nervous system. Uznadze has demonstrated that precisely the same phenomena can be shown in children and animals, such as rats, hens, and monkeys.

Altogether it can be said that the empirical studies carried out over the last forty-five years at Tiflis provide the strongest support for, not to say verification of, Uznadze's concept of the interaction of the organism with its environment. This he perceives as an active dynamic relationship where the individual is motivated by definite, concrete needs and, on the basis of these, establishes a mutual relationship with the environment. The difference between man and other animals in this respect is that, whereas an animal's behaviour is determined entirely by the influence of the environment, man reacts typically to a given phenomena only after assimilating its meaning into consciousness. In fact, illusions of set can be established in man using imaginary balls, by speech alone. Again, the human subject is aware of himself as an individual acting within an environment. By the process of 'objectification' he forms a subjective image of reality in consciousness. This is of vital significance since on this process of objectification depends the further development of the specific peculiarities of human activity – consciousness, speech, thought.

Although at first sight the 'reflex' model of behaviour of Pavlov and the 'set' model of Uznadze seem to be identical there are important differences between them. These centre in the interpretation of the phenomena of irradiation, generalization, need, situational interaction, and Uznadze's concept of objectification. The general picture however is very much the same, and if Pavlov's 'reflex arc' concept is modified in the direction of Anokhin's (1966) revision – the 'acceptor action' model of behaviour – the 'fit' of one model to the other becomes very close indeed.

(iii) Social Psychology in the Soviet Union

Social psychology was placed in the deep freeze in the late twenties and early thirties. The reasons for this are numerous and cogent. In its Russian form, social psychology was associated with the name of Bekhterev who, as we have seen, added 'collective reflexology' as a branch of his theories of the cosmos. With the discrediting of reflexology as a form of 'idealistic energetics', social psychology tended to attract vituperative denunciation by reason of association. But in any case, as developing in Western Europe and America at this time under the aegis of behaviourism, positivism, phenomenalism, pragmatism, not to mention Freudianism, social psychology – like Taylorism in industrial psychology – could correctly be described as an alien importation, hostile to Marxism. The theories of dialectical and historical materialism were centrally concerned with the sorts of issues which social psychology takes under its wing, so that as far as theory was concerned, the Soviet intelligentsia and men of affairs felt no gap in their understanding of reality when social psychology (and sociology) ceased to figure on university syllabuses. Applied social psychology was considered to be the concern primarily of the Party and political activists. The 1936 decree on 'pedological distortions' placed psychology as an academic discipline centrally in the area of educational psychology, turning it away completely from the study of groups, of delinquency, of personal relations, psychopathology, morale, and motivation. With the development of the Stakhanovite movement in industry and society, the substitution of Makarenko's practical techniques and know-how for an empirical study of child and adolescent collectives, the harnessing of the Komsomol and the Young Pioneers as teachers' auxiliaries in establishing discipline and morale in the schools, the development of 'the cult of personality' as an essential prerequisite for the accomplishment of the titanic tasks facing the new society – nobody even thought of the question: who needs social psychology?

This remained the situation until 1963. Soviet social psychology between 1936 and 1963 must be studied as part of the general life and functioning of Soviet society. There were no professional studies made, or if made, published during this period in the area of social psychology. A remarkable compilation of articles had been published in 1949 under the title of *Soviet Socialist Society*: this had prepared the way for the establishment of an independent science of sociology, with its own problems and its own methodology. One of the first fruits of this new climate was the publication of Sakharov's *On the Personality of the Criminal and the Causes of Crime in the USSR*, published in 1961. This book analyses not only the sociological aspects of crime but the psychological as well. But the main outcome of the text on Soviet society was that it suggested the possibility of developing the related field of social psychology, by similar techniques and broadly based on empirical inquiries as in the case of sociology. This, and related questions, were discussed at a conference in Leningrad in 1963. A softening of the line is to be observed in the view expressed in the report of this meeting that it is possible to reject the theory of bourgeois social science while accepting some of its concrete methods:

> Bourgeois science, in its endeavour to fight Marxism, 'psycho-logises' social phenomena. Soviet psychologists, having totally rejected the theory of bourgeois social psychology, can accept some of its concrete investigations. It has become essential at present to develop a Marxist social psychology.[7]

Two years later, after a lapse of thirty years, a book *Problems of Social Psychology* was published. This was a collection of articles by various authors and dealt with general methodology in addi-tion to reporting two sociometric investigations. The subject mat-ter of social psychology was defined as follows:

> Social psychology constitutes a vast arena of social conscious-ness. It directly reflects social existence in the form of needs, tastes, interests, feelings, moods, fantasies, thoughts and views, as well as in the form of the illusions and prejudices of various social groups beginning with the smallest collective – the family – and ending with the largest socio-historical communities – classes, nations, peoples, mankind. All the diverse psychic phenomena and experiences of groups, just as of the unorganized mass of the population, are refracted in the different forms of their behaviour, in spontaneous or conscious actions, and are fixed in habits, customs, mores and traditions.[8]

One of the major problems remains; how to discriminate between the area proper for social psychological studies and that of ideology – or, indeed, whether this distinction should be made, and at what level.

Far from being considered a new revelation, the empirical sociometric studies reported in this book were severely criticized. This was in spite of the fact that Moreno's theoretical position had already been condemned by the authors of these papers. Sociometry was dismissed by the critic as 'a superficial and formal method of research' which leads only to formalist and worthless conclusions:

> Psychological investigations of a socialist collective . . . should reveal the mores, traditions, and common orientation of the

collective, the struggle of internal contradictions within it, the antagonism of progressive and conservative forces. These investigations should show how personality develops under the conditions in a given collective.[9]

In this same year, 1965, Leningrad University set up an Institute for Comprehensive Social Studies. Its defined function is to investigate the whole area of the social studies, both theoretical and practical. Such questions as the causes of high labour turnover, effects of automation on human personality, empirical data on marriage, divorce, and other life situations are studied. The Institute undertakes research on contract. It is organized around nine 'laboratories' and proposes to look again at man and society without preconceptions or fixed ideas. Workers in the Institute are prepared to use, and have actually used, questionnaires, public opinion polls, and other social-psychological instruments which have not been popular in the USSR for over thirty years. The justification of all this activity is that for too long the 'cult of personality' has involved Soviet scientists in marking time, in 'compiling quotations' from Marx, Engels, and Lenin instead of making a conscientious and timely study of contemporary life, its processes, and new developments. It is claimed that the Twentieth Party Congress removed all the obstacles to the development of the social sciences. The pressing problems of everyday life demanded this new approach – industrial management, urbanization and the problems it created, the problem of class differences ('strata' in socialist society) and their elimination, new forms of labour and automation, population changes and migrations, the problems of Communist upbringing and the survival of religious beliefs and rituals (such as baptism), problems of work, health, family life – these all demanded concrete study and data collection, the only sure basis for scientific decision-making.

With these considerations in mind, the Central Committee of the CPSU issued a resolution *On Measures for the Further Development of the Social Sciences*, published in *Pravda* on August 22, 1967. It criticizes the lag in research on fundamental problems; specifically, it says:

Little attention is paid to the quality and profundity of philosophical analyses of modern achievements in the natural sciences, to study of problems of social psychology, of the collective and the individual, of society and the State, and of the

development of socialist democracy during socialist construction.[10]

The significance of this resolution, especially its timing, was profound. For almost a decade empirical sociological studies have been
proceeding into a very wide range of questions, using extremely
refined methods of mathematical analysis of data, some of it
derived from questionnaires, or opinion surveys or from straight-
forward social surveys. Psychological studies of a parallel kind
have been bedevilled by all sorts of theoretical objections about
subjectivism, that it has no real content etc. The resolution of 1967
legitimizes this study and elevates the question of its further development to the level of a matter of State policy. This must inevitably lead to the expenditure of more and more resources in its
development.

However, this does not betoken any surrender to Western
concepts and methods by the Soviet intellectuals. Techniques such
as sociometry, small group interaction analysis, attitude scales,
questionnaires, natural situations (a technique invented by
Lazursky) are used at present on an 'as if' they are true basis, in
an experimental fashion reminiscent of the 1920s and early thirties,
but with rather more of a critical and informed eye. For example,
one research worker, whilst using the sociometric technique feels
it necessary to say that 'the confused mixture of sociological idealism, political reaction, and infantile fantasy contained in Moreno's
writings could not but repel Soviet research workers'.[11] The
system of social-psychology elaborated in Western Europe and
North America is categorized as being based on idealistic philosophy, and is believed to be aimed at the solution of those problems
in which the ruling class is interested. Admissions to the latter
effect are quoted from the professional journals. On their side,
Soviet social psychologists are only too ready to establish that their
work conforms to the demands laid upon them by their society
and leading class – hastening to point out that this class enshrines
the best ideals of the whole of humanity. The theme of the 'New
Soviet Man' was revived in consequence of the theses of the
Central Committee of the CPSU published for the Fiftieth Anniversary of the Socialist Revolution. The interesting new development is that in place of mere assertion, empirical evidence is
available in areas such as the intellectual interests of the Soviet
worker, life of the oil-workers in the Turkmenian Republic, the
workers' evaluation of different life-models and life-styles, choice

of occupation, attitudes to baptism, attitudes to love, marriage, divorce, changes in patterns of skill in the working class, inter-ethnic marriages – all published in the 60s.

Considering the late start in this field of investigation, it is clear that Soviet psychologists will quickly overcome any backlog that exists. The degree of sophistication that exists can hardly be exaggerated, in view of the fact that *theoretical* discussion and analysis of the content of the social sciences is a daily concomitant of everyman's life in the Soviet Union – it is as pervasive as television advertising in North America. No one need feel sorry for the Russians that they have been deprived of television advertising (and other sorts too) for so many years. Neither should their lack of familiarity with Western social realities cause us to shed any tears on their behalf. As they did in 1957, although probably less spectacularly, and in a less public area – the reference is to SPUTNIK I – Soviet research workers are likely to surprise the rest of the world. The vigour with which Soviet psychologists are attacking areas of human behaviour which were ignored for many decades, or which have been in the theoretical doldrums for about the same length of time, is a promise of numerous and fascinating dividends of fresh insights for all of us, if we are prepared to listen.

(iv) Thought and Speech: the Central Problem of Soviet Psychology

For the whole period of its existence and development, no one has seriously questioned the fact that the problem of the relationship between thought and speech, and their connection with other psychic functions, is the central problem in Soviet psychology. It is this centrality of the problem which accounts for the nagging criticism of idealistic ways of conceptualizing the psyche. The trouble with idealism is that it begins by distorting, or falsifying, the total picture of these relationships; the idealists see everything upside-down, in a topsy-turvy world, so that every detail of the composition is necessarily falsified. Therefore, although an empirical science of the thought-process and its development is the *sine qua non*, not any empirical science will do. The test of a true and useful psychology is *not* that it is empirical but that it conceptualizes reality as it is. Soviet psychology claims to have the best, if not the only correct picture of the total reality; this makes it possible to define the real problems, to select the appropriate method, and to test the truth or falsity of the conclusion – at least in principle. Not everybody is competent to carry through the different stages without error, but the accumulated wisdom of the collective of Soviet psychologists, and of other Marxists, operates in the long term to correct any inadequacies.

The processes of thought and speech are seen through the prism of dialectical materialism; in particular the theory is based on the Marxist account of knowledge ('reflection') and the reflex theory of Sechenov and Pavlov. The fundamental theses, which no empirical study can invalidate and which all empirical investigations should take as their starting-point are: knowledge is a reflection of the external world; practice is the criterion of its truth; truth is a process not only for knowing reality but for transforming it; to be capable of transforming reality one must understand its dialectical nature.

In relation to the problems of thought and speech certain psychologists are given outstanding attention since, in their work, they exemplify these basic truths and advance our understanding of them. This is the significance of Vygotski. More than any other psychologist, in relation to thought and speech, he set Soviet psychology off on Marxist lines. Not only did he centre his work in this area, his investigations established the basic principles of Marxism in regard to the development of the human child. He completely refuted the idealistic notion that speech, logical thought, memory etc. are in any sense 'innate', or that they 'mature' in some way in the absence of social experience. In a series of experimental studies he demonstrated the real nature of the higher mental processes, showing how they evolve under the influence of education. He elucidated the way in which the child's consciousness develops by assimilating adult experience and by taking over the historically developed culture of the human group. Thought, memory, speech – these basic processes all start out as forms of concrete behaviour in which the child imitates the adults. In the course of development, these overt activities and external forms of behaviour become more and more complex, and at the same time more and more internalized. What idealist philosophy for centuries has taken to be inherent, spontaneously developing forms of mental life turn out to be strictly determined, concretely based developing formations arising out of the socialization of the child.

The idealists manage to forget, or to overlook, the social environment as well as the environment of concrete artefacts created by man in the course of history; they even manage to ignore the whole history of childhood. Thus they fail to understand that in reality the mental processes which differentiate man from other animals originate in the activities carried on by the child under adult supervision in a human environment. Vygotski's work demonstrated the truth of Marx's view of the integral character of thought and speech. Still higher mental functions are the result of formal instruction where materials are selected, ordered, and presented by adults.

Leontiev, Smirnov, Zinchenko, and many others have filled in details of this picture. For example, the origin and growth of the active, selective memory characteristic of humans has been traced out and shown to consist of a system of internal mental processes, social in origin, and established on the basis of a complex system of verbal connections. In recent years, Galperin, Zaporozhets, Elkonin, and others, have shown how even more complex processes, such as concept formation and acts of will, arise out of the concrete activities of childhood.

These studies continually demonstrate the truth of Vygotski's paradigm: that the history of mental processes is that they are initially concrete acts, which, thanks to verbalization through social (adult) intervention, become internalized. This is how consciousness is built up as a reflection of reality: the child proves the reality, the truth, the 'this-sidedness' of his thought through concrete activities. This is ultimately the only way, since the thoughts transmitted by adults are themselves the embodied practice of millennia of human activity and need to be related to concrete activity. This contribution of Vygotski and his work, which is continuing, is the central question in Soviet psychology, and the discovery of these principles represents one of its most important achievements.

The connection between thought (and other mental processes such as perceptions, attention, logical memory, and voluntary action) and brain functioning is established through the work of Pavlov and his disciples, especially Krasnogorski. But Soviet psychologists do not regard thinking as identical with the conditional reflex activity of the brain in the narrow sense, as a process entirely of associations. Rubinstein in fact at one time expressed the view that thinking, and other higher mental processes, are not association processes but are specifically psychic processes. Whereas associations are accidental and contingent, thinking is the reflection of necessary and essential connections and relations of objective reality. However, it is now realized that Sechenov's and Pavlov's model of the reflex was more subtle that had been realized, and was complex enough to represent the thought-process. The second signal system concept of Pavlov contributed a new dimension to brain functioning – abstraction and generalization of the characteristically human kind became possible.

Luria has used neurologically impaired subjects to discover the relationships between thought, speech, and the brain. He has demonstrated in detail how the brain enables us to receive information from the external world, to create a subjective image of it, to predict the effects of our interaction with it, to evaluate the results of our actions, in short, to regulate our behaviour. This conception of the brain as the supreme regulator of conduct ('nervism') has been built up and verified on the basis of exact studies of the brain. The discoveries of neuro-surgery, neurology, and psychology over more than forty years provide an integral picture isomorphic with that of Vygotski. The study of brain damage, and the restoration of impaired functions through a process of re-education, confirms the theoretical principles underlying these explanations of the higher mental processes.

(v) Soviet Work on Individual Differences

The study of individual differences is regarded in the Soviet Union as being one of the most basic tasks of psychology. However, the method of using short, standardized tests to obtain a quantitative measure of the individual's traits, abilities, or personality is not used, being regarded as fundamentally unsound. The vast majority of such tests lack any scientific foundation and are harmful in practice. This theoretical posture has been maintained in the Soviet Union since 1936 – standardized tests, whether they be of the Binet type, or Rorschach, or Cattell, throw no light on individual differences.

The aim of Soviet work is to achieve the most accurate study of individual differences, based on an analysis of the typological properties of higher nervous activity. A modified Pavlovianism is the frame of reference for this work. It has been proceeding since the 1940s under Teplov's general leadership. He has defined the task (1960) to be not simply to preserve Pavlov's theories but to develop them, clearly recognizing and respecting the basic foundations of his teaching. This means that the attachment to the Hippocratic typology (choleric, sanguine, melancholic, phlegmatic) must be severed – this for two reasons: (i) there are clearly more than four types of human temperaments, and there is evidence of this being true also of dogs; (ii) more basic to Pavlovian typology is his concept of the *properties* of the nervous system, from which a general typology should be developed. It was because the idea of four types was developed by Pavlov (1927) before the concept of a typology based on the properties of the nervous system, objectively established, that Pavlov continued to use his initial typology through the 1930s. Synthesis had preceded analysis. The transfer of this erroneous classification to man wrought great harm. Teplov definitively repudiated the Pavlovian theory of four types in 1963 on the grounds that no advance was possible until this was done. Biryukova (1961) had earlier identified eight basic types amongst Soviet athletes; Krasupsky (1963) had found forty-eight different nervous types in a sample of 116 dogs investigated at the Koltushi laboratory. Teplov pointed out that there was not even a mention of the four temperaments in the works of Hippocrates!

It was Pavlov's great merit to recognize that a typology could be based precisely on the combinations, or 'complexes', of the characteristic properties of the nervous processes. At the end of his scientific labours, in his paper on *General Types of Higher Nervous Activity in Animals and Man* (1935), Pavlov recognized three basic properties of the nervous system which should be used as the basis of the description of types: (i) the strength of neural processes, (ii) the mobility of these processes, and, (iii) the balance of excitation and inhibition. Teplov defines the task as being to study the relationships between different properties, and to select those various combinations of qualities which appear to be the most 'natural' or 'typical'. This problem, he agrees, has not yet been solved. But he revises the basic properties, as defined by Pavlov, on the grounds that experimental work indicates that 'equilibrium' involves two things, endurance and speed of conditioning and the speed of alteration (Nebylitsyn, 1963). These facts have been verified on both animals and human beings – the animals including such species as cows, rabbits, mice, dogs. There are four primary properties of the nervous system – strength, mobility, lability, and dynamicity, plus two secondary features, one being an interaction of dynamicity with each of the other three basic qualities and the other an interaction of strength with arousal and inhibition. Schematically, these can be shown as follows:

Fig. 3   Schematic properties of the nervous system

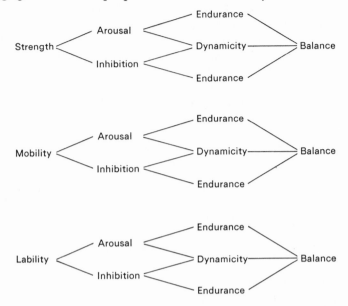

A complete programme of tests, devised by Podkopayev (1952), consists of twelve quantitative measures involving conditioning, de-conditioning and re-conditioning procedures, with bromides and caffeine being taken by the subject at the appropriate stages. It is here that the great bottleneck has developed in this area of research as it takes several weeks, sometimes months of work with *each* subject even using the newest techniques (EEG, photo-chemistry, etc.) to identify the type to which he or she belongs.

But this is regarded as being absolutely basic research since the study of individual differences can make no progress beyond mere description, until we understand the nature of the basic properties of the nervous system, how they combine to produce the various kinds of temperaments and how temperament is related to will, character, abilities, and personality. Teplov was not averse to the use of statistical methods in psychology, provided the measures were soundly based and meaningful in themselves. Correlational analysis had been used in seeking to answer basic questions by Federov (1961) and Kokorina (1963). More recently, under Teplov's supervision, factor analysis has been used by Nebylitsyn (1960; 1963) in seeking to validate the empirical tests used for nervous system 'typing'.

The significance of these individual differences in the mode of functioning of the central nervous system for the psychology of abilities, personality, and character is clear enough, although detailed connections have to be made out – they cannot simply be deduced. In Teplov's view, it is not possible to reduce even separate, simple elements of ability to specific properties of the nervous system. Man's abilities are formed according to specific psychological laws. A knowledge of individual differences is essential if we are to provide the best method of instruction and rearing for each individual. But these 'types' cannot be diagnosed on the basis of conversations with the subject, nor on direct observation of his behaviour. Extensive clinical interviews by experienced Pavlovians, using 'real-life' indices of strength, equilibrium, and mobility, are of some help, but merely as hypotheses requiring verification by direct study of the central nervous system.

(vi) Soviet Evaluations of the Past History of Psychology

As an evolutionary philosophy, Marxism places great emphasis on the study of origins and development. Indeed no phenomenon is regarded as understood if we cannot trace it to its starting-point and through its dialectical development. The ideas in a particular scientific discipline, such as psychology, can only be properly understood in the context of the period in which they were put forward, since an idea which may be true and progressive in a certain period alters its character and may become false and reactionary in another.

As we have endeavoured to explain, Russian psychology developed in a particular social, economic, and ideological context. Under Peter, it began to assume a modern, scientific visage. In its Soviet form it represents a new phenomenon, uniquely different from other psychologies, with its own basic assumptions, its specialized content, its own particular laws of development. While it is not simply a unilinear continuation of the preceding history of Russian materialist philosophy and of West European Marxism, neither is it completely fenced off from these earlier developments. The unique genius of Lenin and Pavlov was erected on the ideas, the aspirations, the practical know-how of men and women living in their own era: even more so on the work of their predecessors. The polemics in which they engaged had been fought already over the same issues but on other battlefields; they were to be fought again over the same ground as before but with new protagonists.

One of the unique features of Russian psychology is its tendency towards a single-minded decision for a no-holds-barred fight to a finish on the ideological issue. Materialism, *sans phrases*, without compromise – this has been the declared agenda since 1863; since 1917 the agenda has been revised only by the addition of the word 'dialectical'. The great materialist tradition, stemming from Bacon, Locke, Hobbes and Holbach, was assimilated and expressed in a characteristic idiom by Russian thinkers – unqualified, direct, as a confrontation.

Unfortunately, until very recently the history of these developments has been treated in an extremely one-sided way. There seem to be two main reasons for this: first, the hatred of materialism in general and of Communist ideas in particular has created an iron curtain of misunderstanding amongst the academic historians of Russian thought. One is forced to agree with Lenin's thesis that, in this area at least, a battle to the death has been joined, and that only the feeble-minded can fail to see this and be non-partisan. The second problem for the historian is that Russian history has been interpreted, since Catherine the Great's time, from a *non*-Russian, which means an *anti*-Russian, standpoint. The fact that Catherine was a German princess, and that all the administrative organs of the State, including the archives, were effectively under strong German control for considerable periods should be remembered. There were historians who were also Russian patriots, but their views were either unknown because of their alien tongue, or discounted since the 'cosmopolitans' already occupied the field. Lomonosov's quarrel with Müller in the Academy of Sciences was precisely on this issue – the refusal of West Europeans to admit any originality or independent status to the Russian people. Falsification of the views of Russian thinkers, such as Lomonosov, Radishchev, Chernishevski, Sechenov, and Pavlov, still continues. This is due partly to ignorance but, more importantly, the obdurate habit of refusing to apply the same standards of scholarship to Soviet Russian matters as to other academic areas. Russian *emigrés,* irrespective of their credentials and tendency, are accepted as interpreters of the Russian 'soul' or 'mind' – although their fundamental principle of evaluation is that which was succinctly stated almost two millennia ago: 'What good can come out of Galilee?'

Ananiev was the first Marxist to attempt an explanation of the development of Russian psychology: this was in 1938. Between 1939 and 1945 he published a series of articles in which he sought to establish the progressive character of Russian psychological thought. In 1947, his outline of the history of Russian psychology in the eighteenth and nineteenth centuries provided many novel facts and interpretations, refuting the view that Russian science was backward in this area. Independently, Kerrovich worked over the same ground and came to similar conclusions. Although Ananiev's book was a pioneer effort, or perhaps *because* it was a pioneer effort, it contained certain errors and loosenesses of interpretation which were pointed out at the time.

The eighteenth century was an interesting period in many ways. It was then that Russian psychology made considerable progress, although not yet an independent discipline separated from philosophy. This period has been studied especially by Kostyuk (1952), Sokolova (1957), and their associates. During this period we meet such figures as Tatishchev, Lomonosov, Kozelsky, Novikov, Skovorodova, and Radishchev, in addition to a remarkable group of Moscow professors. Although, as we have seen, these thinkers cannot be considered materialists in the proper sense of the word, being deistic rather than atheistic in their thinking, they stated various theses which have been caught up and integrated in Soviet psychology of the present day. Lomonosov, for example, attempted to develop a realist interpretation of sensations as the motion of material particles. He gave an explanation of colour-vision on the basis of a tri-component system. He characterized the thought-process as a complex movement from appearance (sensation) to essence (concept). Concepts were explained as reflections in consciousness of objects and their interrelations. He put forward a number of valuable ideas on the nature of speech, of its many-sided connections with thought and the emotions. The conception of the passions, and other mental phenomena, as vital properties of man which develop under the influence of living conditions is also to be found in his writings.

As one of the founders of Moscow University, Lomonosov's ideas continued to influence leading thinkers there. An atheistic and materialistic tendency is to be found in the writings of Anichkov. He asserted the dependence of the 'soul' on the state of the organism. He also suggested that all our cognitive activity proceeds in, and belongs to, the brain and its associated nerves. As we have seen, this idea was vehemently denied as late as the middle of the next century by leading idealist and liberal thinkers, and is so denied even today. According to Gurova, Skiadan was the first person to indicate that the cerebral cortex was the organ of the higher mental processes: he too was a professor at Moscow. He took it to be his particular task to discover the material, physiological basis of psychic processes as early as 1778.

Even Skovorodova, the 250th anniversary of whose birth was celebrated in 1972, put forward some progressive ideas in the course of developing his confused, contradictory, and original system of thought. He rejected the notion of innate ideas, following Locke, and discovered the source of our knowledge in the external world. Like Socrates, with whom he is often compared, he pointed the need to pass from mere contemplation of phenomena to the discovery of their essence. Acts of the will arise out of necessity which operates not only in the life of man, but in all nature. His views have been examined in detail by Kostyuk, as well as by Sokolova.

It was in the person of Radishchev, however, that psychology in Russia in the eighteenth century reached its highest level. Like later writers under the conditions of Tsarism and as one who had already suffered exile for his ideas, he conceals his own views in his writings on man by presenting arguments for both idealism and materialism, for theism as well as atheism. He leaves it to any possible reader of his private writings to choose whichever view appeals to him. In the course of exploring the arguments for and against the immortality of the soul, he develops the thought that the 'soul' is a property, or 'product' of the brain. If so, he argues, then the soul and body must come into existence and disappear together. He noted the similarity between man and animals, but pointed out the differences: that man has an upright posture, a different kind of thumb or hand, articulate speech, and a different kind of intellect. Whilst emphasizing the sensory basis of our thought-processes, Radishchev refused to identify thinking with sensation. In fact, he developed what must be considered an original system of psychological thought for his period.

Throughout the first half of the nineteenth century, the progressive trend in psychology was maintained by teachers and writers amongst whom Galich, Lyubovsky, Lody, Mukhin, Dyadkovsky, and Filomafitsky must be numbered. Galich, the teacher of Pushkin, worked out a scheme of development of man's perceptions. His main sphere of interest, however, lay in the 'motivational-dynamic' trend which has been a leading theme in Russian psychology ever since. Lyubovsky published a *Short Handbook of Experimental Psychology* in 1815. This was conceived by him as a text which should break with the religious dogmas of the spirituality and immortality of the soul, these forming the major premise of most translated texts on psychology available at the time. His other major motive was to provide a work which was founded on native conditions and ideas, rather than on foreign imports (mainly German idealistic philosophy). He was one of the first Russian psychologists to put forward the explanation of memory and other mental processes on the basis of associationism. Lody, in criticizing Kant's views, developed the thesis that not only sensory but also intellectual perception is a reflection of objectively existing things. He believed that we form concepts by means of comparison, abstraction, and generalization of the general signs of these objects. He anticipated Vygotski in his interest in thought and language and the connections between them. He also anticipated Vygotski in the emphasis he laid on the leading role of instruction in sciences on the development of the child's intellectual capacities.

As we have already noted, not only those psychologists mentioned above, but also the three professors of physiology at Moscow University – Mukhin, Dyadkovsky, and Filomafitsky – laid the basis for many of the ideas which were caught up in the remarkable synthesis made by Sechenov in his monograph *Reflexes of the Brain*. It is clear that this work was based on this forgotten school of progressive thought. The influence of these three physiologists on Sechenov was revealed for the first time only in 1957 by Shumilin. These early nineteenth-century thinkers sought to extend the natural–scientific mode of explanation to human mental activity. Mukhin, rejecting the theory of phrenology, that is, that human behaviour is determined by inherited anatomical peculiarities, was on the point of recognizing the supreme role of the central nervous system in the vital activity of the organism. He was the first physiologist to establish the significance of *inhibition* in the nervous system, explaining it as a process of non-conduction of the impulse through the nerve fibres. He pictured association as a material process depending on actual physiological connections of the neural paths and centres. Dyadkovsky sharply rejected vitalism; he rejected Wolff's conception of 'faculties', and Schelling's transcendentalism. These tendencies were the popular anti-scientific intellectual currency of the period. He linked the organic and inorganic worlds in an evolutionary scheme in which sensation, irritability, and different forms of sensitivity arise in stages as properties of matter. He recognized the reflex function of the nervous system and, even before Sechenov, recognized that the brain also was involved in reflex activity. The idea that mental phenomena were capable of analysis apart from cerebral functioning, he maintained, was false and 'wild'. It was Filomafitsky who, before Pavlov, visualized the nervous system as the organ which integrated the organism with its environment. In experiments with frogs, he anticipated Sechenov's discovery of central inhibition, taking the view that the brain exerts an inhibiting effect on the reflex activity of the spinal cord (1840). According to Shaskolskaya (1949), he anticipated Pavlov in creating a gastric fistula in the dog for lecture-demonstrations of the digestive process. He put forward the idea that 'every voluntary action is reflex in character'. If Sechenov is 'the father of Russian physiology' then Filomafitsky (1807–1849) is clearly the grandfather.

The second half of the nineteenth century in Russian psychological thought is dominated by the ideas of Belinsky (died 1848), Gertsen, Chernishevski, and Dobrolyubov. As we have seen, these thinkers continued and developed the materialist tradition in psychology in opposition to the dualism of the orthodox, State-sponsored incumbents of university chairs of philosophy, logic, and psychology. They sponsored the realist school in Russian literature of the nineteenth century and guided its development from Pushkin to Tolstoy, Turgeniev, and Ostrovsky. Gertsen (or Hertzen in its Latinized form) decisively rejected psychophysical dualism and spoke for a psychology which would understand human personality as 'the product of physiological *and* historical necessity'. This is probably the briefest possible formulation of the major thesis of current Soviet psychology. For Gertsen, the concept of action is *the* central psychological concept. According to Lenin, his *Letters on the Study of Nature* (1845) 'placed him on a level with the greatest thinkers of his time'.[12] They certainly played an important part in the development of progressive thought in Russia. Chernishevski's views have been analysed at considerable length by many Soviet writers, since 1939. He developed his philosophy in opposition to the leading schools of professional psychology – Katkov, Yurevich etc., as well as against thinkers who were not officially favoured but who developed an anti-monistic line of thought, such as Lavrov. According to Chernishevski, the most essential points for psychology are: the recognition of causality as an absolute principle; the resistance of external reality as the matrix of human activity. This means that man acts on his environment to change it. But the environment exerts a resistance to change unless the human agent is acting in accord with the laws of the medium. External reality is the medium or matrix within which, and against which, man exercizes his powers. Concurrently with the successful change produced in external reality, man himself changes. Chernishevski also emphasized as basic principles of psychology: psycho-physical monism; thought as the mediated reflection in man's consciousness of the regularities of the external world; man's activity in thinking whereby he alters nature according to his vital needs. His associate Dobrolyubov also consistently applied materialist principles in the elucidation of the social realities of his time.

Other minor figures, associated with Chernishevski and the journal *Sovremennik*, like Antonovich, Pisarev, and Shelgunov, also contributed to this line of thought. But, of course, it was Sechenov, directly influenced by these currents, who made the radical breakthrough in his *Reflexes of the Brain* (1863). The close similarity between his views and those of the English associationist, George Henry Lewes (*The Physiology of Common Life*, 1859), should be noted. The Russian translation of Lewes's book occasioned a violent controversy in which Antonovich castigated the anti-Science views of Golitsky, Yurevich, and Katkov.

As far as Sechenov is concerned, every aspect of his thought has been exhaustively studied in over sixty articles and books written in connection with the fiftieth anniversary of his death in 1905. A contrast is drawn between *Reflexes of the Brain* (1863) and Wundt's *Vorlesungen über die Menschen – und Thiereseele* (1863) – the first with its monism and advocacy of objective method, the second with its Kantian agnosticism, psychophysical parallelism, and advocacy of the subjective method (*Selbstbeobachtung*). Similar attention, not quite so marked, has been paid to psychologists who are outside the main stream of Soviet psychology, such as Ushinsky (1824–1870), and minor figures like Lesgaft (1837–1909), Potebnya (1835–1891), Lange (1858–1921), and many other Russian contributors to psychological science. The psychological views of leading writers of the nineteenth century, such as Gogol, Shevchenko, Franko, Goncharov, Tolstoy, and Gorky have been elucidated and extensively discussed.

As a multi-national state, the Soviet Union includes many old-established nations, a large number with a long history of independent culture. Considerable attention has been devoted to the views of native thinkers of non-Russian nationality, especially in connection with the relationship of their views to the systematic

positions adopted by Soviet psychology. Indeed, a large proportion of the historical work referred to above has been carried out
by Ukrainian psychologists, such as Kostyuk, Pelekh, Rayevsky.
Georgian psychology in its historical development has been written
up by Prangishvili. Special studies have been made of the views
of eighteenth and nineteenth century Georgian thinkers, such as
Orbeliani, Bagration, Dodashvili, Kikodze, and others. Similarly,
Armenian contributions have been evaluated. Mazmanyan has
written on the history of psychological thought in Armenia, special
attention being paid to Nazaryanets (1812–1879), Popovyanets,
and Bagatryan. The views of the celebrated novelist and poet
Abovyan (1805–1848), regarded as the founder of Armenian
literature, have been analysed. Nabaldyan (1829–1866) is regarded as the founder of materialist psychology in Armenia. In
Soviet Azerbaydzhan, the writings of ibn-Sina (Avicenna 980–
1037) and of Nasireddin Tusi (1201–1274), his disciple, have been
scrutinized for their spontaneous materialist tendency. Similar
studies have been made in the history of Kazakh, Estonian, and
Lithuanian psychology.

Different anniversaries, of the Revolution, of the births or deaths
of figures celebrated in the history of Soviet psychology – such as
Marx, Lenin, Pavlov, Vygotski, Ushinsky etc. – are marked by
sheafs of articles, sometimes by books of interpretation, bio-
graphies, collected writings etc. On the centenary of Lenin's
birthday in April 1970, for example, practically the whole of the
journal *Voprosy Psikhologii* was devoted to articles on different
aspects of his theory of reflection.

References

1. Platonov *Psychology as you like it.*
2. I. Sechenov *Reflexes of the Brain.* 1961: 34.
3. I. P. Pavlov *Sobranie Sochineniya* 1951 **3**: 244.
4. B. G. Ananiev 1959–60 **2**: 250–251.
5. V. M. Yakushev 1966: 180.
6. A. S. Prangishvili, in Ananiev 1961 **2**: 181.
7. Vedenov *Sovietskaya Pedagogika* 1966 (4): 34; cf. *Soviet
   Education* 1966 (5): 23.
8. *Problems of Social Psychology* (1965), quoted by Vedenov,
   1966: 36.
9. Vedenov *Sovietskaya Pedagogika* 1966 (4): 35.
10. *Pravda* Soviet Education 1966 (5): 23. Aug. 22, 1967.

11. Kerbikov, in M. Cole and I. Maltzman (eds.) *Handbook of Contemporary Soviet Psychology* New York: Basic Books. 1969: 389.
12. V. I. Lenin *Selected Works* (2 vols.) London: Lawrence and Wishart. 1946 **1**: 633–638.

Reading List

Books in English
Anan'ev, B. G. *et al.* (1961, 1962) *Psychological Science in the USSR* (2 vols.) Washington: U.S. Joint Publ. Res. Serv.
Anon (1966, 1967) *Psychological Research in the USSR* (2 vols.) Moscow: Progress Publishers.
Gray, J. A. (1964) *Pavlov's Typology* London: Pergamon Press.
Ostrander, Sheila and Schroeder, L. (1970) *Psychic Discoveries Behind the Iron Curtain* Englewood Cliffs, N.J.: Prentice-Hall.
Slobin, D. I. (ed.) (Spring – Summer, 1966) Handbook of Soviet Psychology, Spec. Issue of *Soviet Psychology and Psychiatry* **4** (3–4).
Winn, R. B. (ed.) (1961) *Psychotherapy in the Soviet Union* New York: Philosophical Library.
Books in Other Languages
Mecacci, L. (ed.) (1971) *Soviet Psychology in Western Countries* Rome: Instituto di Psicologia.
Smirnov, A. A. (ed.) (1970) *Osnovy Psikhologii* (vol. 1) Moscow: Prosveshcheniye.
Sokolova, M. V. (1961) *Iz Istorii Russkoi Psikhologii* Moscow: RSFSR Acad. Ped. Sci.

Chapter 10 *Summary: Russian Psychology and its Soviet Form*

1. Science was especially difficult to cultivate in Tsarist Russia due to the relentless and all-powerful influence of custom, the dominant role of conservative social forces such as religion, the patriarchal and extended family, the unanimity principle in village government, the communal land relationships and arrangements, the illiteracy of the mass of the population, and the absence of an educated public opinion.

2. At the same time the actual contribution of Russian scholars is denigrated since, especially from Catherine II's time, the history of the Russian State and of Russian ideas has been interpreted by foreigners, cosmopolitans or *emigrés*, whose aim has been to 'interpret' Russia to Western Europe. Thus, scientific ideas are normally lifted out of context, assimilated to West European ideas, originality is denied, and the actual development of native concepts is twisted and misunderstood.

3. It is one of the leading characteristics of Russian intellectuals, under the conditions of Tsarism, to develop their ideas to the extreme logical limit. Whatever may be true of the history of Western Europe and America, it is certainly true that philosophical, social, and historical studies have been an arena where war to the death has been declared between the official establishment and modern science and philosophy.

4. The Orthodox Church existed as an extension and support of the civil arm. It bore the character of a religious 'reflection' of the

autocracy and bureaucracy. The priests supported the most conservative State policies, they actively persecuted dissenters and
radicals, they fostered anti-Semitism, and acted as agents of the
secret police.

5.   From the tenth century until the Revolution, the dominant
thought-patterns of the mass of the Russian people were drawn
from Greek Christianity. The dogmas of the Church have been
the matrix within which concepts of science, art, and literature
germinated and developed. Russia did not benefit from either the
European Renaissance or from the Reformation: in spite of many
contradictions and retrogressive tendencies, these did nurture the
free life of the intellect in the West.

6.   Russian thought is steeped in the notion of a physical, supernatural unity generated by communal life – in the *Mir*, the family,
State, and Church. This feeling for the *kollektiv* – any group en-
dowed with a common purpose, mutual trust, and empathic unity
– explains the outrage expressed by Russian thinkers of all per-
suasions (Khomyakov, Hertzen, etc.) when brought face-to-face
with Western individualism.

7.   The influences which eventually put an end to the monolithic
system of State power, ecclesiastical monopoly, and serf exploitation are diverse and complex. Religious dissent, the innovations
of Peter I, the peasant wars, new concepts of science and freedom
of inquiry derived from study in Western Europe – these gave rise
to an independent, secular culture without which a science of
psychology is impossible.

8.   Psychology developed in opposition to Orthodox 'anthropology'. The basic tenets of the established religion devalued empirical inquiry, and the special problems of psychology had been
pre-empted for centuries by detailed doctrines about 'the Soul'.
These doctrines claimed the sanction of Divine Truth and debarred secular investigation. The inquirer in these areas (e.g.
Sechenov) was immediately involved in a confrontation with
Church and State. The first psychologists were, willy-nilly, radicals
if not revolutionaries.

9.   Dating from about 1789, the situation of the scholar, whether
historian, scientist, or philosopher, was parlous indeed. It was

possible to be sentenced to death for writing a book (Radishchev, 1790), for discussing a letter (Dostoievski, 1849), for distributing a manifesto (Ushakov, 1863). Many scientists were under police surveillance, their books and journals were subject to seizure and censorship. For example, Sechenov could not publish his monograph on Cerebral Reflexes under its original title, while many passages had to be changed to pass the censor. Radical writers were arrested, beaten, exiled to Siberia. As late as Easter 1917, the writings of scientists were censored and conferences could not meet. There was a determined war against unorthodox opinions. Under Tsarism, this meant scientific knowledge in general, and non-Biblical concepts of behaviour in particular.

10.   The result of this war was the effective polarization of Russian thought into two camps – the radical, atheistic, and materialist school versus conservative, religious, dualistic obscurantism. Caught between these were numerous liberal, humanistic, uncommitted, neutral tendencies. These were basically alien imports from an alien world.

11.   It is possible to recognize the development of the scientific tendency in the study of human behaviour along the line:

Tatishchev   Chernishevski
Kantemir→Lomonosov→Radishchev→Belinsky→Dobrolyubov
Prokopovich   →Sechenov→Pavlov.

A parallel line of development which runs from:

Bacon→Locke→Holbach→Feuerbach→Marx

was also assimilated into Russian psychology. The key link was Lenin.

12.   The tendencies expressed in the work of the nineteenth century radical intelligentsia are still the hallmarks of Soviet psychologists. These are now expressed in terms of *partisanship,* that is, a rejection of basic assumptions hostile to Marxism; *monism,* that is, the assertion of the unity of psychical and somatic processes; *materialism,* that is, the assumption that we have exact knowledge of a physical and psychological reality which exists independently of man's perceptions of it; *dialectics,* that is, the notion that everything is in flux with no self-existent, autonomous entities which are unchangeable; the *activity* of man who, as a species and as

individual, acts to change reality and in doing so is himself changed.

13. These principles rule out as idealistic misconceptions a great number of concepts which remain influential in non-Soviet psychology – 'intelligence', 'instinct', 'drive', 'subjective states' etc. – if these are perceived as independent, explanatory constructs. By education and social action 'human nature' can be changed to an infinite degree. Human behaviour is in no way limited by biological factors or innate 'powers' – man-in-the-group can act on barriers imposed by the here-and-now environment.

14. Soviet psychology therefore works within the constraints of the Bolshevik interpretation of the Marxist theory of human nature. Empirical studies arise out of this context of agreed assumptions and cannot, in principle, contradict them. Scientific method is understood in this sense. While, at certain times and in certain places, work is done which violates one or other of these basic assumptions (e.g. ESP experiments), this happens and is permitted to happen to discover whether or not some *practical* and *immediate* advantage might be derived. The experiments are not intended to be taken as a general refutation of a philosophical position, or to mark a reversion to a pre-1917 *laissez-faire* régime tolerating spiritistic, animistic, or religious (idealistic) conceptions – on the contrary.

15. A considerable variety of Soviet materials exists in the form of research reports of empirical studies, in virtually all areas of psychology. A special kind of rigour is developed in relation to problems which have a considerable bearing on practical life. In this area especially, we have a great deal to learn from Soviet psychology. But we cannot simply ignore the basic theoretical positions on which this work is based. Soviet psychologists would indeed assert that this is precisely what we have to learn.

Chapter 11 *Comparative Perspectives: British, American, and European Psychology*

The understanding of Soviet psychology is facilitated by comparing it with the other schools of thought – in particular with the various systematic positions to be found in Western Europe, Britain, and North America. There is another reason for placing it in this context. As we have attempted to show, the essential nature of Soviet psychology cannot be understood without some basic knowledge of the historical roots from which it developed. This includes not only the Russian influences of a historical, social, and intellectual kind; it also involves consideration of the development of psychology in Western Europe. In this concluding chapter we will attempt to point to the historical connection between Soviet and European psychology, indicating at the same time the main sources of the theoretical impasse between these protagonists.

Unfortunately, like the history of science in general, the development of psychology is unknown to the great majority of those who teach the subject. The accepted version is confused and tendentious. The main reason for this is that psychology as a science was beset in Western Europe by exactly the same problems as in Eastern Europe. Religious philosophers and political interests bedevilled not only the definition of the subject matter of psychology, they also obscured the record of how it developed. A process of selective emphasis gave rise to a distorted view which functioned to salvage the established religious ideology. It also cluttered up public discourse, contaminating the language with eclectic jargon. Political, religious, and philosophical preoccupations diverted attention from the real issues. They ensured that the radical, scientific approach towards the definition of the subject matter of psychology (behaviour) and towards its method (objectivity, acceptance of causality, monism) should be passed over, or become so twisted up in transmission by careless or unsympathetic middlemen that it was not available to the student of the subject as a viable alternative to the anti-scientific positions assumed by the established authorities.

Let us begin then by making some important distinctions. These should serve to clear the air of a great number of major irrelevancies and arguments. Psychology, as the science of human behaviour, is concerned with man as an object, with man as he is and as he acts in the world of nature and society. As science, psychology is not involved either in establishing or refuting the theological view of man, except in so far as the theologian may *illicitly* proceed from *a priori* principles to dogmatize about the empirical realities of behavour. Empirical psychology can study the origins and development of religious ideas in the normal and pathological individual, but it cannot provide us with a criterion with which to decide on the truth of religious views or of the existence and nature of a supernatural order. In this respect, the psychologist is neither better off, nor worse off, than the ordinary citizen. He is guided in these questions by the normal criteria of evidence and logical argument. In spite of the etymology of the word, psychology has nothing to do with the study of souls. It is concerned with applying the same rules as appertain in other branches of science to the systematic analysis of behaviour-patterns to discover the nature of the causal process at work.

In the modern period, the history of psychology, so defined, really begins with Helmholtz. His stand with Brücke in the 1840s against vitalism, and his enunciation of the principle of conservation of energy (1847), provided a general scientific base for the study of behaviour. In the same way, his investigation of the speed of the nervous impulse (1850) and his analysis of vision (1856) and tone-sensations (1863) provided a model of systematic, objective, causal explanation.

Helmholtz's influence is pervasive in modern psychology. The areas he studied and the methods he used are the undisputed territories gained for science. At various times, the founders of the various theoretical positions available in modern psychology worked with him, or with his direct associates. Sechenov spent time, not only with Helmholtz, but with Brücke, du Bois Reymond, and Ludwig. Contemporary Soviet psychology springs directly from this school. It differs from most other systems in that it has not deviated from the original Helmholtzian experimental methodology and conceptual scheme. Ebbinghaus continued and developed the objective method in his celebrated studies on memory (1885). In the meantime Wundt, who served for a time as Helmholtz's assistant, had set up an experimental laboratory at Leipzig (1879) but had already abandoned Helmholtz's monistic view in favour of mentalism. Freud, who had been Brücke's assistant in Vienna, also abandoned monism for dualism about 1897.

Another seminal influence in the development of a scientific psychology was, of course, Charles Darwin. His two books (*Origin of Species,* 1859; *Descent of Man,* 1872) placed the human species within the natural world, subject to the same laws as other organisms. His studies of the development of his own children, comparing this with the maturation of the young of other anthropoids, introduced the methods of the natural sciences into the study of human behaviour. G. H. Lewes, an intimate friend of Herbert Spencer, was very much under the influence of Darwinian and Spencerian evolutionism. His writings turned Pavlov towards the study of physiology as his life-work. Darwin and Lewes, who influenced Sechenov, must be regarded as important guiding spirits of present-day Soviet psychology. As well as Lewes, mention may be made of Romanes, Lloyd Morgan, and Hobhouse as founders of animal psychology and the pioneers of the radical behaviourism approach. The phrase 'radical behaviourism' was actually coined by Hobhouse (1929) to describe 'the one and only method in psychology'.

We can briefly characterize the development of psychology during the nineteenth century in Europe in terms of two contrasting tendencies which were at war with each other. The protagonists were fully aware of the nature of the struggle. On the one hand were the various evolutionary schools. These pictured man as given by nature, as governed by scientific law, and capable of being studied empirically to provide accurate information about behaviour. Thus behaviour was perceived as being, at least in principle, predictable because *caused.* On the other side were the various schools derived from Descartes and closely associated with philosophical movements of continental idealism (Kant, Schelling, Hegel). These thinkers and their disciples were anxious to save religious belief from the materialist, sceptical, humanistic critique. These conflicting schools, of course, had roots in earlier developments. The conflict, conceptualized as being between 'science' and 'religion', was generated afresh in each generation. As far as psychology was concerned, the basic conflict was between the rationalist, mentalistic deductive mode sponsored by Descartes and the *a posteriori*, empirical method of Francis Bacon. The relationship of the various schools to each other are shown in the charts.

This is a very schematic description of the connection between certain 'schools' of psychology and the tendencies in philosophy from which these 'schools' are derived. It is given to indicate the kind of context necessary by means of which a rationale can be worked out to understand (a) *what* it is Soviet psychologists reject, and (b) *why* they do so. This is not to imply that this writer is expressing a judgement on the matters under dispute, it is merely to assert that it is necessary to understand what the dispute is about.

The fact is that Soviet psychology is in dispute with *all* the tendencies represented. It adopts a fundamentalist position *vis-à-vis* other schools. To start with, 'mentalism' is rejected in its entirety as being anti-scientific in practice and basically erroneous in theory. It is anti-scientific by virtue of an inherent *idealism* (which assumes an independent, autonomous existence for 'mind') or by virtue of some kind of psychophysical *dualism* (which persists in giving some kind of limited autonomy to 'mind'). Contemporary mentalistic psychologies, the varieties of which are too numerous to mention, tend to eschew theory. They assume an eclectic posture. This is, of course, an anti-theoretical position. It is very fashionable, especially in America. Eclecticism is regarded by Soviet psychologists as an attempt to maintain all the comforts of unreason whilst claiming the status and prestige of intellectuals. Semantically speaking, Soviet psychologists translate 'eclectic' as meaning 'unprincipled.'

For different reasons most of the varieties of behaviourism are rejected by Soviet psychologists as presenting too simplistic a view of human behaviour. Speech and thinking, as activities closely associated with the central nervous system, are the areas where the dispute is centred. The influence of human history and human society on the forms, and even the process of thought, are emphasized as the missing elements in the non-Soviet approach to these problems.

Having said all this, so to speak from *inside* Soviet psychology, the question must be asked as to what is lacking, or defective, in this school.

Fig. 4   Mentalistic psychologies: time chart

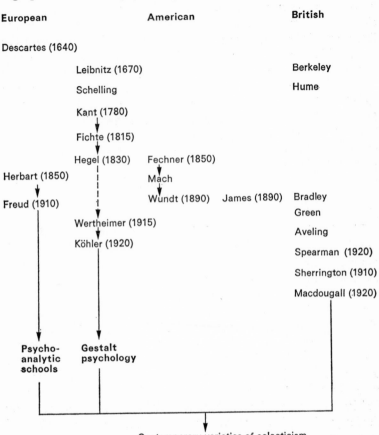

Contemporary varieties of eclecticism

From the point of view of Western psychology, the major deficiency of Soviet psychology lies in its theoretical exclusiveness and intolerance of alternative views. The major emphasis in the Soviet system, in every area of its functioning, is on *consensus*. The collective decision has an overriding authority. The correct response to truth as declared by the State power, speaking on behalf of the community, is submission. Individual or minority views opposed to the collective perception have to be reassessed with a view to changing them. The individual dissident, whether his disagreement is intellectual, moral, or practical, is expected to conform to the declared consensus. Persuasion is used in the first instance, but violence is not ruled out. This is clear from the history

Fig. 5 Radical behaviourist lineages: time chart

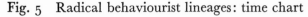

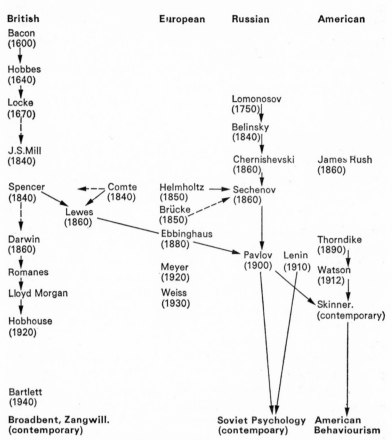

of psychology in the USSR. The ultimate criterion of truth is social utility – but not in the narrow sense of the immediate polical present reality. In spite of Western commentaries on Soviet discussions to the contrary, narrow factional struggles within the Soviet Communist Party (CPSU) have very little effect on Soviet intellectual life. There is a broad movement of thought which is guided in a general direction by Party policies. But, with one or two exceptions (the cases of Lysenko and Marr are flagrant violations of this generalization) there is no day-to-day, detailed direction of intellectual work. Nor is the direction in the hands of a handful of political desperadoes. The future must be safeguarded in the present: this implies that social utility must recognize: (i) the primacy of the objective reality over subjective evaluations; (ii) the ultimate victory of truth over error; (iii) the need for action to change events. Taken together with other principles, these recognitions add up to something very similar to the scientific approach, as this is understood everywhere.

However, the Leninist conception of society, of truth, and of intellectual work results in the short run in the persecution of minority and individualistic views. The conviction that a particular group is the custodian of a body of declared truths to which all must pay allegiance inevitably generates discrimination and violence against dissenters. This has been the case throughout history. It is true of the history of the Soviet State, as it is of the history of Soviet psychology. In defence of many private injustices and public policies, one can point to the 'cordon sanitaire' set up by the Allied powers in 1918, to the 'Cold War' generated for similar purposes by the same groups in 1945, to the siege conditions which have beset the Soviet State since its inception. But having said everything one can in mitigation of the crimes committed by the State against individuals and against large communities, the fact remains that Soviet intellectuals have paid a heavy price in loss of occupation, exile, material suffering, and death itself for the maintenance of this monolithic system of State power and ideas. There is no need to underline the similarities between the present régime and the arbitrary bureaucratic behaviours and thought processes under the Tsars. These have no doubt suggested themselves to the reader at the appropriate points in the foregoing narrative. 'Orthodoxy, autocracy, and national character' was the slogan which aptly described the demands made on intellectuals under the Tsars. The words have changed their meaning – the content is different as a result of the Revolution. But the slogan still characterizes those features of the régime which give concern even to sympathetic observers.

Bibliography

(English translations, where available are shown in brackets)

Airopetyants, E. and Bykow, K. M. (1945) Physiological Experiments and the Psychology of the Subconscious. *Journal Phenomenol. Research* **5**: 577–593.

Alekseev, N. A. (ed.) 1939 *Protsess N. G. Chernyshkevskogo, arkhyvnye dokumenty.* Saratov: Ogiz.

Aluf, A. (1932) *The Development of Socialist Methods and Forms of Labour.* Moscow: Foreign Workers Pub. Soc.

Amlinsky, I. E. (ed.) (1950) *Nauchnaya sessiya posvyashchennaia problemam fiziologicheskogo ucheniya Akad. I. P. Pavlova* (*Scientific session dedicated to the problems of the physiological teaching of Acad. I. P. Pavlov*). Moscow: Akad. Nauk SSSR.

Ananiev, B. G. (1948) *Uspekhi Sovetskoi Psikhologii.* Leningrad: Lenizdat.

Anan'ev, B. G. *et al.* (1959–1960) *Psikhologicheskaya Nauka v SSSR* (The Science of Psychology in the USSR) Moscow: Acad. Ped. Sci. (2 vols.).

Anan'ev, B. G. *et al.* (eds.) (1955) *Materialy Soveshchaniya po Psikhologii.* Moscow: Acad. Ped. Sci.

Anan'ev, B. G. and Lomov, B. F. (eds.) (1961) *Problemy Vospriyatiya Prostranstva i Prostranstvennykh Predstavlenii* Moscow: Acad. Ped. Sci.

Andreev, B. S. (1959) *Lechenie snom pri nevrozakh* Leningrad. Translated by B. Haigh as *Sleep Therapy in the Neuroses* (1960) New York: Consultants Bureau.

Anokhin, P. K. and Strij, E. (1934) The Study of the Dynamics of the Higher Nervous Activity *Fiziol. Zh. USSR* **17**: 1225–1237. (*Psych. Abst.* (1935) **9**: 3629).

Anokhin, P. K., in O'Connor, N. (ed.) (1961) *Recent Soviet Psychology* New York: Liveright.

Anokhin, P. K. (1966) New Aspects of the Study of the Work of the Brain. *Revue Roumaine de Neurologie* **3**: 7–14.

Anokhin, P. K. (1967) Brain Research *Soviet Psychology* **5**: 14–23 (*Am. Psychologist* **17**: 155–56).

Anon. (Spielrein, I. N.) (1930) Industrial Psychology in Russia. *J. Nat. Inst. Ind. Ps.* **5**: 221–222.

Antonov, N. P. (1953) Dialectical Materialism – the Theoretical Basis of Psychology (in Russian) *Voprosy Filosofii* **6**.

Antsiferova, L. I. (1956) Neobehavioristic Theory and Jean Piaget's Concept of Operations (in Russian) *Voprosy Psikhologii* **2**: 165–172.

Arkhangel'skii, S. N., Endovitskaya, E. T., and Neverovich, Ya.Z. (1958) *Naglyadnye Posobiya i Opyty v Kurse Psikhologii* Moscow: Uchpedizdat.

Artemov, V. A. (1942) Twenty-five Years of Soviet Psychology (in Russian) *Sovetskaya Pedagogika* **6**: 24–30.

Asratyan, E. A. (1955) Switching in Conditioned Reflex Activity as a Basic Form of its Changeability (in Russian) *Voprosy Psikhologii* **1**: 49–57.

Astrup, C. (1962) *Schizophrenia: Conditional Reflex Studies* Springfield, Ill.: Thomas.

Babkin, B. P. (1938) Experimental Neuroses in Animals and their Treatment by Bromides *Edin. Med Jour.* **45**: 605–619.

Babkin, B. P. (1946) Sechenov and Pavlov *Russian Rev.* **5**: 24–35.

Banshchikov, V. M. and Rapaport, A. M. (1951) Therapy in Psychiatric Hospitals of the USSR (in Russian) *Nevropatologiya i Psikhiyatriya* **20**: 32–47.

Basov, L. *Psychology, Reflexology and Physiology* (in Russian) Leningrad: Inst. Sc. Pedagogics.

Bassin, F. V. (1960) A Critical Analysis of Freudianism; Rejoinder to Professor Musatti *Soviet Review* **1**: 3–13, 27–44.

Bauer, R. A. (ed.) (1962) *Some Views on Soviet Psychology* New York: American Psychological Association.

Bekhterev, V. M. (1927) Vladimir Bekhterev *Die Med. der Gegenwart* 1–52.

Bekhterev, V. M. (1918) *General Principles of Human Reflexology* London: Jarrolds.

Bekhterev, V. M. (1908) Die objective Untersuchung der neuropsychischen Tätigkeit *Cong. Int. Psychiat. Neurol.*, Amsterdam, 20–27.

Bekhterev, V. M. (1913) Sur la Psycho-réflexologie, ou Psychologie objective *Arch. Internat. Neurol.* **1**: 273–287.

Bekhterev, V. M. (1924) Die Ergebnisse des Experiments auf dem Gebiete der Kollektiven Reflexologie *Zscht. f. angew. Psychol* **24**: 305–354.

Bekhterev, V. M. (1915) La Localisation des psycho-réflexes dans l'écorce cerebrale. *Scient.*, 20, 444–457.

Bekhterev, V. M. (1913) Qu'est ce que la psycho-réflexologie? *Arch. Internat. Neurol* **2**: 76–92.

Bekhterev, V. M. (1912) Über die Hauptäusserungen der neuropsychischen Tätigkeit der objektive Studium derselben (Zur Psycho-reflexologie) *Zsch. f. Psych* **60**: 280–301.

Bekhterev, V. M. *Conduction Paths of the Brain and Spinal Cord* Russian ed. 1888 Saint Petersburg; German ed. 1900 Berlin; French ed. 1900 Lyons.

Bekhterev, V. M. (1903–7) *Bases of the Teaching Concerning the Functions of the Brain* (Russian) Saint Petersburg.

Bekhterev, V. M. *Psychic Activity and Life* Russian ed. 1904 St. Petersburg; French ed. 1907 Paris; German ed. 1909 Wiesbaden.

Bekhterev, V. M. *General Principles of Human Reflexology* Russian ed. 1918 St. Petersburg; English ed. 1933 London: Jarrolds.

Bekhterev, V. M. (1921) *Collective Reflexology* (Russian) Petrograd.

Bekhterev, V. M. (1925) *Psychology, Reflexology and Marxism* (Russian) Leningrad.

Belik, A. P. (1961) *Estetika Chernyshevkogo* Moscow: Vysshaya shkolay Publishing House.

Belinsky, V. G. (1948) *Selected Philosophical Works* Moscow: Foreign Languages Pub. House.

Belinsky, V. G. (1948–51) *Sochineniya* (3 vols.) Moscow: Izd. Akad. Nauk SSSR.

Bel'chikow, Yu. A. (1962) *Obshchestvenno-politicheskaia lektsiya V. G. Belinskogo* Moscow University Publishing House.

Berdyaev, N. (1948) *The Russian Idea* London: G. Bles.

Bereday, G. Z. F. *et al.* (1960) *The Changing Soviet School* Cambridge, Mass.: Riverside Press.

Bereday, G. Z. F., Penna, J. (eds.) (1960) *The Politics of Soviet Education* New York: Fredrick A. Praeger, Pub.

Beritashvili, J. S. (Beritov, J. S.) (1961) *Uchenie o prirode cheloveka u drevnei Gruzii* (IV-XIV vv.) Tbilisi, Georgia, USSR: Univ. of Tiflis.

Beritashvili, J. S. (1951) Decree of the Scientific Council on the Work of Beritashvili (Beritov) (in Russian). *Zhurnal Vysshei Nervnoi Deyatel 'nosti* **1**: 145.

Beritov, J. S. (1924) On the Fundamental Processes of the Cortex of the Cerebral Hemispheres. *Brain* **47**: 109–148; 358–376.

eritoff, J. S. (1935) Studies on the Individual Behavior of Dogs *J. Psysiol. USSR* (English ed.) **19**: 47–55.

Beritov, J. S. (1927) Über die individuell-ergebene Tätigkeit des Central-nervensystems. *J. Psychol. Neurol.* (Leipzig) **33**: 113–335.

Berlyne, D. E. (1963) Psychology in the USSR *Canadian Psychologist* **4**: 1–13.

276 SOVIET PSYCHOLOGY: HISTORY, THEORY, CONTENT

Berman, H. J. and Hunt, D. H. (1950) Criminal Law and Psychiatry: The Soviet Solution. *Stanford Law Review* **2**: 635–663.

Bervi-Kaidanova *An Historical Outline of Russian Education* (MS copy n.d.) University of Alberta Education Library (3 vols.).

Baron, H. (1963) *Plekhanov: The father of Russian Marxism.* Stanford University Press.

Biryukov, D. A. (1953) Some Problems of the Comparative Physiology and Pathology of the Higher Nervous Activity (in French) *Raison* **7**: 33–37.

Blakeley, T. J. (1962) *Soviet Philosophy.* Dordrecht, Holland: D. Reidel Publishing Co.

Blakeley, T. J. (1964) *Soviet Theory of Knowledge* Dordrecht, Holland: D. Reidel Publishing Co.

Bochenski, J. M. and Blakeley, T. J. (eds.) (1961) *Studies in Soviet Thought* Dordrecht, Holland: D. Reidel Publishing Co.

Bogoslovskii, N. V. (1957) *Nikolai Gavrilovich Chernyshevskii 1828–1889* Moscow: Young Guard Publishers.

Bogoyavlenskii, D. N. and Menchinskaya, N. A. (1959) *Psikhologiya Usvoeniya Znanii v Shkole* Moscow: Acad. Ped. Sci.

Boiko, E. I. (ed.) (1961) *Studies in Higher Neurodynamics as Related to Problems of Psychology* Washington: Office Tech. Serv. (MS translation).

Borovski, V. M. (1929) Psychology in the USSR *J. Gen. Ps.* **2**: 177–186.

Bowditch, H. P. and Warren, J. W. (1890) The Knee-Jerk and its Physiological Modifications *J. Physiol.* **11**: 25–64.

Bowen, J. (1962) *Soviet Education: Anton Makarenko and the Years of Experiment* Madison: Univ. Wisconsin Press.

Bowman, H. E. (1954) *Vissarion Belinski; A Study in the Origins of Social Criticism in Russia* Cambridge, Mass.: Harvard Univ. Press.

Brackhill, Y. (1960) Experimental Research with Children in the Soviet Union: Report of a Visit. *Am. Psychologist* **15**: 226–33.

Brazier, Mary (1951) *Electrical Activity of the Nervous System* London: Pitman.

Brazier, Mary (ed.) (1961) *Brain and Behavior* (vol. 1) Washington: Am. Institute Biol. Science.

Bronfenbrenner, U. (1962) Soviet Methods of Character Education: Some Implications for Research. *Am. Psychologist* **17**: 550–65.

Bronfenbrenner, U. (1970) *Two Worlds of Childhood: U.S. and U.S.S.R.* New York: Basic Books.

Brožek, J. (1963) Contemporary Psychology in the Soviet Union: Some General Characteristics and Selected Areas of Research, in Marx, M. H. and Hillix, W. A. (eds.) *Systems and Theories in Psychology* New York, N.Y.: McGraw-Hill Book Co. 438–455.

Brožek, J. (1962) Current Status of Psychology in the U.S.S.R. *Annual Review of Psychology* **13**: 515–66.

Brožek, J. (1964) Recent Developments in Soviet Psychology. *Annual Review of Psychology* **15**: 493–594.

Brožek, J. (ed.) (1971) *Selected Aspects of Contemporary Psychology in the USSR: A Symposium* (Monogr. Soviet Med. Sciences). New York: Fordham Univ. Press.

Bykov, K. M. (1935) Studies in the Physiology of Digestion of Man. *J. Physiol. USSR* (English ed.) **19**: 63–80.

Bykov, K. M. (1947) *Novoe v uchenie Pavlova o vysshei nervnoi de 'yatelnosti* Moscow: Pravda Publishers.

Bykov, K. M. (1953) New Data on the Physiology and Pathology of the Cortex (in French). *Raison* **7**: 5–32.

Bykov, K. M. (1954) *The Cerebral Cortex and the Internal Organs* (translated from the 3rd Russian edition) Moscow: Foreign Languages Publication House (1959).

Bykov, K. M. (ed.) (1958) *Textbook of Physiology* Moscow: Foreign Languages Pub. House.

Chernakov, E. T. (1948) Against Idealism and Metaphysics in Psychology (in Russian). *Voprosy Filosofii* **3**: 301–315.

Chernishevski, N. G. (1953) *Selected Philosophical Works* Moscow: Foreign Languages Pub. House.

Chernishevski, N. G. (1939–1953) *Polnoe Sobranie Sochineniya* (16 vols.) Moscow: Culture and Literature Pub. House.

Clardy, J. V. (1965) *The Philosophical Ideas of Alexander Radishchev* London: Vision P.

Counts, G. S. (1957) *The Challenge of Soviet Education* N.Y.: McGraw-Hill.

Dairi, N. G. (1963–4) New Techniques for Checking Knowledge. *Soviet Education* **6** (3): 42–54.

Davidenkov, S. N. (1939) Nevrozy. *Bolshaya Sovetskaya Entsiklopedia* **41**: 444.

Davidenkov, S. N. (1963) Nevrozy. Leningrad: State Publishing House for Medical Literature.

Deineko, M. (1963) *Public Education in the USSR* Moscow: Progress Publishers.

DeGeorge, R. T. (1966) *Patterns of Soviet Thought*. Univ. Michigan Press.

Delafresnaye, J. F. (ed.) (1961) *Brain Mechanisms and Learning: A Symposium* Oxford: Blackwell Sci. Publ.

DeWitt, N. (1961) *Education and Professional Training in the USSR*. Washington, DC: US Government Printing Office.

Dicks, H. V. (1952) Observations on Contemporary Russian Behavior. *Human Relations* **5**: 111–175.

Diserens, C. M. (1925) Psychological Objectivism. *Psychol. Review* **32**: 121–152.

Dmitryev, A. A. and Kochigine, A. M. (1955) The Importance of Time as Stimulus of Conditioned Reflex Activity. *Psych. Bull.* **56**: 106–32.

Dobrolyubov, N. A. (1934–1939) *Polnoye Sobranie Sochineniya* (9 vols.) Moscow: Culture and Literature Publ. House.

Dobrolyubov, N. A. (1948) *Selected Philosophical Essays* Moscow: Foreign Languages Publ. House.

Drabovitch, W. (1935) Freud et Pavlov. *Évolution psychiatrique* 21–35.

Dunn, L. M. and Kirk, S. A. (1963) Impressions of Soviet Psycho-educational Service and Research in Mental Retardation. *Exceptional Children* **29**: 299–311.

Edelstein, P. (1948) Conference of Physiologists and Psychiatrists (in Russian). *Nevropat. i Psikhiatrya* **17**: (2).

Efimov, W. W. and Tschernomordik, O. S. (1931) Zur Berufskunde des Rationalisators. *Ind. Psychotechnic* **8**: 338–344.

Eliasberg, L. (1932) Bericht Ueber den Internationalen Kongress fuer Psychotechnik. *Psychotechn. Zeitschrift* 18–24.

El'konin, D. B. (1960) *Detskaya Psikhologiya* Moscow: Uchpedgiz.

Engels, F. (n.d.) *Ludwig Feuerbach and the Outcome of Classical German Philosophy* London: Lawrence and Wishart.

Engels, F. (1955) *The Dialectics of Nature* London: Lawrence and Wishart.

Esipov, B. P. (1961) *Samodeyatel'naya rabota uchashchikhsya v protsesse obucheniya* Moscow: Izvestiya Acad. Ped. Sci.

Evgeniev, B. (1949) *Aleksander Nikolaevich Radishchev, 1749–1802.* Moscow: Young Guard Publ. House.

Fearing, F. (1930) *Reflex Action: A Study in the History of Physiological Psychology* Baltimore: William and Wilkins.

Feuer, L. S. (ed.) (1959) *Marx and Engels: Basic Writings on Politics and Philosophy* N.Y.: Doubleday Anchor.

Filosofskaya Entsiklopedia (1964) (3 vols.) Moscow: Institute of Philosophy.

Fink, Y. (1954) I. P. Pavlov and Scientific Psychology (in Russian) *Ofakim* **8**: 157–171.

Fitzpatrick, W. H. and Delong, C. W. (1961) *Soviet Medical Research Related to Human Stress: A Review of the Literature* Washington: U.S. Public Health Service Publishers.

Florovsky, G. (1937) *Puti Russkovo Bogoslaviya* Paris: YMCA Press.

Fol'bort, G. V. (ed.) (1960) *Problems of the Physiology of the Processes of Fatigue and Recovery* Washington: Office Tech. Serv.

Foley, J. P. (1933) The Cortical Interpretation of Conditioning. *J. Gen. Ps.* **9**: 228–232.

French, T. M. (1933) Interrelations between Psychoanalysis and the Experimental Work of Pavlov. *Amer. J. Psychiatry,* **89**: 1165–1203.

Friede, B. (1936) La Psychotechnique en URSS. *Monde* (304).

Fulton, J. F. (1949) *Physiology of the Nervous System* Oxford Univ. Press.

Galperin, P. I. (1966) The Method of 'Sections' and the Formation of Mental Actions by Stages in the Investigation of Children's Thinking (in Russian). *Voprosy Psikhologii* **11**: 128–135.

Gantt, W. H. (1958) *Physiological Bases of Psychiatry.* Springfield, Ill.: Thomas.

Gantt, W. H. (1960) Pavlov and Darwin, in S. Tax (ed.) *Evolution after Darwin* **2**: 219–38. Chicago: University of Chicago Press.

Gerasimow, W. P. (1954) The Essence of Pavlov's Teaching (in German), in *Zur Psychologie des Vorschulalters* Berlin: Volk & Wissen.

Gindikin, V. I. (1962) A Contribution to the Investigation of Certain Factors making for the Appearance of Psychopathic Conditions. *Soviet Psychology and Psychiatry* **1** (1): 42–50.

Gilyarovski, V. A. (1942) *Psychiatry* (in Russian) Moscow: Medgiz.

Gilyarovski, V. A. (1961) Chapter on Soviet Union, in L. Bellak *Contemporary European Psychiatry* New York: Grove Press.

Giorgini, R. (1935) Considerazione sulle teoria dei reflessi condizionati. *Riv. Neurol.* **8**: 262–292.

Glinka, M. E. (1961) *M. V. Lomonosov* (in Russian) Moscow-Leningrad: Acad. Sciences Pub. House.

Gordon, W. W. (1951) The Pavlov Conference. *Soviet Studies* **3**: 34–59.

Graborov, A. H. (1961) *Ocherki po oligofrene pedagogiki* Moscow: Uchpediz.

Grashchenkov, N. I. and Shmaryan, A. S. (1947) Thirty Years of Soviet Neurology and Psychiatry (in Russian). *Nevropatologiya i psikhiatriya* **16** (5): 3–18.

Grashchenkov, N. I. (1949) K stoletiyu so dnya rozhdeniya I. P. Pavlova. *Nevropatologiya i Psikhiyatriya* **18**: 3–23.

Grybek, I. A. (1954) Investigation of the Interaction of the First and Second Signal Systems employing the Method of a Laboratory (Artificial, Experimental, Unknown) Language (in Russian). *Zh. vyssh. nervn. Deiatel'nosti.* **4**: 457–464.

Gurevich, B. H. (1959) Cybernetics and Certain Modern Problems of the Physiology of the Nervous System. *J. Nervous and Mental Diseases* **128**: 169–78.

Gul'yanov, E. V. (1959) *Psikhologiya obusheniya pis'mu* Moscow: Acad. Ped. Sci.

Guthrie, E. R. (1934) Pavlov's Theory of Conditioning. *Psychol. Review* **41**: 199–206.

Gvozdev, A. N. (1961) *Voprosy izucheniya detskoi rechi* Moscow: RSFSR Acad. Sciences.

Hamel, I. A. (1919) A Study and Analysis of the Conditioned Reflex. *Psychol. Monogr.* **27** (118): 1–65.
Hanfmann, Eugenia (1953) Concept Formation Test, in A. Weider (ed.) *Contributions Toward Medical Psychology: Theory and Psychodiagnostic Methods* **2**: 731–40. New York: Ronald Press Co.
Hanfmann, Eugenia and Kasanin, J. (1942) Conceptual Thinking in Schizophrenia (Monogr. 67). New York: Nervous and Mental Disease Monographs.
Hans, N. (1963) *The Russian Tradition in Education* London: Routledge and Kegan Paul.
Hecker, J. (1933) *Moscow Dialogues* London: Chapman and Hall.
Hecker, J. (1934) *Russian Sociology* London: Chapman and Hall.
Haumant, E. (1913) *La Culture Française en Russie*: 1700–1900 (2nd ed.) Paris: Hachette.
Hecht, D. (1947) *Russian Radicals Look to America*: 1825–1894 Cambridge, Mass.: Harvard Univ. Press.
Hertzen, A. (1956) *Selected Philosophical Works* Moscow: Foreign Languages Pub. House.
Hertzen, A. (1954) *Polnoe Sobraniya Sochineniya* (30 vols.) Moscow: Acad. Sciences Pub. House.
Hertzen, A. (1968) *My Past and Thoughts* London: Chatto.
Hilgard, E. R. (1937) The Relationship between the Conditional Response and Conventional Learning Experiments. *Psych. Bull.* **34**: 61–102.
Hudson, P. S. and Richens, R. H. (1946) *The New Genetics in the Soviet Union* London: C'wealth Plant Breeding Institute.

Ignat'ev, E. I. (1960) *Psikhologiya mladshego shkol'nika* Moscow: Acad. Ped. Sci.
Ignat'ev, E. I. (ed.) (1960) *Voprosy Psikhologii Lichnosti* Moscow: Uchpedizdat.
Ignat'ev, E. T. (1965) *Psikhologiia* Moscow: Prosveshchenie.
Ischlondsky, N. E. (1930) *Neuropsyche und Hirninde* (2 vols.) Berlin: Urban und Schwarzenberg.
Ivanov, N. (1959) The Training of Soviet Engineers, in G. R. Kline (ed.) *Soviet Education* New York: Columbia University Press.
Ivanov-Smolensky, A. G. (1927) *Neurotic Behavior and the Teaching of Conditioned Reflexes. Am. J. Psychol.* **84**: 483–488.
Ivanov-Smolensky, A. G. (1927) *Etudes experimentales sur les enfants et les aliénes selon la methode des reflexes conditionels. Ann. med. psychol.* **12**: 140–150.
Ivanov-Smolensky, A. G. (1927) On the Methods of examining

Food Reflexes in Children and in Mental Disorders. *Brain* **50**: 138–141.

Ivanov-Smolensky, A. G. (1928) The Pathology of Conditioned Reflexes of the So-called Psychogenic Depression. *J. Nervous and Mental Diseases* **67**: 346–350.

Ivanov-Smolensky, A. G. (1935) Experimental Study of the Child's Higher Nervous Activity. *J. Physiology USSR* (English ed.) **19**: 149–155.

Izakson, I. (1932) For Propaganda for the Socialist Organization of Labour (in Russian). *Voprosy Truda* **7**: 59–64.

Jasper, H. M. and Smirnov, G. D. (1960) The Moscow Colloquium on Encephalography of Higher Nervous Activity. *Intern. J. Electroenceph. and Clin. Neurophysiol.* (Supplementary Volume) **13**.

Joravsky, D. (1966) Soviet Ideology. *Soviet Studies* **18** (1): 2–19.

Jordan, Z. A. (1963) *Philosophy and Ideology* Holland: D. Reidel Publishing Co.

Journals: *Unter dem Banner des Marxismus*
       Sovietskaya Pedagogika
       Soviet Psychology
       Soviet Psychiatry
       Soviet Education
       Current Digest of the Soviet Press

Jurinetz, W. (1925) Psychoanalyse und Marxismus. *Unter dem Banner des Marxismus.*

Jurovsky, Anton (1952) The Fundamental Problem of Contemporary Psychology (in Czech). *Psychol. Časopis* **1**: 17–28.

Kahane, E. (1966) *The Thought of Claude Bernard* New York: American Institute of Marxist Studies.

Kairov, I. A. (ed.) (1960) *Pedagogicheskii Slovar'* (2 vols.) Moscow: Acad. Ped. Sci.

Kalinowsky, L. B. (1960) Impressions of Soviet Psychiatry. *Comparative Psychiatry* **1**: 35–41.

Kasatkin, N. I. (1932) Pavlov's Theory of Schizophrenia. *Arch. Neurol. Psychiat.* **28**: 210–218.

Kasatkin, N. I. and Lurkova, A. M. (1935) On the Development of Conditioned Reflexes. *J. Exp. Ps.* **18**: 1–19.

Kassoff, Allen (ed.) (1966) *Prospects for Soviet Society* New York: Am. Council on Foreign Relations.

Kavetskii, R. E., Solodyuk, N. F., Vouk, S. I., Krasnogorskaya, M. S. and Dzoeva, T. A. (1961) *Reaktivnost' organizma i tip nervnoi sistemy* Kiev: Acad. Sciences, Ukr. SSR.

Keller, F. J. and Viteles, M. S. (1937) *Vocational Guidance Throughout the World* London: Jonathan Cape (chapter on S.U.).

King, J. (ed.) (1963) *Communist Education* London: Methuen.

Kitson, H. D. (1931) Report on the Seventh International Conference on Psychotechnique. *J. App. Psychol* **15**: 593–596.

Kline, N. S. (1960) The Organization of Psychiatric Care and Psychiatric Research in the Union of Soviet Socialist Republics. *Ann. N.Y. Acad. Sciences* **84**: 147–224.

Kline, G. L. (ed.) (1957) *Soviet Education* New York: Columbia University Press.

Kline, N. S. (ed.) (1961) *Pavlovian Conference on Higher Nervous Activity. Ann. N. Y. Acad. Sciences* **92**: 813–1198.

Kniazkov, S. A. and Sebrov, N. I. (1910) *Ocherk istorii narodnogo obrazovaniya v Rossii do epokhi reforma Aleksandra II* Moscow: Uchpedgiz.

Koch, S. (1959) *Psychology: A Study of Science* New York: McGraw-Hill.

Kohnstamm, G. A. (1967) Teaching Piagetian Thought Operations to Preoperational Children (in Russian). *Sovietskaya Pedagogika* (1): 33–35.

Kolbanowski, W. (1952) *The Psychology of Personality in Works of A. S. Makarenko* (in German). Berlin: Volk und Wissen.

Komm, A. G. (1957) The Problem of the Psychology of Intelligence in the Works of Jean Piaget. *Voprosy Psikhologii* **3** (1): 157–164.

Konorski, J. (1950) Mechanisms of Learning. *Symposia Soc. for Exp. Biology* Cambridge University Press IV: 409–431.

Konorski, J. and Miller, S. (1937) On Two Types of Conditioned Reflex. *J. Gen. Ps.* **16**: 264–272.

Konorski, J. and Miller, S. (1937) Further Remarks on Two Types of Conditioned Reflex. *J. Gen. Ps.* **17**: 405–407.

Konorski, J. and Miller, S. (1930) *Méthode d'examen de l'analyseur moteur par les réactions salivo-motrices*. Paris: CR Soc. Biol. **104**: 907–910.

Konstantinov, N. S. (ed.) (1952) *Ocherki po istorii pedagogiki: sbornik statyei* Moscow: Uchpedgiz.

Konstantinov, N. S. *et al.* (1956) *Istoriya pedagogiki* Moscow: Uchpedgiz.

Konstantinov, F. B. (1950) *The Role of Socialist Consciousness in the Development of Soviet Society* Moscow: Foreign Languages Pub. House.

Konstantinov, F. B. (ed.) (1960) *Filosofskaya Entsiklopediya* (2 vols.) Moscow: State Scientific Publishing House.

Korinskaya, V. A. and Pancheshnikova, L. M. (1964) Experiment in Creating Objective Measures for Evaluating the Knowledge, Skills and Habits of Pupils. *Soviet Education* **7** (2): 43–52.

Kornilov, K. N. (1930) Psychology in the Light of Dialectical Materialism in C. Murchison *Psychologies of 1930* Worcester, Mass.: Clark University Press. 243–278.

Kornilov, K. N., Smirnov, A. A. and Teplov, B. M. (1948) *Psikhologiya* Moscow: Uchpedgiz.

Kornilov, K. N. (1955) On the Tasks of Soviet Psychology (in Russian). *Voprosy Psikhologii* **1** (1): 16–28.

Kostyleff, N. (1910) Les Travaux de l'école de psychologie russe: Étude objective de la pensée. *Rev. Phil.* **70**: 483–507.

Kostyleff, N. (1914) Bechterew et le psychologe de demain *Rev. Phil.* **77**: 147–169.

Kostyleff, N. (1914) *Le méchanisme cerébrale de la pensée* Paris: Felix Alcan.

Kostyleff, N. (1947) *La réflexologie et les essais d'une psychologie structurale* Neuchatel: Delachaux et Niestlé.

Kostyuk, G. S. (1955) On the Question of the Lawful Principles of Psychology (in Russian). *Voprosy Psikhologii* **1**: 18–28.

Kostyuk, G. S. (ed.) Voprosy psikhologii usvoyeniya uchashchimsiya yazyka (in Ukrainian). Kiev: *Nauchnye Zapiski Research Inst. Psychol., Ukrainian SSR.*

Krasnogorski, N. I. (1908) Conditioned Reflexes in Children (in Russian). *Russ. Vrach* **37**: 930–932, 969–974.

Krasnogorski, N. I. (1909) Über die Bedingungsreflexe im Kindesalter *Jb. Kinderheilkunde* **69**: 1–24.

Krasnogorski, N. I. (1931) Über die Grundmechanismen der Arbeit der Grosshirnrinde bei Kindern. *Jb. Kinderheilkunde* **78**: 373–398.

Krasnogorski, N. I. (1923) Die Schlag und die Hemmung. *Monatsschrift. f. Kinderheilkunde* **25**: 372–386.

Krasnogorski, N. I. (1925) The Conditioned Reflex and Children's Neuroses. *Am. J. Dis. Child* **30**: 753–768.

Krasnogorski, N. I. (1930) Psychology and Psychopathology in Childhood as a Branch of Pediatric Investigation. *Acta Paediatr. Stockholm* **11**: 481–502.

Krasnogorski, N. I. (1933) Physiology of Cerebral Activity in Children as a New Subject of Pediatric Investigation. *Am. J. Dis. Child* **46**: 473–494.

Krasnogorski, N. I. (1958) *Higher Nervous Activity in the Child* (in Russian) Leningrad: Uchpedgiz.

Kreindler (1947) *Les Réflexes Conditionnels* Bucharest: Editions d'Etat.

Krushinskii, L. V. (1960) *Animal Behavior: Its Normal and Abnormal Development* (trans. B. Haigh from *Formirovanie povedeniya zhivotnykh v norme i patologii* Moscow). New York: Consultants Bureau, 1962.

Kubie, L. S. (1935) Über die Beziehung zwischen dem bedingten Reflex und der psychoanalytischen Technik. *Imago* **21**: 44–49.

Koupalov, P. (1949) Un Grand Savant Russe: I. P. Pavlov. *La Pensée* **27**: 42–58.

Kupalov, P. S. (ed.) (1949) *Lektsii I. P. Pavlova po fiziologii: 1912–1913 gg* Moscow: Acad. Sciences Pub. House.

Kupalov, P. S. (1954) Theory of Types of Higher Nervous Activity in Animals (in Russian). *Zh. vyssh. nervn. Deiatel' nosti* **4**: 3–19.

Lang, M. (1959) *The First Russian Radical: Alexander Radishchev* London:

Lashley, K. S. (1929) *Brain Mechanisms and Intelligence* Chicago: Univ. Press.

Lashley, K. S. (1930) Basic Neural Mechanisms in Behavior. *Psychol. Review* **37**: 1–24.

Laszlo, E. (1967) *Philosophy in the Soviet Union: A Survey of the Mid-sixties* N.Y.: Praeger.

Lebedev, A. A. (1962) *Geroi Chernyshevskogo* Moscow: Sovet. pisatel'.

Lavretsky, A. (1968) *Belinsky, Chernyshevsky i Dobroliubov v bor'be za realism* Moscow: Khudozhestvennaya Literatura.

Leff, G. (1961) *The Tyranny of Concepts* London: Merlin Press.

Lebedinsky, M. (1931) Two Congresses (in Russian). *Front Nauki i tekhniki* **10**: 67–71.

Leites, N. S., Razmyslov, P. I. and Redko, A. Z. (1955) Conference on Psychology in Montreal (in Russian) *Voprosy Psikhologii* **1**: 117–128.

Lektorsky, V. A. and Sadovsky, V. N. (1961) Basic Ideas of J. Piaget's 'Genetic Epistemology' (in Russian). *Voprosy Psikhologii* **1** (4): 167–178.

Lenin, V. I. (1941–1950) *Sochineniya* (4th edition, 35 volumes) Moscow: Marx-Lenin Institute.

Lenin, V. I. (1938) Dialectics (vol. 6) *Five Essays on Tolstoy* New York: Critics' Group.

Lenz, A. K. (1935) Les Réflexes conditionnels salivaires chez l'homme sain et aliénes et leur rapprochement avec les données de la conscience: Récherches experimentales. *Encephalon* **30**: 394–440.

Leontiev, A. N. (1949) The Most Important Tasks of Soviet Psychology (in Russian). *Sovietskaya Pedagogika* **1**: 76–85.

Leontiev, A. N. (ed.) (1954) *Doklady na soveshchanii po voprosam psikhologii* Moscow: Akad. Pedagog. Nauk RSFSR.

Leontiev, A. N. and Luria, A. R. (1957) The Fifteenth International Congress on Psychology (in Russian). *Voprosy Psikhologii* **3** (6): 146–158.

Leontiev, A. N. (ed.) (1958) *The Orienting Reflex* (in Russian) Moscow: Akad. Pedag. Nauk RSFSR.

Leontiev, A. N. and Zaporozhets, A. V. (1960) *Rehabilitation of Hand Function* (trans. B. Haigh) New York: Pergamon.

Leontiev, A. N. (1959) *Problemy Razvitiya Psikhiki* Moscow: Acad. Ped. Sci.

Leontiev, A. N. (1961) Intellectual Development of the Child, in

R. B. Winn (ed.) *Soviet Psychology: A Symposium* New York: Philosophical Library.

Leontiev, A. N. (1960) The Formation of Abilities *Problems of Psychology* **1** (1): 1–12 (English, ed. N. O'Connor).

Leontiev, A. N., Luriya, A. R. and Smirnov, A. A. (1966) *Psychological Research in the USSR* (2 vols.) Moscow: Progress Pub.

Letiche, J. M. (ed.) (1964) *A History of Russian Economic Thought* Berkeley, California: Univ. of California Press.

Levin, Deana (1964) *Soviet Education* New York: Monthly Review Press.

Leytes, N. S. (1962) Individual Differences in Aptitudes, in *Psychological Science in the USSR* **2**: 103–127 Washington D.C.: US Joint Publ. Res. Serv.

Liddell, H. S. (1934) *The Conditioned Reflex*, in F. A. Moss (ed.) *Comparative Psychology* N.Y.: Prentice Hall, 247–296.

Liddell, H. S. (1938) The Experimental Neurosis and the Problem of Mental Disorder. *Amer. J. Psychiatry* **94**: 1035–1043.

Linhart, J. (1951) *Pavlov's Teaching and Psychology* (in Czech). Prague: Osveta.

Linhart, J. (1953) Higher Nervous Activity of the Child, Part I of General Principles of the Higher Nervous Activity of Children (in Czech) Prague: Statni pedagogičke nakladatelstvi.

Linhart, J. (1954) Pavlov's Teaching and Pedagogical Disciplines (in Czech). *Psychol. Časopis* **2**: 3–13.

Lomov, B. F. (1961) The Sixteenth International Congress of Psychology (in Russian). *Voprosy Psikhologii* **7** (1): 171–180.

London, I. D. (1951) Contemporary Psychology in the Soviet Union *Science* **114**: 227–233.

London, I. D. (1952) The Scientific Council on Problems of the Physiological Theory of Academician I. P. Pavlov: A Study in Control. *Science* **116**: 23–27.

London, I. D. (1954) Research on Sensory Interaction in the Soviet Union. *Psych. Bull.* **51**: 531–568.

London, I. D. (1961) Psychiatry; Psychology, in M. T. Florinsky (ed.) *McGraw-Hill Encyclopedia of Russian and the Soviet Union* 461–64. New York: McGraw-Hill.

Loucks, R. B. (1933) An Appraisal of Pavlov's Systematisation of Behavior from the Experimental Standpoint. *J. Comp. Psych.* **15**: 1–47.

Loucks, R. B. (1937) Reflexology and the Psychobiological Approach *Psychol. Review* **44**: 320–328.

Lovibond, S. H. (1954) The Object Sorting Test and Conceptual Thinking in Schizophrenia *Austral. J. Psychol.* **6**: 52–70.

Lungwitz, H. (1931) Kritische Bemerkungen zur Reflexologie. *Psychiat. Neur. Woch.* **33**: 311–317.

Luria, A. R. (1928) Psychology in Russia *J. Genet Ps.* **35**: 347–355.

Luria, A. R. (1928) Die moderne Russische Psychologie und die Psychanalyse. *Int. Z. für Psychoanalyse* **12**: 40–53.

Luria, A. R. (1928) Die moderne Psychologie und der dialektische Materialismus. *Unter dem Banner des Marxismus.*

Luria, A. R. (1929) The Conjunctive Motor Method and its Application to Research in Affective Reaction (in Russian). *Proc. Moscow Inst. Expt. Ps.* **3**.

Luria, A. R. (1932) *The Nature of Human Conflict* N.Y.: Liveright.

Luria, A. R. (1932) The Crisis in Bourgeois Psychology. *Psikhologiya* **5**: 63–95.

Luria, A. R. (1961) *The Role of Speech in the Regulation of Normal and Abnormal Behaviour* N.Y.: Pergamon Press.

Luria, A. R. (1962) *Vysshie korkovye funkstii cheloveka i ikh narusheniya pri lokal'nykh porazheniyakh mozga* Moscow: Moscow University.

Luria, A. R. (1961) An Objective Approach to the Study of the Abnormal Child. *Am. J. Orthopsychiat* **31**: 1–16.

Luria, A. R. (1966) Brain and Mind. *Soviet Psychology and Psychiatry* **4**: 3–4, 62–69.

Luria, A. R. (1966) *Higher Cortical Functions in Man* (trans. B. Haigh) New York: Basic Books.

Luria, A. R. (1970) *Traumatic Aphasia: Psychology and Treatment* New York: Humanities Press.

Luria, A. R. and Yudovich, F. Ya. (1959 *Speech and the Development of Mental Processes in the Child* London: Staples Press.

Luria, A. R. and Vinogradova, O. S. (1959) An Objective Investigation of the Dynamics of Semantic Systems. *Brit. J. Psychol.* **50**: 89–105.

Luria, A. R. (1963) *The Mentally Retarded Child* Oxford: Pergamon Press.

Luria, A. R. (1970) *Rehabilitation of Brain Function after Brain Injury* New York: Pergamon Press.

Lustig, B. (1963) Therapeutic Methods in Soviet Medicine *Monogr. Soviet Med. Science* No. 3. New York: Fordham Univ.

Lynn, R. (1966) *Attention, Arousal and the Orientation Reaction* London: Pergamon Press.

Lynn, R. (1963) Russian Theory and Research on Schizophrenia. *Psych. Bull.* **60**: 486–98.

Maiorov, F. P. (1933) Complete Facts concerning Higher Nervous Physiology (in Russian). *Trud. Fiziol. Lab. Pavlova* **5**: 255–320.

Makarenko, A. S. (1954) *Kniga dlia roditelei* (*A Book for Parents*) Moscow: State Publishing House.

Makarenko, A. S. (1953) *Flagi na bashniakh* (*Learning to Live: Flags on the Battlements*) Moscow: State Publishing House.

Makarenko, A. S. (1957–1958) *Sochineniya* (7 vols.) Moscow: State Publishing House.

Maksimov, A. A. (ed.) (1953) *Filosofskie voprosy sovremennoi fiziki* Moscow: Akad. Nauk SSSR.

Mal'kova, M. (1962–63) In the Schools of America. *Soviet Education* **5** (1–2): 50–63.

Mansurov, N. S. (1965) Soviet Psychology and Pedagogical Science (in Russian). *Sovietskaya Pedagogika* 9.

Manuilenko, S. W. (1954) Pavlov's Theory of Two Signal Systems and their Significance for the Rearing of Children in the Pre-school Age (in German). *Zur Psychologie des Vorschulalters* Berlin: Volk & Wissen.

Marinesco, G. and Kreindler, A. (1933) Des Réflexes Conditionels. *J. de Psychol.* **30**: 855–886.

Marinesco, G. and Kreindler, A. (1934) Rapports des Réflexes conditionels avec l'évolution biologique du névrose et des endocrines. *J. de Psychol.* **31**: 206–272.

Marinesco, G. and Kreindler, A. (1935) *Des Réflexes conditionnels, études de physiologie normale et pathologique* Paris: Alcan.

Marx, K. and Engels, F. (1964–66) *Werke* (39 vols.) Berlin: Dietz-verlag.

Marx, K. and Engels, F. (1947) *The German Ideology* New York: International Publishers.

Mateer, F. (1918) *Child Behavior: a Critical and Experimental Study of Young Children by the Method of Conditioned Reflexes* Boston: Badger.

Matiushkin, A. M. and Sokhin, F. A. (1963) All-Union Conference on Philosophical Problems of the Physiology of Higher Nervous Activities and Psychology. *Soviet Psychology and Psychiatry* **1**: 3–13.

Mazmanyan, M. A. (ed.) (1960) Proceedings of the Second Trans-causasian Conference of Psychologists. *Voprosy Psikhologii.*

Mazour, A. G. (1937) *The First Russian Revolution, 1825: the Decembrist Movement, its Origins, Development and Significance.* Berkeley: University of California Press.

Medynski, E. N. (1936) *Istoriya Russkoi Pedagogiki* Moscow: Uchpedgiz.

Menchinskaya, N. A. (1962) Problem-solving Studies, in *Clinical Psychology* (Proc. Fourteenth Intern. Congr. Appl. Psychol., Munksgaard, Copenhagen) **4**: 140–53.

Menshutkin, B. N. (1952) *Russia's Lomonosov.* Princeton, N.J.: Princeton Univ. Press.

Merkulov, V. L. (1960) *Aleksei Alekseevich Ukhtomskii* (1875–1942) Moscow-Leningrad: USSR Acad. Sci.

Miller, Eleanor O. (1965) New Use for the Vigotsky Blocks. *J. Clin. Psychol.* **11**: 87–89.

Mintz, A. (1958) Recent Developments in Psychology in the USSR. *Ann. Rev. Psychol.* **9**: 453–504.

Mintz, A. (1959) Further Developments in Psychology in the USSR. *Ann. Rev. Psychol.* **10**: 455–87.

Mokhov, F. (1933) *The Protection of Labour in the U.S.S.R.* Moscow-Leningrad: Co-op. Soc. For. Workers in the USSR.

Morkovin, B. V. (1961) Mechanisms of Compensation for Hearing Loss: Theories and Research in the Soviet Union. *J. Speech Hearing Disorders* **26**: 359–67.

Murray, H. A., May, M. A. and Cantril, H. (1959) Some Glimpses of Soviet Psychology. *Am. Psychologist* **14**: 303–7.

Murray, H. A. (1960) Historical Trends in Personality Research, chapter 1 in H. P. David and J. C. Brengelmann *Perspectives in Personality Research* New York: Springer.

Musatti, C. L. (1960) An Answer to F. V. Bassin's Criticism of Freudianism. *Soviet Review* **1**: 14–27.

McFarland, R. A. (1935) Psychological Research in Soviet Russia. *Scientific Monthly* (N.Y.) **40**: 177–181.

McLeish, J. L. (ed.) (1955) *Soviet Education Bulletin* London: SCR (duplicated).

McLeish, J. (1952) Foundations of Soviet and Western Psychiatry: A Review of Recent Literature. *Anglo-Soviet Journal* **13**: 17–21.

McLeish, J. (1950) Aspects of Soviet and American Psychology *Soviet Studies* **1**: 343–346.

McLeish, J. (1951) Psychology in the Soviet Union *Quarterly Bulletin British Psychological Society* **12**: 47–52.

Papernova, B. (1933) Women in Socialist Construction on Equal Terms with Men. *Soviet Culture Review* **2**: 25–33.

Parmigiani, P. (1953) Particular Aspects of Sleep Cure in Russian Psychiatric Literature (in Italian – English summary). *Neurone* **2**: 49–56.

Parsons, H. L. (1964) Value and Mental Health in the Thought of Marx. *Phil. and Phenom. Res.*, **24** (3) 355–365.

Pavlov, I. P. (1951) *Polnoe Sobranie Sochinenii.* Acad. Sci., USSR, Moscow, 5 vols.

Pavlov, I. P. (1927) *Conditioned Reflexes.* Oxford University Press, London.

Pavlov, I. P. (1928) *Lectures on Conditioned Reflexes.* International Publishers, N.Y., vol. **2** (1941).

Pavlov, I. P. (1930) A Brief Outline of the Higher Nervous Activity. in C. Murchison: *Psychologies of 1930*, pp. 207–220. Clark Univ. Press, Worcester, Mass.

Pavlov, I. P. (1955) *Selected Works* (English edition). Moscow: Foreign Languages Pub. House.

Pavlov, I. P. (1960) *Conditioned Reflexes: An Investigation of the Physiological Activity of the Cerebral Cortex* (trans. G. V. Anrep) New York, N.Y.: Dover Publications.

Pavlov, I. P. (1961) *Psychopathology and Psychiatry: Selected Works* Moscow: Foreign Languages Pub. House.

Payne, T. R. (1966) On the Theoretical Foundations of Soviet Psychology. *Studies in Soviet Thought* **6** (2): 124–134.

Perepel, E. (1939) The Psychoanalytic Movement in the USSR. *Psychoanalytic Review* **26**: 299–300.

Perevalova, L. A. (1964) *Pedagogicheshie vzglady M. V. Lomonosova* Moscow: Izdat. Prosv.

Petrushevskii, S. A. (1951) Pavlov's Teaching and the Marxist–Leninist Theory of Reflection (in Russian). *Voprosy dialekticheskogo materializma* **3**: 296–327.

Pevzner, M. S. (1961) *Oligophrenia: Mental Deficiency in Children* (English trans.) New York: Consultants Bureau.

Piaget, J. (1956) Basic Problems of Genetic Epistemology (in Russian). *Voprosy Psikhologii* **2** (3): 30–47.

Piaget, J. (1962) *Comments on Vygotsky's Critical Remarks* Cambridge, Mass.: M.I.T. Press.

Pick, H. L. (Jr.) (1961) Research on Taste in the Soviet Union in M. R. Kare and B. P. Halpern (eds.) *The Psychological and Behavioral Aspects of Taste* 117–26. Chicago: Univ. Chicago Press.

Pinskii, B. I. (1962) *Psikhologicheskie osobennosti deyatel'nosti umstvenno otstalykh skol'nikov* Moscow: RSFSR Acad. Ped. Sci.

Pipes, R. (1966) *Karamzin's Memoir on Ancient and Modern Russia. A Translation and Analysis.* New York: Atheneum.

Pirogov, N. I. (1941) *Sochineniya* Leningrad: Uchpedgiz.

Plekhanov, G. V. (1938) *Sochineniya, History of Russian Social Thought* Moscow: State Publishing House, vols. 20, 21, 22 (ed. David Ryazanov).

Plekhanov, G. V. (1934) *Essays in the History of Materialism* (trans. Ralph Fox) London: John Lane.

Plekhanov, G. V. (1969) *Fundamental Problems of Marxism* New York: International Publishers.

Plekhanov, G. V. (1946) *Beitrage zur Geschichte des Materialismus: Holbach, Helvetius, Marx* Berlin: Verlag Neuer Weg.

Plekhanov, G. V. (1959) *Izbrannye filosofskie proizvedeniya* (5 vols.) Moscow: Ogiz.

Plekhanov, G. V. (1958) *Literatura i estetika* Moscow: Gos. izd-vo Khudozk-lit-ry.

Plekhanov, G. V. (1957) *O religii i tserkvi; izbrannye proizvedeniya* Moscow: Izd-vo Akademii nauk SSSR.

Plekhanov, G. V. (1956) *The Development of the Monist View of History* Moscow: Foreign Language Pub. House.

Poliansky, F. Ia. (1965) *Plekhanov i russkaya ekonomicheskaya mysl.* Moscow: Izd-vo Moskovskogo Universiteta.

Pobyedonostsev, K. P. (1960) *Psikhologiya tvorcheskogo myshleniya* Moscow: Acad. Ped. Sci.

Prangishvili, A. S. (1962) General Psychological Theory of Set, in

Psychological Science in the USSR **2**: 179–199. Washington: Office Tech. Serv.

Ramul, K. A. (1958) *Demonstratsionnyie Opyty po Psikhologii* Tartu State University, Tartu, Estonian SSR.

Radishchev, A. N. (1949) *Izbrannyie Sochineniya* Moscow: Acad. Sci.

Randall, F. B. (1967) *N. G. Chernyshevskii* New York: Twayne Publishers.

Razran, G. H. S. (1930) Theory of Conditioning and Related Phenomena. *Psychol. Review* **37**: 25–43.

Razran, G. H. S. (1933) Conditioned Responses in Animals other than Dogs: A Behavioral and Quantitative Critical Review of Experimental Studies. *Psych. Bull.* **30**: 261–324.

Razran, G. H. S. (1933) Conditioned Responses in Children. *Archives of Psychology.* **148**:–120.

Razran, G. H. S. (1935) Psychology in the USSR. *J. Phil.* **32**: 19–24.

Razran, G. H. S. (1935) Conditioned Reflexes: An Experimental Study and a Theoretical Analysis. *Arch. Psychol.* (N.Y.) **28** (191).

Razran, G. H. S. (1937) Conditioned Responses: A Classified Bibliography. *Psych. Bull.* **34**: 191–256.

Razran, G. H. S. (1942) Current Psychological Theory in the USSR. *Psych. Bull.* **39**: 445–446.

Razran, G. H. S. (1949) Stimulus Generalization of Conditioned Responses. *Psych. Bull.* **46**: 337–365.

Razran, G. H. S. (1971) Russian Contributions to American Psychology, in L. B. Murphy and G. Murphy (eds.) *The World of Mind*. N.Y.: Knopf.

Razran, G. H. S. (1957) Recent Russian Psychology: 1950–1956. *Contemporary Psychology* **2**: 93–101.

Razran, G. (1961) Recent Soviet Phyletic Comparisons of Classical and of Operant Conditioning: Experimental Designs. *J. Comp. Physiol. Psych.* **54**: 357–65.

Razran, G. H. S. (1964) Growth, Scope and Direction of Current Soviet Psychology. *American Psychologist* **19** (5): 342–9.

Raeff, M. (1966) *Origins of the Russian Intelligentsia*. New York: Harcourt Brace Jovanovich.

Redl, Helen B. (1966) *Soviet Educators on Soviet Education* London: Collier-Macmillan.

Reich, W. (1929) Dialektische Materialismus und Psychoanalyse *Unter Dem Banner Des Marxismus* (7–8).

Reinvald, N. I. (1964) On Medical Psychology for Physicians (in Russian). *Voprosy psikhologii* **9** (2).

Rives, S. M. (1948) The Characteristics of Will of the New Soviet Man (in Russian). *Sovietskaya Pedagogika* **12**: 12–26.

Richet, G. (1925) *Réflexes psychiques, réflexes conditionels, automatisme mentale* Petrograd: Pavlov's Jubilee Volume.

Roginsky, Y. Y. (1961) Racial Differentiation and the Psyche, in Contemporary Raciology and Racism. *Intern. J. Am. Linguistics* **27**: 44–69.

Ronco, P. G. and Sawyer, H. L. (1962) A Survey of Russian Literature related to Human Factors Engineering. *Human Factors* **4**: 107–23.

Rosenthal, J. S. (1932) Typology in the Light of the Theory of Conditioned Reflexes *Char. and Personality* **1**: 56–69.

Rosenzweig, M. (1960) Pavlov, Bechterev and Twitmeyer on Conditioning. *Am. J. Psychol.* **73**: 312–16.

Rostow, W. W. (1953) *The Dynamics of Soviet Society* New York: W. W. Norton.

Rubinshtein, S. L. (1944) Soviet Psychology in Wartime. *Philos. Phenom. Res.* **5**: 181–198.

Rubinshtein, S. L. (1948) Psychological Science and Education *Harvard Ed. Rev.* **18**: 158–170.

Rubinshtein, S. L. (1946) Consciousness in the Light of Dialectical Materialism. *Sci. and Soc.* **10**: 252–261.

Rubinshtein, S. L. (1959) *Printsipy i Puti Razviti Psikhologii* (*Principles and Paths of the Development of Psychology*) Moscow: Acad. Sci. 354.

Rudnev, P. (1963) Party and Public Education *Soviet Education* **6**: 14–33.

Sadovsky, V. N. and Yudin, G. A. (1966) Jean Piaget – Psychologist, Logician, Philosopher (in Russian). *Voprosy Psikhologii* **11** (4): 106–120.

Sapir, J. (1929) Freudismus, Soziologie, Psychologie. *Unter dem Banner des Marxismus.*

Sarkisov, S. A. (1950) The Teachings of I. P. Pavlov on Central Nervous Activity and Problems of the Structure of the Brain (in Russian). *Voprosy Filosofii* **3**: 124–142.

Schniermann, A. L. (1928) Present Day Tendencies in Russian Psychology. *J. Gen. Ps.* **1**: 397–404.

Schniermann, A. L. (1930) Bekhterev's Reflexological School, in C. Murchison *Psychologies of 1930* 221–242 Worcester, Mass.: Clark University Press.

Schultz, R. S. and MacFarland, R. A. (1935) Industrial Psychology in the Soviet Union. *J. App. Psychol.* **19**: 265–308.

Sechenov, I. M. (1952) *Selected Physiological and Psychological Works.* Moscow: Foreign Languages Pub. House.

Sechenov, I. (1935) *Selected Works* Moscow: State Publishing House.

Sechenov, I. M. (1961) *Refleksy golovnogo mozga* Moscow: USSR Acad. Sci.

Sechenov, I. M. (1952–56) *Izbranniye proizvedeniya* (ed. Koshtoyanz) (2 vols.) Moscow: Politizdat.

Sechenov, I. M. (1952) *Fiziologiya nervnoi systseny: izbranniye trudy* (5 vols.) Moscow: State Publishing House for Medical Lit.

Shore, M. J. (1947) *Soviet Education: Its Psychology and Philosophy* N.Y.: Philosophical Library.

Shul'gin, V. N. (1956) *Ocherki zhizni i tvorchestva N. G. Chernyshevskogo* Moscow: State Publishing House.

Shumilin, I. N. (1962) *Soviet Higher Education* Münich: Carl.

Sidorov, M. I. (1957) *G. V. Plekhanov i voprosy istorii russkoi revolutsionno-demokraticheskoi mysli XIXv* Moscow: Izd-vo Akademii nauk, SSSR.

Shcherbatov, M. M. (1969) *On the Corruption of Morals in Russia* (1786–1787) (ed. A. Lentin) Cambridge University Press.

Shemyakin, F. N. (ed.) (1960) *Myshlenie i Rech'* Moscow: Acad. Ped. Sci.

Sherrington, C. S. (1906) *The Integrative Action of the Nervous System* New Haven: Yale University Press.

Shevarev, P. A. (ed.) (1962) *Vospriyatie i Myshlenie* Moscow: Izvestiya, Acad. Ped. Sci.

Simon, B. (ed.) (1963) *Educational Psychology in the USSR* London: Routledge and Kegan Paul.

Skinner, B. F. (1931) The Concept of the Reflex in the Description of Behavior. *J. Gen. Ps.* **5**: 427–458.

Skinner, B. F. (1937) Two Types of Conditioned Reflex: A Reply to Konorski and Miller, *J. Gen. Ps.* **16**: 272–279.

Skinner, B. F. (1938) *The Behavior of Organisms: An Experimental Analysis* New York: Appleton-Century.

Skinner, B. F. (1957) *Verbal Behavior* New York: Appleton-Century-Crofts.

Skovoroda, G. S. (1961) *Tvory* (2 vols.) Kjiv: Izd-vo Ukr. SSR: Akad. Nauk. (in Ukrainian).

Skudina, M. M. (1960) The Gifted Child. *Soviet Education* **3** (12): 56–60.

Slavina, L. S. (1954) Specific Features of the Intellectual Work of Unsuccessful Scholars (in Russian).*Sovietskayapedagogika.* **5**:91–101.

Smirnov, A. A. (1966) *Soviet Psychology and its Development* An Address to the Eighteenth International Congress of Psychology in Moscow.

Smith, H. M. (1949) *Torchbearers of Chemistry* New York, N.Y.: Academic Press (for Lomonosov).

Smolitskii, V. G. (1968) *Iz ravelina: o sud'be romana N. G. Chernyshevskogo, 'Chto delat'?'* Moscow: Kniga.

Snejnevsky, A. V. (1951) Principles of Prophylaxis of Psychic Diseases in the Soviet Union. *Proc. Fourth Int. Congr. Ment. Hlth.* 308–314.

Sokolov, E. H. (1955) Higher Nervous Activity and the Problem of Perception (in Russian). *Voprosy Psikhologii* **1** (1): 58–65.

Sokolov, E. N. (1960) Neuronal Models and the Orienting Reflex, in Mary A. B. Brazier (ed.) *Central Nervous System and Behavior* 187–239. New York: Josiah Macy, Jr., Foundation.

Sokolov, E. N. (1963) Higher Nervous Functions: the Orienting Reflex. *Ann. Rev. Physiol.* **25**: 545–80.

Sokolov, E. N. (1963) *Perception and the Conditioned Reflex* New York: Pergamon Press.

Sokolov, E. N. (ed.) (1959) *The Orienting Reflex and the Problems of Higher Nervous Activity* (in Russian) Moscow: Akad. Pedagog. Nauk.

Sokolova, M. V. (1963) *Ocherki istorii psikhologicheskikh vozzrenii v Rossii v XI-XVIII vekakh* Moscow: Akad. Pedagog. Nauk RSFSR.

Sokolansky, I. A. and Meshcheryakov, A. I. (1962) *Obuchenie i vospitanie slepoglukonemykh* Moscow: Acad. Ped. Sci.

Somerville, J. (1947) *Soviet Philosophy* N.Y.: Philosophical Library.

Speransky, A. D. (1944) *A Basis for a New Theory of Medicine* N.Y.: International Publishers.

Spielrein, I. N. (1931) Die Psychotechnik in der Soviet Union. *Annals of Business Economy* **4**: 342–353.

Spielrein, I. N. (1931) On the Turn in Psychotechnics. *Sov. Psihkot.*

Spielrein, I. N. (1933) Zur Theorie der Psychotechnic. *Zeit. fur ang. Ps.* **44**.

Spirkin, A. G. and Brunow, E. P. (1953) *Pavlov's Theory of the Signal Systems* (in German) Berlin: Volk und Gesundheit.

Stagner, R. (1931) Conditioned Reflex Theories of Learning. *Psychol. Review* **38**: 42–59.

Stalin, J. V. (1939) *History of the Communist Party of the Soviet Union (Bolsheviks)* Moscow: K.P.S.S.

Stalin, J. V. (1952) *Collected Works* Moscow: Foreign Languages Pub. House.

Stalin, J. V. (1946–51) *Sochineniya* Moscow: State Publishing House for Political Literature.

Stalin, J. V. (1947) *Leninism* Moscow: Foreign Languages Pub. House.

Stoletov, V. N. (ed.) (1949) O polozhenie v biologicheshikh naukakh (The Situation in Biological Science). *Report of a Discussion at the Academy of Agricultural Science* Moscow: State Publishing House for Agricultural Literature.

Teplov, B. M. (1950) *Psikhologiya* Moscow: Uchpedgiz.

Teplov, B. M. (ed.) (1956, 1959, 1963) *Tipologicheskie osobennosti vysshei nervnoi deyatel'nosti cheloveka* Moscow: Acad. Ped. Sci.

Teplov, B. M. (1961) *Problemy individual 'nykh razlichii* Moscow: Acad. Ped. Sci.

Teplov, B. M. (1962) Investigation of the Properties of the Nervous System as a Path leading to the Study of Individual Differences, in *Psychological Science in the USSR* Washington: Office Tech. Serv. **2**: 2–62.

Thorndike, E. L. (1898) Animal Intelligence: An Experimental Study of the Associative Processes in Animals. *Psychol. Monog.* **2** (8): 1–109.

Tizard, J. (1958) Children in the USSR: Work on Mental and Physical Handicaps. *Lancet* **II**: 1325–30.

Tomaszewski, T. (1949) *Principles of Psychology in the USSR* (in Polish) Warsaw: Czytelnik.

Trotsky, L. D. (1926) *Sochineniya* (Kultura perekhodnovo Vremeni) **21**: 430–431.

Tsereteli, S. B. (1966) On the Concept of Dialectical Logic (in Russian) *Voprosy Filosofii* **19** (3): 31–38.

Tsvetayev, D. V. (1890) *Protestanty i Protestantizm v Rossii do epokhi preobrazovani* Moscow.

Twitmyer, E. B. (1902) *A Study of the Knee-Jerk* Philadelphia: Winston.

Ulam, A. B. (1965) *The Bolsheviks* New York: Macmillan.

Ushinski, K. D. (1948) *Sochineniya* (4 vols.) Moscow: Uchpedgiz.

USSR Gosplan (1933) Results of the Fulfilment of the First Five Year Plan for the Development of the National Economy of the USSR Moscow: State Planning Institute.

Utkin, I. A. (ed.) (1960) *Theoretical and Practical Problems of Medicine and Biology in Experiments on Monkeys* (trans. R. Schachter) New York, N.Y.: Pergamon Press.

Uznadze, D. N. (1939) Investigations in the Psychology of Set. *Acta Psychologica* **4**: 323–61.

Uznadze, D. N. (1958) *Experimental Investigations in the Psychology of Set* (in Russian) Tbilisi: Academy of Sciences.

Valentiner, T. (1932) Die I Internationale Psychotechnische Konferenz in Moskau. *Zeit. fur ang. Ps.* **41**: 187–213.

Vasil'ev, L. (1962) *Vnushenie na rasstonianii: Zametki fiziologa* Moscow: State Publishers of Political Literature.

Venable, V. (1966) *Human Nature, the Marxian View* London: Meridian Books.

Vigoorova, F. (1954) *Diary of a School Teacher* Moscow: Foreign Languages Pub. House.

Viteles, M. S. (1938) Industrial Psychology in Russia. *Occupational Psychology* **12**: 87–103.

Vladimirov, G. E. and Vladimirova, E. A. (1960) The Biochemical Characteristics of the Brain under the Action of Positive and Negative Conditioned Stimuli, in T. B. Tower and J. P. Schade (eds.) *Structure and Function of the Cerebral Cortex* New York: Elsevier. 405–416.

Vodolazov, G. G. (1969) *Ot Chernyshevskogo k Plekhanovu: Ob osobennostiakh razvitiia sotsialistisheskoi mysli v Rossi* Moscow: Moscow University Press.

Volgyesi, F. A. (1955) Development of Hypnotherapy according to J. Braid's Discoveries and I. P. Pavlov's Teaching (in German). *Psychiat. Neurol. med. Psychologie* (Leipzig) **7**: 129–145.

Voronin, L. G. (1962) Some Results of Comparative Physiological Investigations of Higher Nervous Activity. *Psych. Bull.* **59**: 161–95.

Voronin, L. G. and Sokolov, E. N. (1960) Cortical Mechanisms of the Orienting Reflex and its Relations to the Conditioned Reflex, in Electroencephalography of Higher Nervous Activity. *Clin. Neurophysiol. Suppl.* (H. H. Jasper and G. D. Smirnov, eds.) **13**: 335–46.

Vucinich, A. (1960) Mathematics in Russian culture. *J. History of Ideas* **21** (2): 161–179.

Vul'fson, B. L. (1966) Freudianiam and Bourgeois Pedagogy. *Soviet Education* **8** (3): 3–14.

Vygotski, L. S. (1934) Learning and Mental Development in School, in B. Simon and Joan Simon (eds.) *Educational Psychology in the USSR* London: Routledge and Kegan Paul.

Vygotski, L. S. (1934) Thought in Schizophrenia. *Arch. Neurol. Psychiat.* **31**: 1063–77.

Vygotsky, L. S. (1960) *Razvitie vysshikh psikhicheskikh funktsii* Moscow: Acad. Ped. Sci.

Warren, H. C. (1921) *A History of the Association Psychology* N.Y.: Scribner.

Watson, J. B. (1916) The Place of the Conditioned Reflex in Psychology. *Psychol. Review* **23**: 89–116.

Watson, J. B. (1926) Behaviorism: A Psychology based on Reflexes. *Arch. Neurol. Psychiat.* **15**: 185–204.

Widy-Wirski, F. (1951) Pavlov and Sherrington (in Polish). *Polski Tyg. Lek.* **6**: 104–108.

Winn, R. B. (ed.) (1961) *Soviet Psychology: A Symposium* New York: Philosophical Library.

Wolman, B. B. (1960) *Contemporary Theories and Systems in Psychology* New York: Harper.

Wortis, J. (1950) *Soviet Psychiatry* Baltimore: Williams and Wilkins.

Yarmolenko, A. V. (1961) *Ocherki psikhologii slepoglukhonemykh* Leningrad: Leningrad University.

Yakushev, V. M. (1966) The Theory of Set in the Light of Reflex Theory. *Soviet Psychology and Psychiatry* **4**: 90–95.

Yaroshevski, M. G. (1948) American Bourgeois Psychologists in the

Struggle to Destroy Consciousness (in Russian). *Voprosy Filosofii* **1**: 280–293.

Yerkes, R. N. and Morgulis, L. (1909) The Method of Pavlov in Animal Psychology. *Psych. Bull.* **6**: 257–273.

Yudin, T. I. (1951) *Essays on the History of Russian Psychiatry* (in Russian) Moscow: Medgiz.

Zaporozhetz, A. V. (1955) *Psikhologiia (Psychology)* Moscow: State Textbook Pub. House.

Zaporozhetz, A. V. (1955) The Development of Voluntary Movement (in Russian). *Voprosy Psikhologii* **1** (1): 42–48.

Zaporozhetz, A. V. and Sokolov, E. N. (1955) The Fourteenth International Congress of Psychology. *Voprosy Psikhologii* **1**: 116–123.

Zaporozhetz, A. V. and Leontiev, A. N. *Rehabilitation of Hand Function* New York: Pergamon Press.

Zeigarnik, B. V. (1958) *Narusheniya myshleniya i psikhicheski bol'nykh* Moscow: State Res. Inst. of Psychiat. Mn. Health.

Zeigarnik, B. V. (1962) *Patologiya myshleniya* Moscow University Press.

Zenkovsky, V. V. (1951) *Das Bild von Menschen in der Ostkirche* Stuttgart: Evangelische Verlagswerk.

Zenkovsky, V. V. (1953) *History of Russian Philosophy* (2 vols.) London: Routledge and Kegan Paul.

Index

abstraction, mental process of, 250
activity, 211, 264–5; in mental development, 172, 249; as source of emotions, 235; unity of consciousness and, 170, 181–2
Adler, A., 104
Adrian, E. D., 228
agnosticism, 2, 86, 190
agriculture: genetics and, 190–5; under Tsarism, 11, 24
Akhmatova, Anna, 185
Alexandrov, A. A., 187
analysers, sensory (in cerebral cortex), 77, 80; motor-speech, 225; visual, 219–20
analysis-synthesis, in cerebral cortex, 91, 93
Ananiev, B. G., 170, 217–18; *The Achievements of Soviet Psychology* by (1947), 169, 198, 254–5
Andreyev, B. S., 177
Anichkov, 255
animals: features of nervous activity shared by man and, 93; mental development in, 171; phenomena of 'set' in, 242; 'psychology' of, 204–5; sleep therapy for neurosis in, 177; speech distinguishes man from, 118; typology of nervous system in, 251; *see also* dogs
anniversaries, publications to celebrate, 260
Anokhin, P. K., 237, 242; at Pavlov discussion, 204, 205, 206
'anthropologism' of Feuerbach, 111, 144
anthropology, modern: emphasizes cultural environment, 121

Antonovich, 259
apes, work on, 171, 208
Aristotle, 34, 38
arithmetic, remedial teaching for children backward in, 178, 222
Armenia, psychology in, 260
army, as progressive sector of society at one stage of Tsarism, 23
Asratyan, E. A., 177, 204, 205, 206
association, principle of: in conditional reflexes, 74, 75, 81
athletes, types of, 251
autocracy, under Tsarism, 15, 48, and now, 272
Aveling, F., 270
Avenarius, R., 86, 135
Azerbaydzhan, psychology in, 260

Babkin, B. P., 112
Bacon, F., 30, 264, 269, 271
Bakunin, M., 18, 40
Bartlett, F. C., 271
Bayle, Pierre, 32
Bazarov, 85
behaviour: Pavlov's reflex theory of, 73–4, 81; Pavlov's work from 1929 as study of, 208; science of, 2, 3, 68, 105, 267; thought, memory, and speech as forms of, 248; in Western psychology, considered as resultant of rational and irrational forces, 232; Western two-factor theory of, 149, 160
behaviourism, American, 4, 66, 104, 111; criticisms of, 99, 139–40, 141, 269; discredited, 159